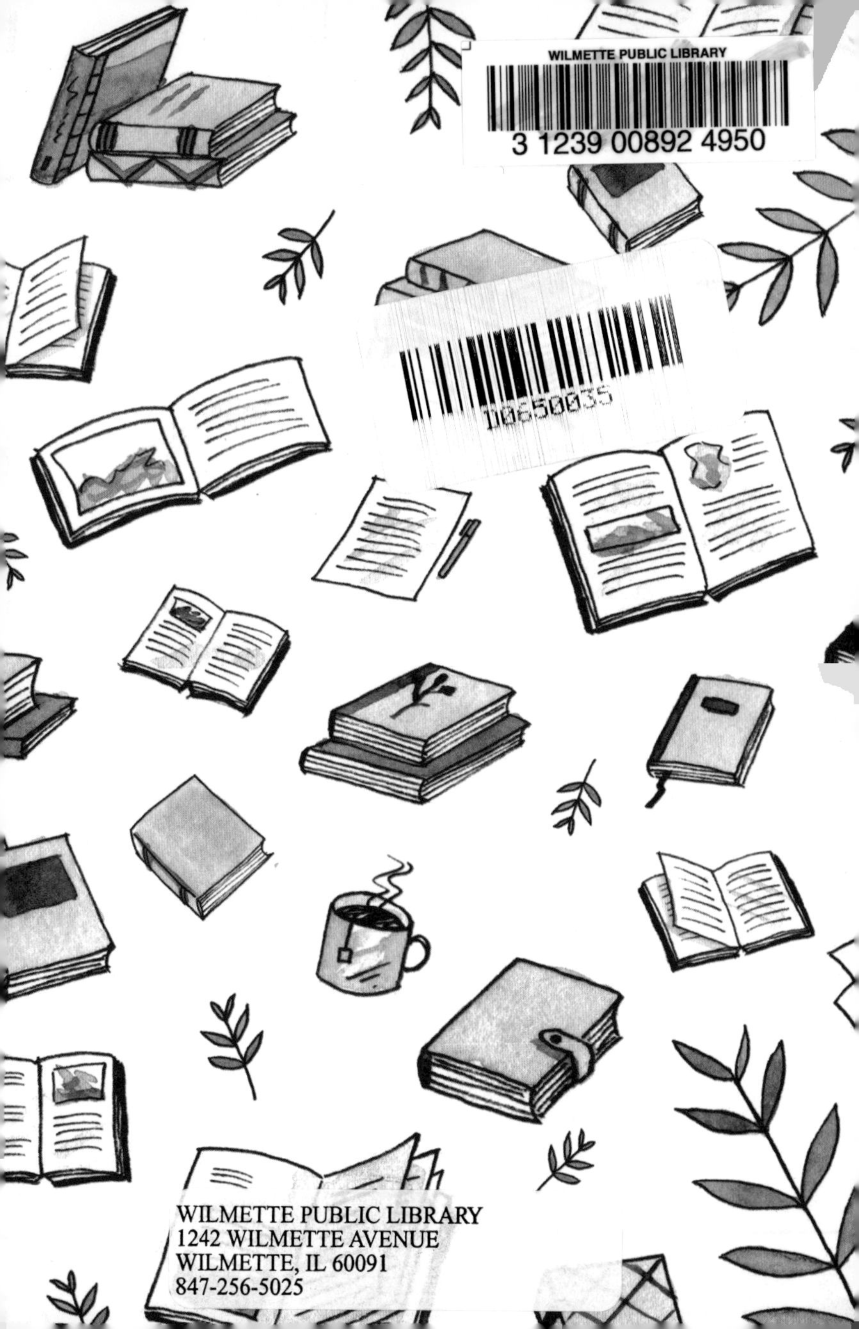

# Book Love

## Debbie Tung

Andrews McMeel
PUBLISHING®

To my parents.
Thank you for giving me the love of reading.


And to my little superstars, Arwen and Evan.
May your lives always be filled with the magic of books.

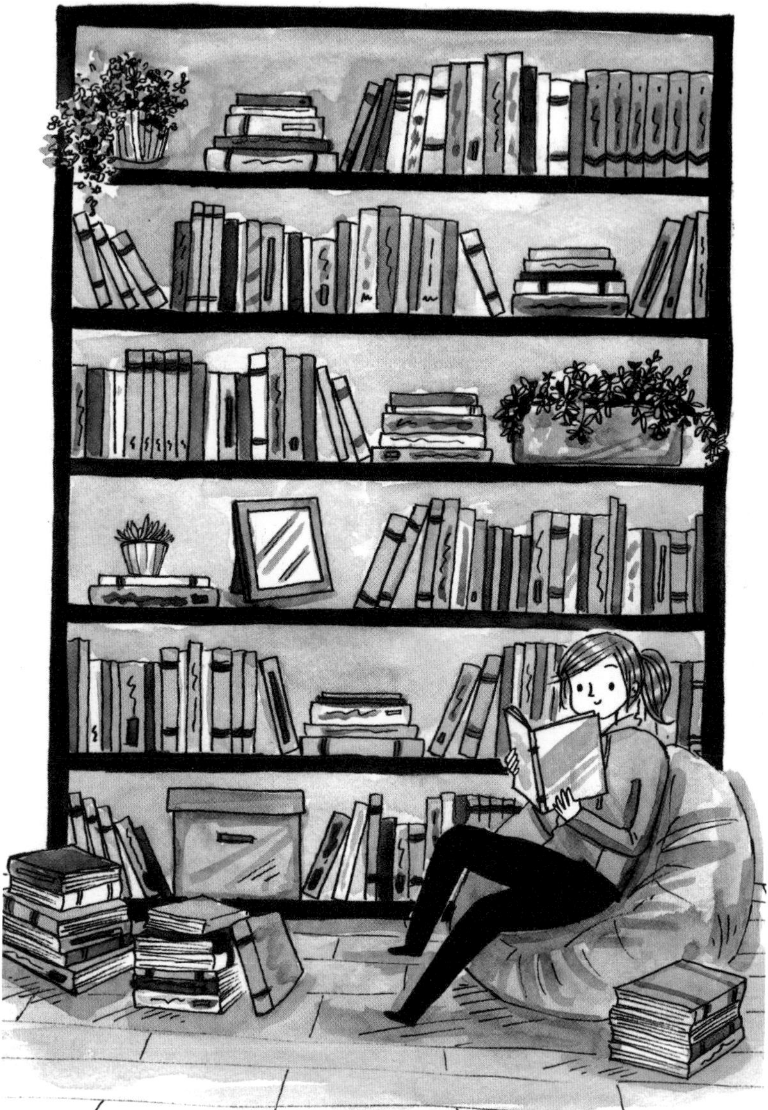

Books can take you

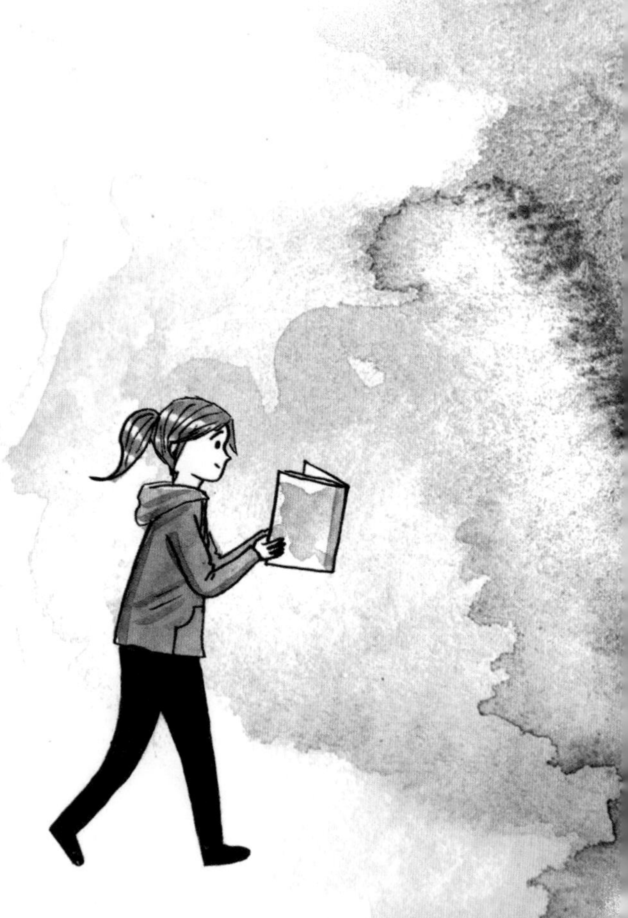

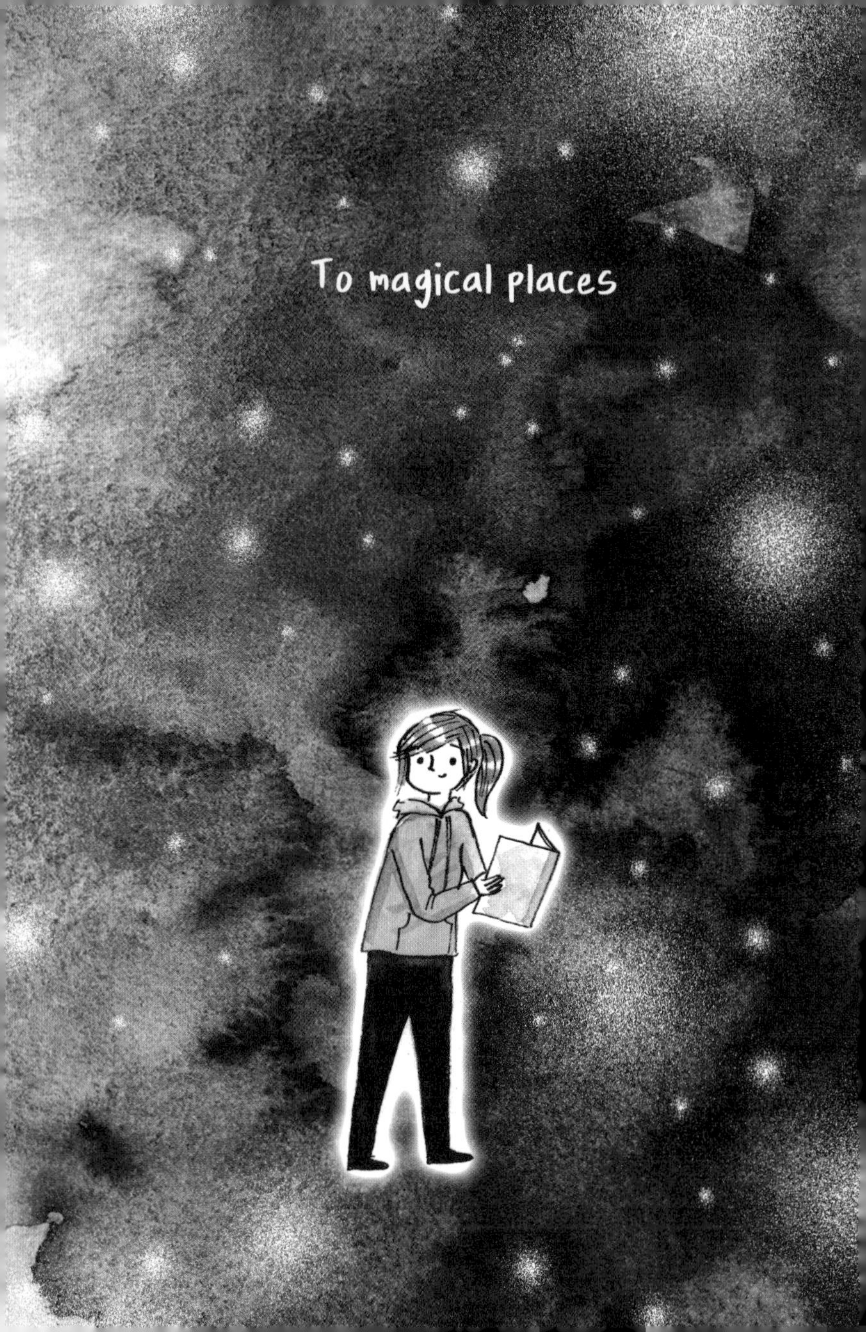
To magical places

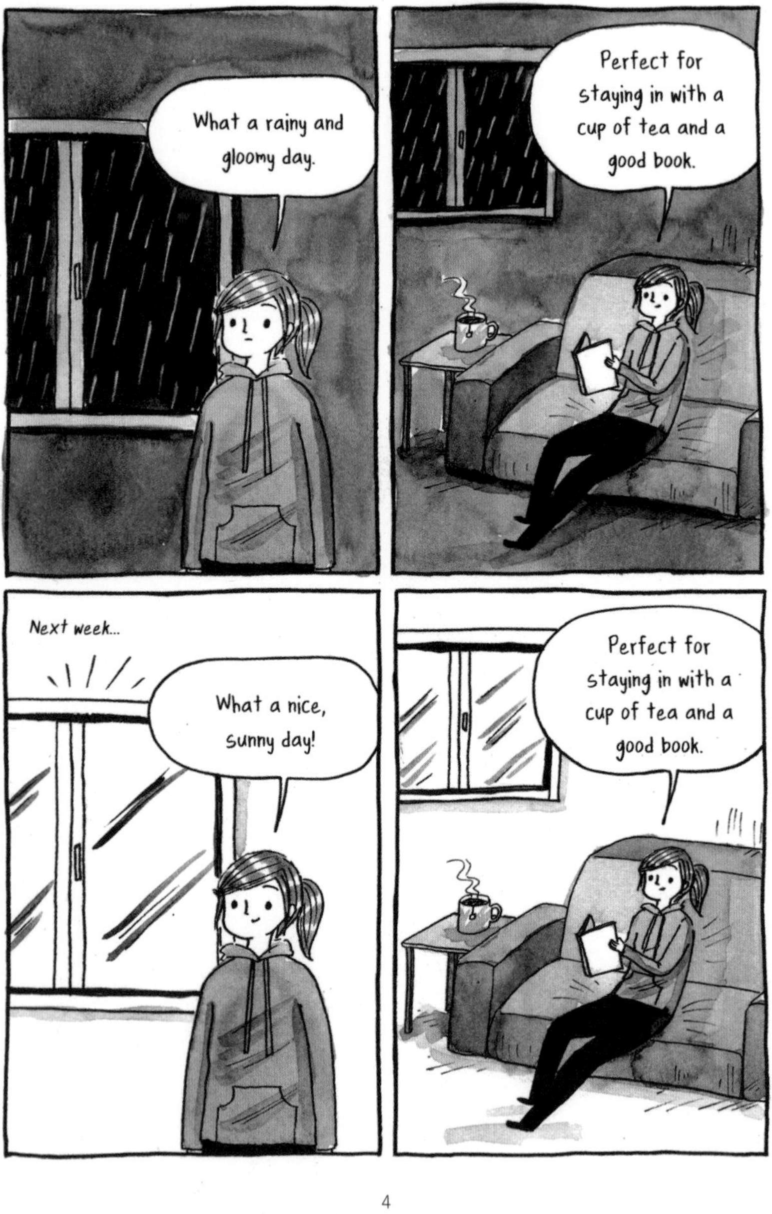
What a rainy and gloomy day.
Perfect for staying in with a cup of tea and a good book.
Next week...
What a nice, sunny day!
Perfect for staying in with a cup of tea and a good book.

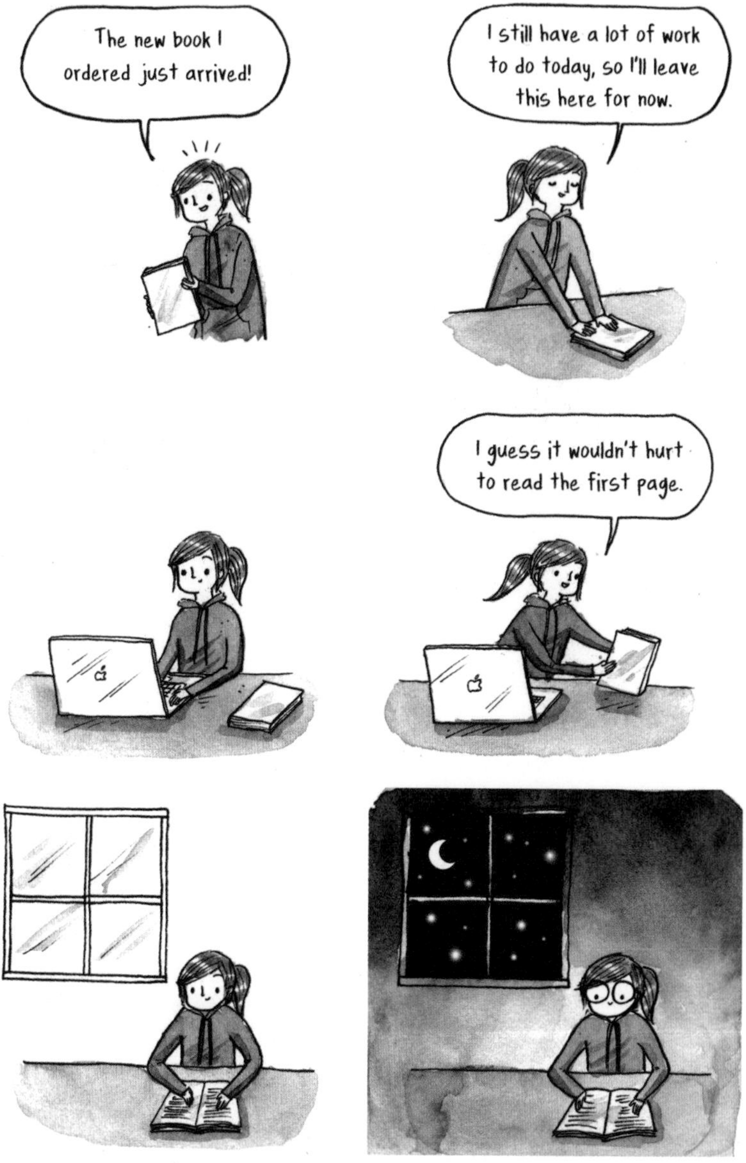
The new book I ordered just arrived!
I still have a lot of work to do today, so I'll leave this here for now.
I guess it wouldn't hurt to read the first page.

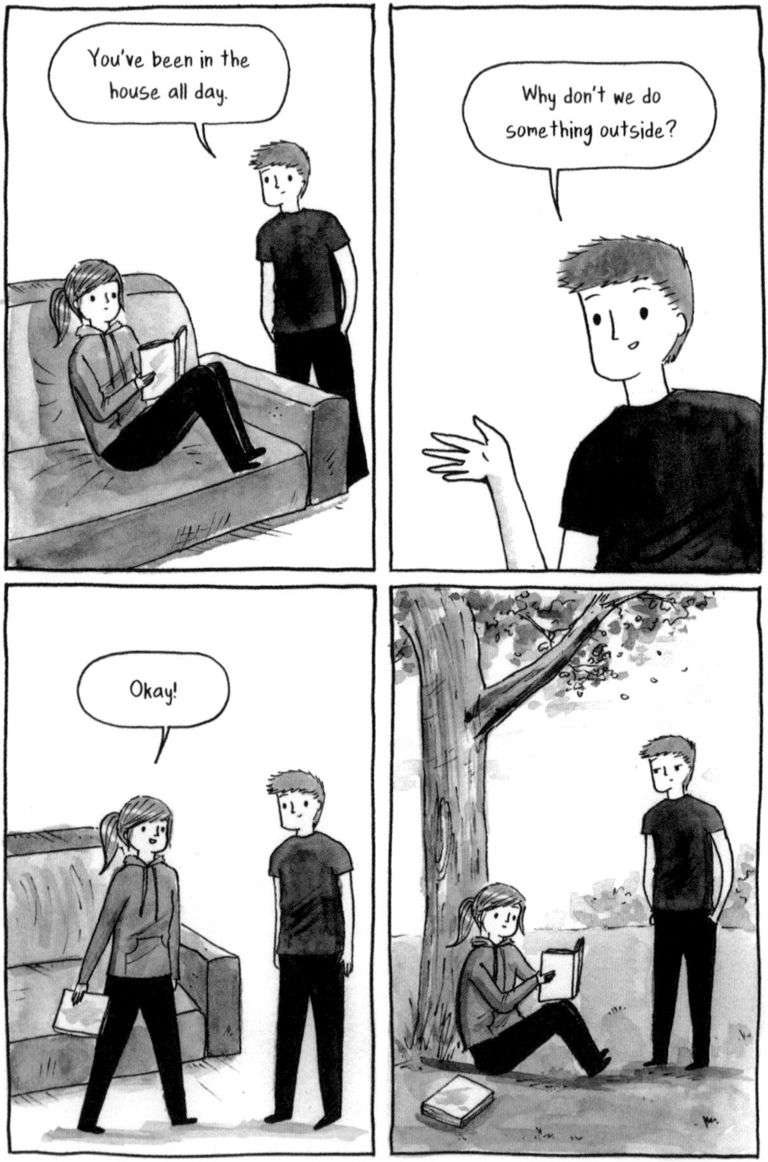
You've been in the house all day.
Why don't we do something outside?
Okay!

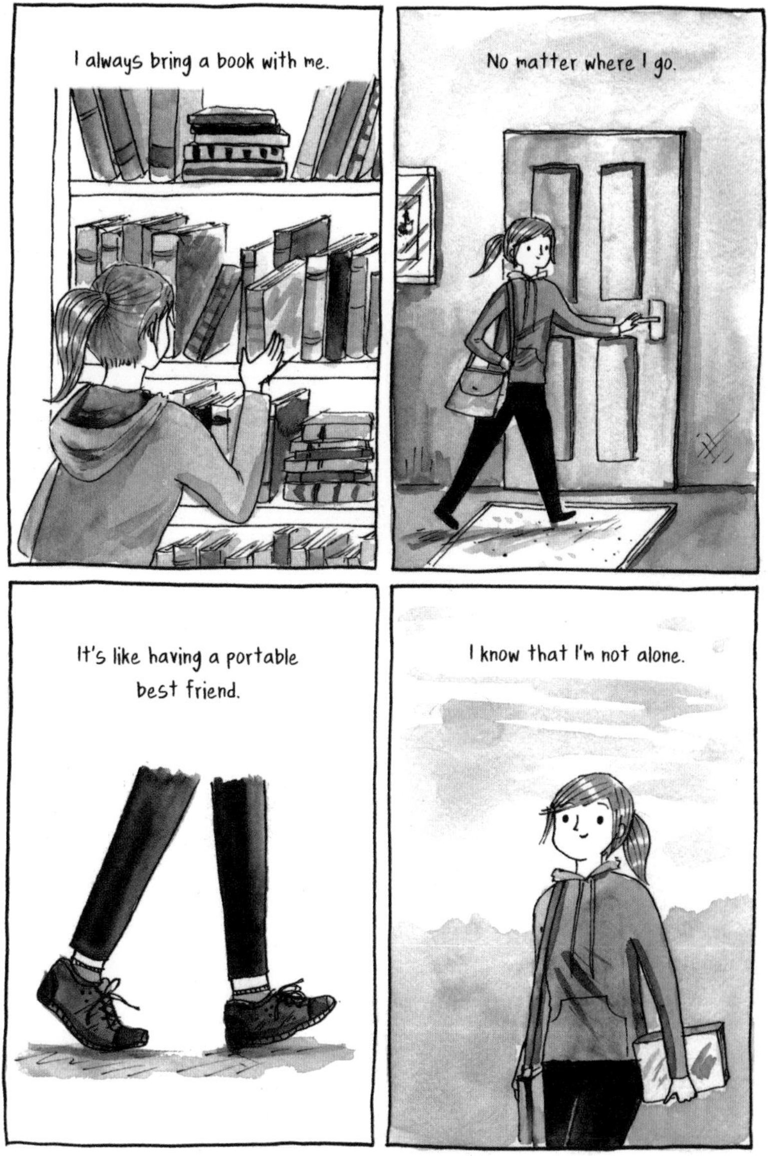
I always bring a book with me.
No matter where I go.
It's like having a portable best friend.
I know that I'm not alone.

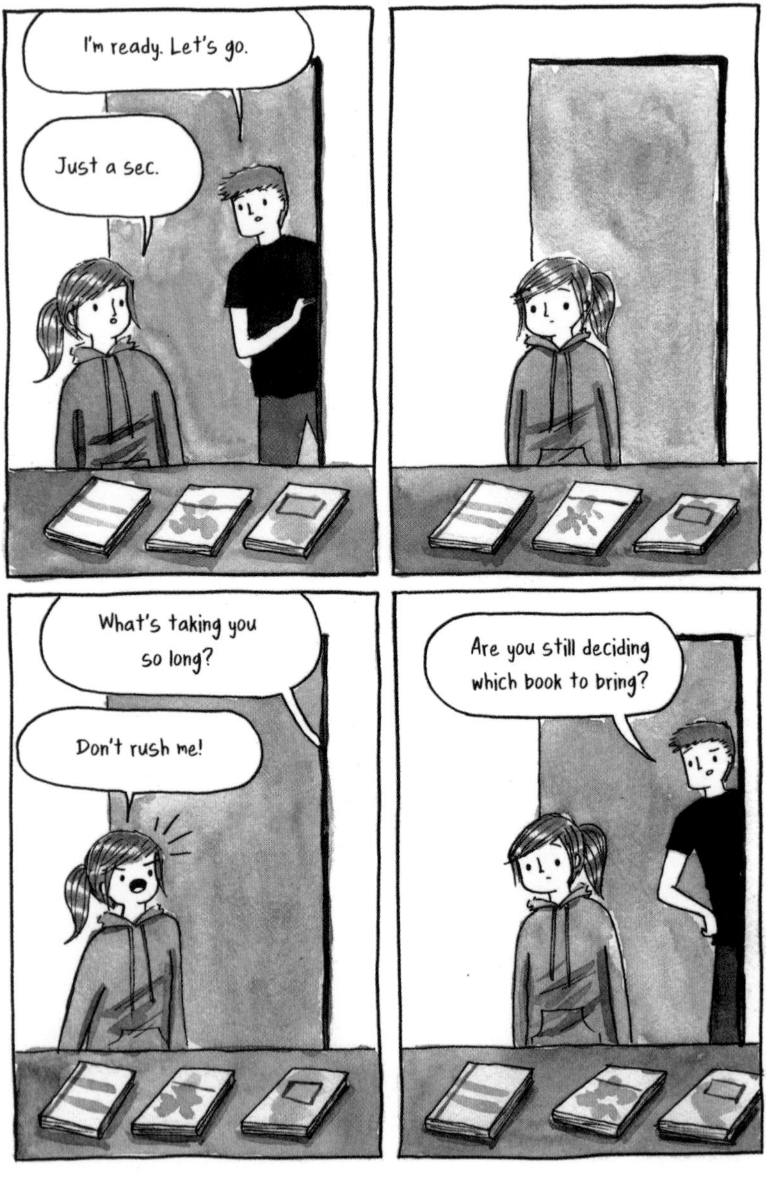
I'm ready. Let's go.
Just a sec.
What's taking you so long?
Don't rush me!
Are you still deciding which book to bring?

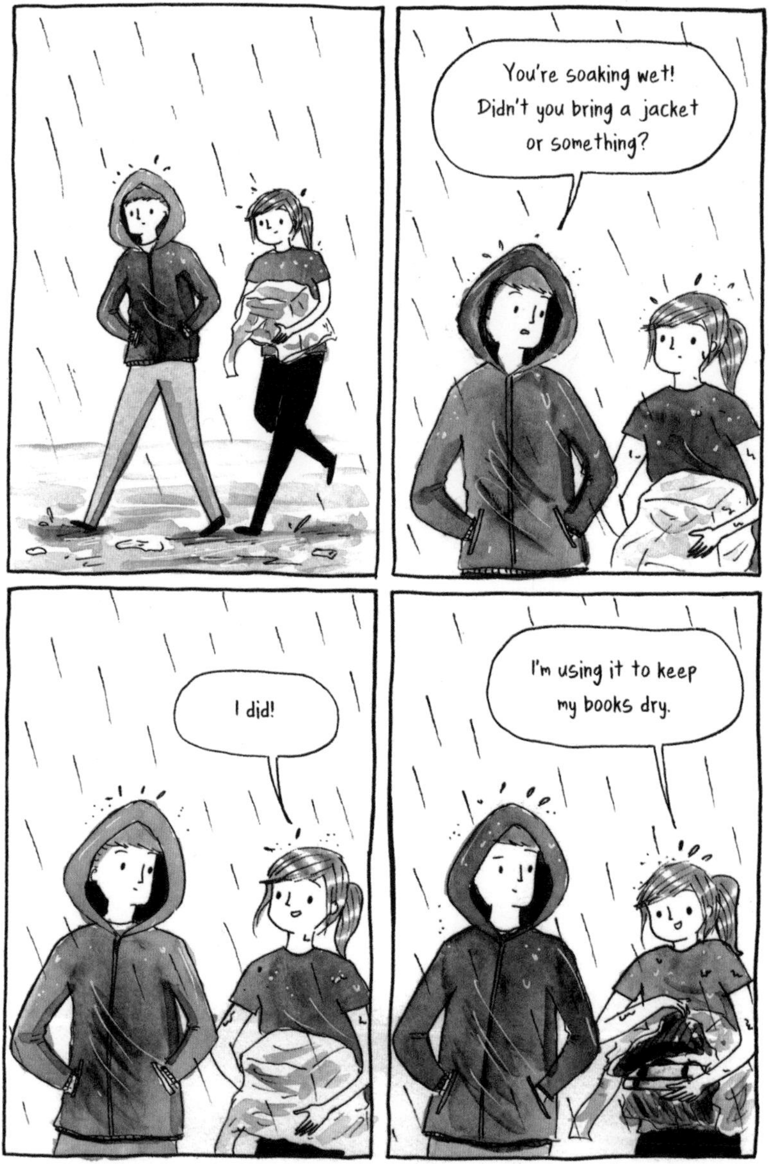
You're soaking wet! Didn't you bring a jacket or something?
I did!
I'm using it to keep my books dry.

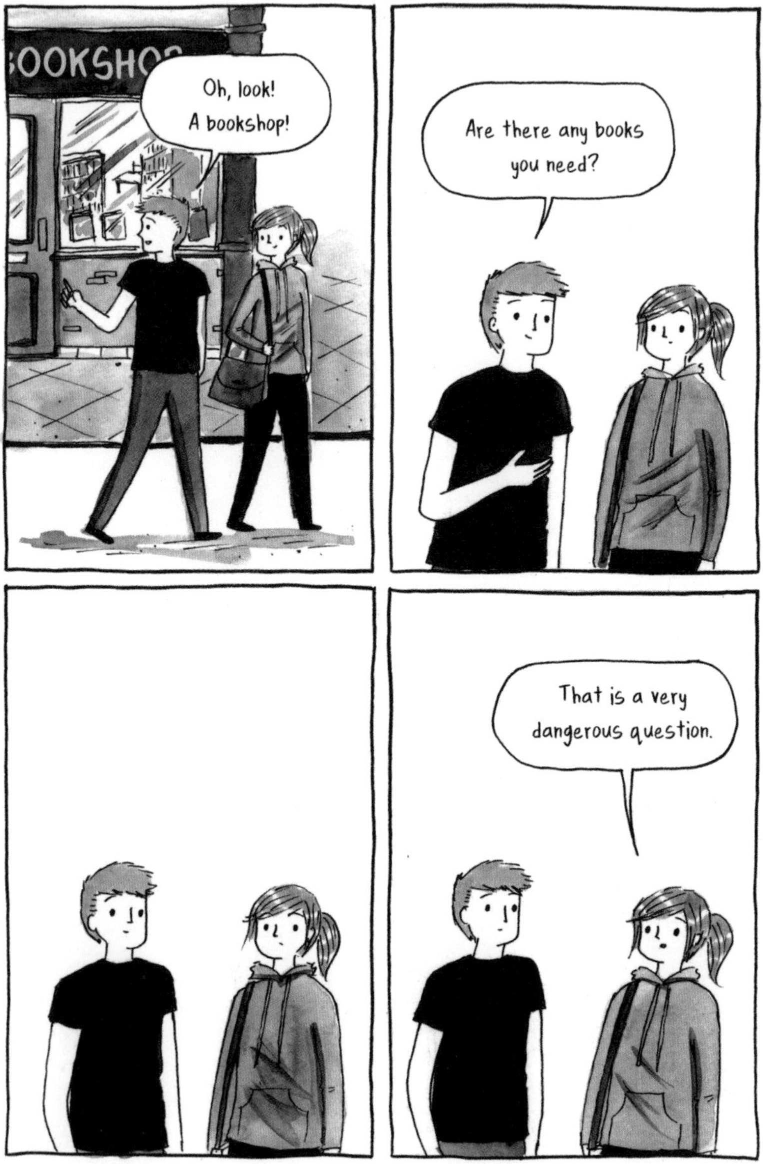
BOOKSHOP
Oh, look! A bookshop!
Are there any books you need?
That is a very dangerous question.

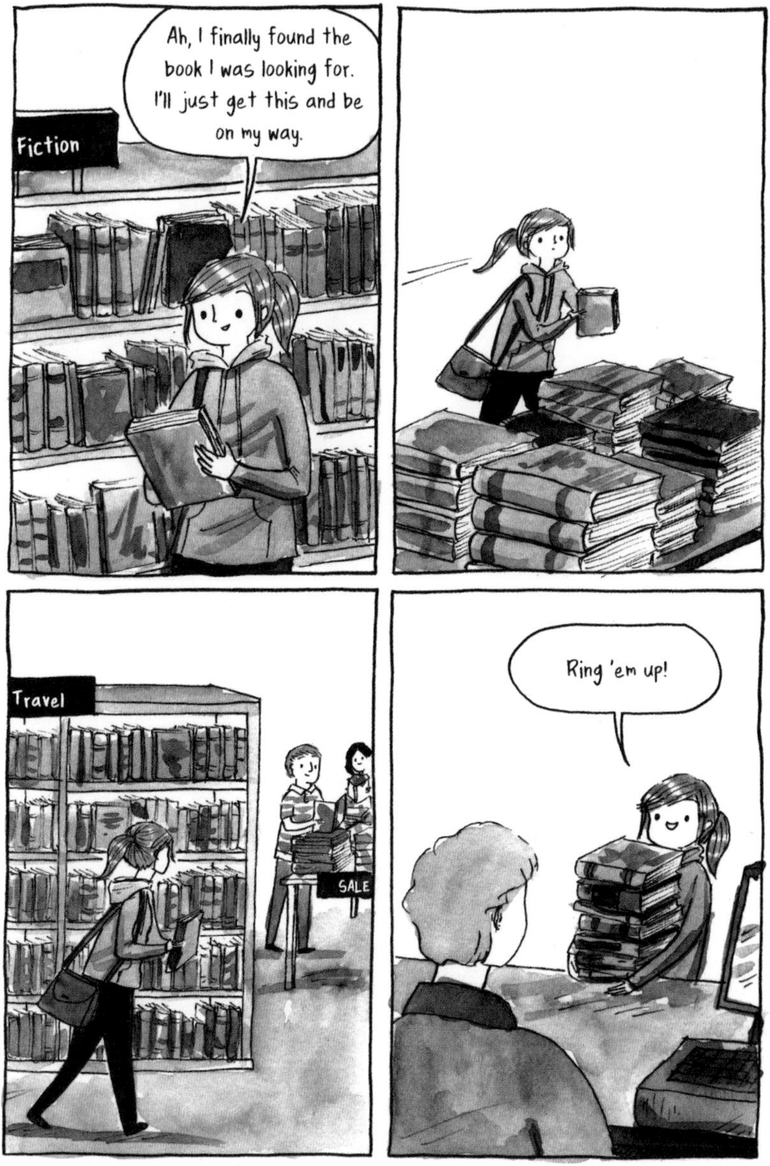
Fiction
Ah, I finally found the book I was looking for. I'll just get this and be on my way.
Travel
SALE
Ring 'em up!

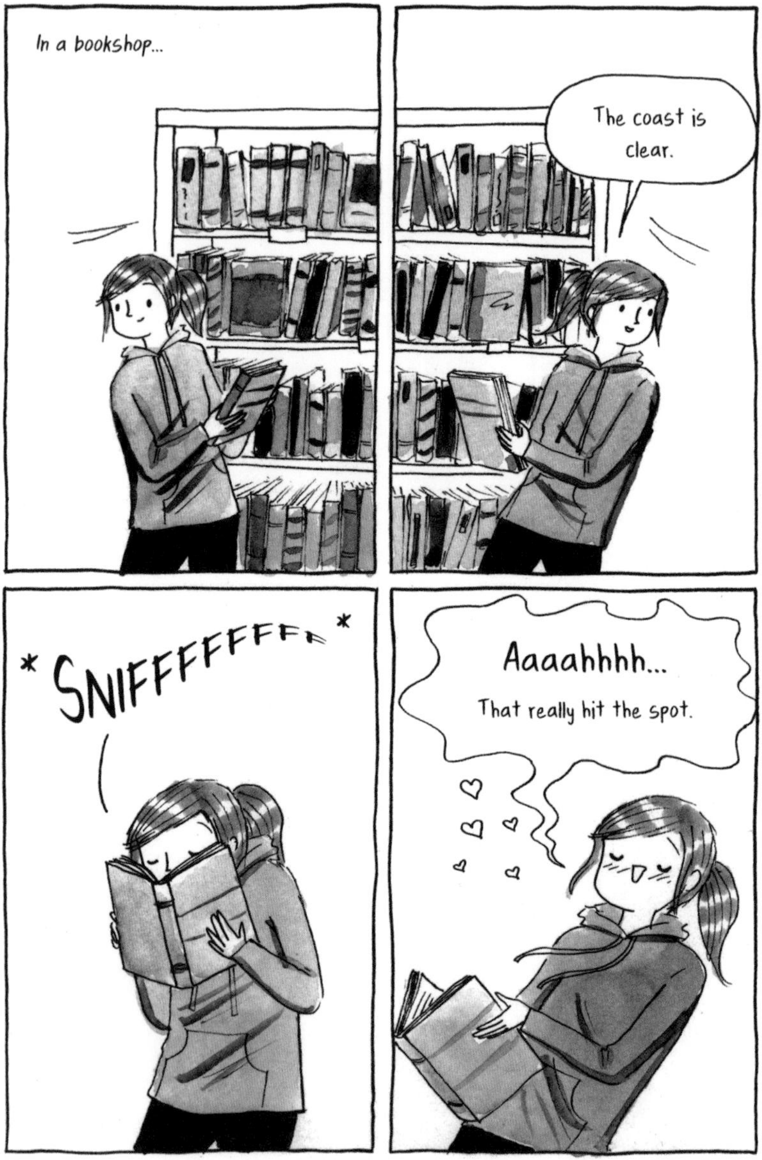
In a bookshop...
The coast is clear.
*SNIFFFFFFF*
Aaaahhhh...
That really hit the spot.

# The Process of Buying a New Book

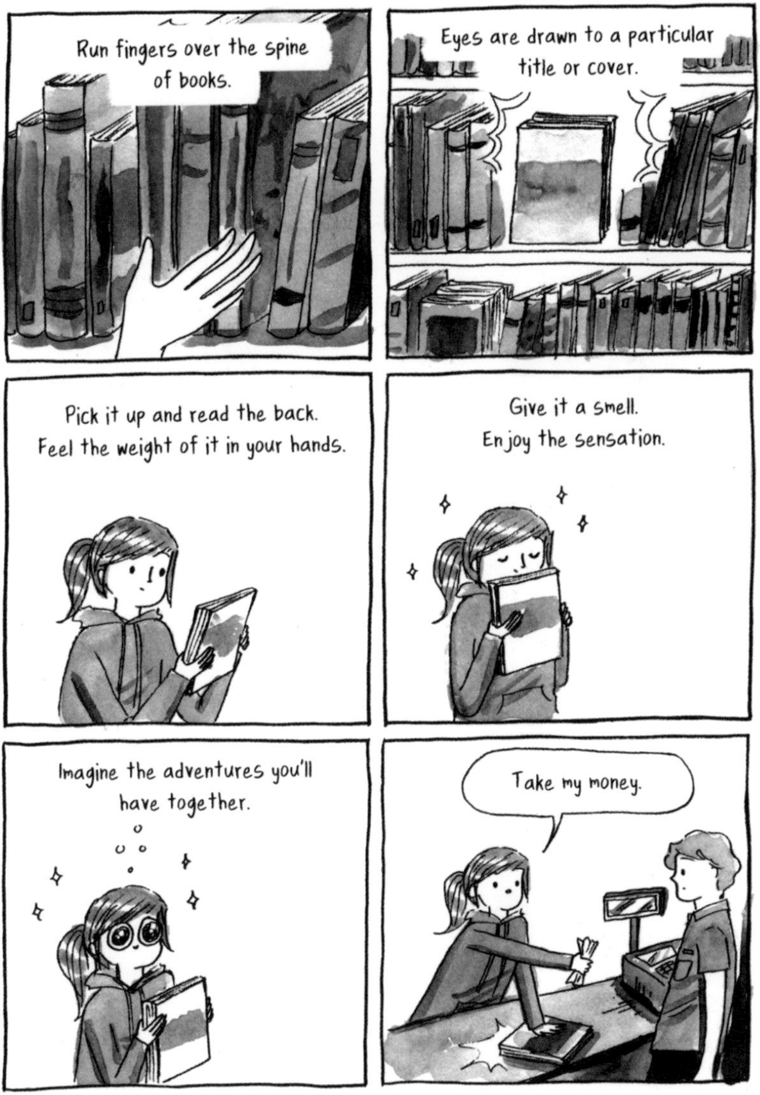
Run fingers over the spine of books.
Eyes are drawn to a particular title or cover.
Pick it up and read the back. Feel the weight of it in your hands.
Give it a smell. Enjoy the sensation.
Imagine the adventures you'll have together.
Take my money.

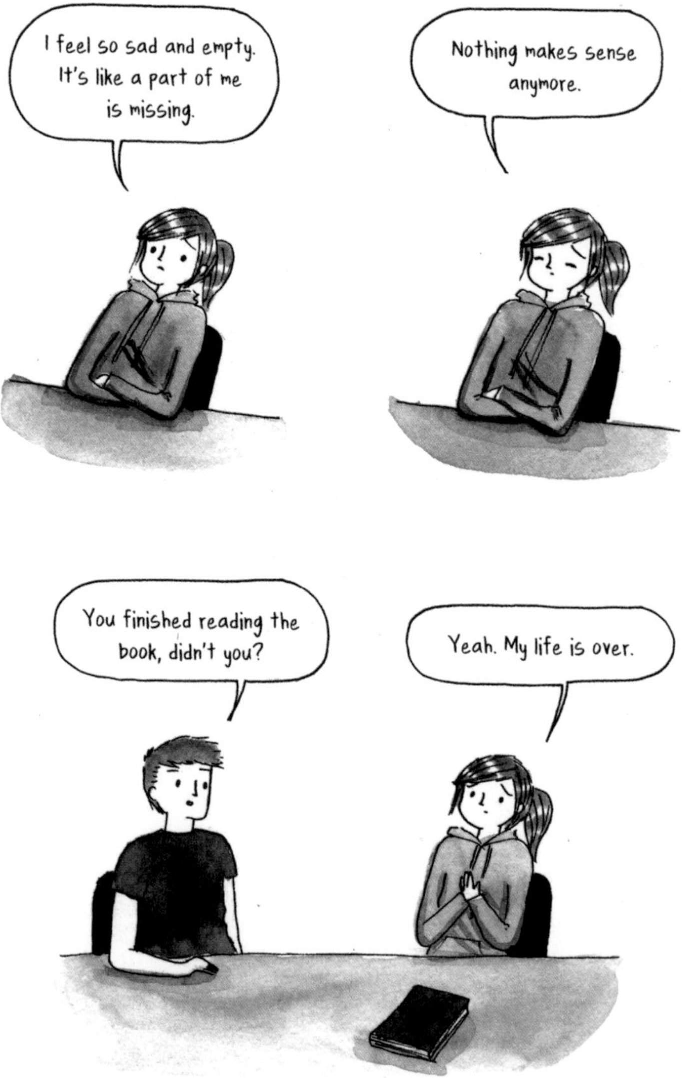
I feel so sad and empty. It's like a part of me is missing.
Nothing makes sense anymore.
You finished reading the book, didn't you?
Yeah. My life is over.

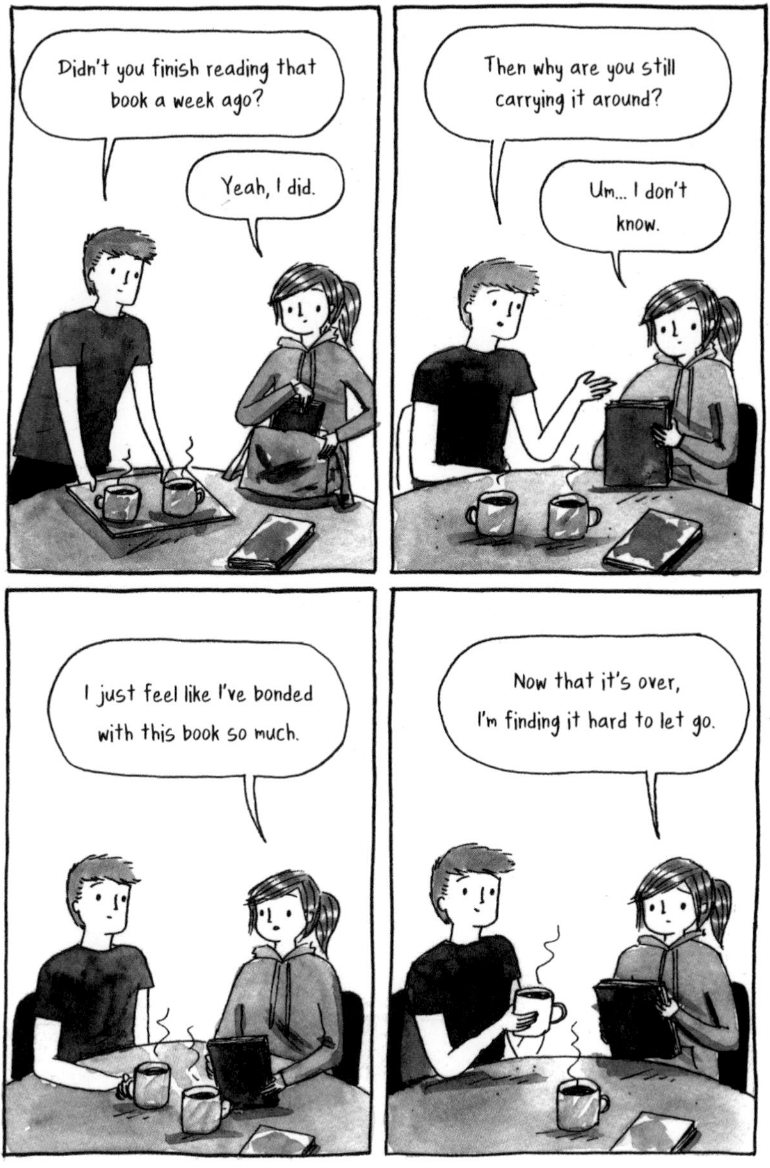
Didn't you finish reading that book a week ago?
Yeah, I did.
Then why are you still carrying it around?
Um... I don't know.
I just feel like I've bonded with this book so much.
Now that it's over, I'm finding it hard to let go.

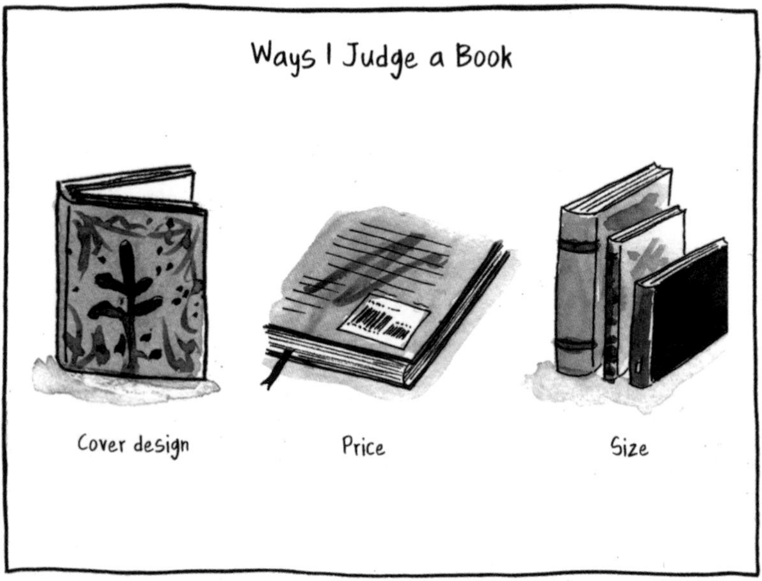
Ways I Judge a Book
Cover design
Price
Size

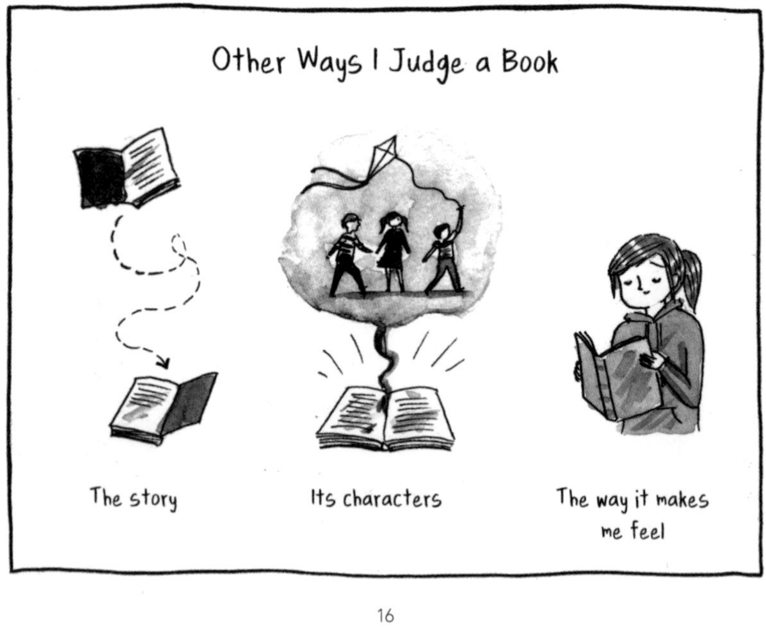
Other Ways I Judge a Book
The story
Its characters
The way it makes me feel

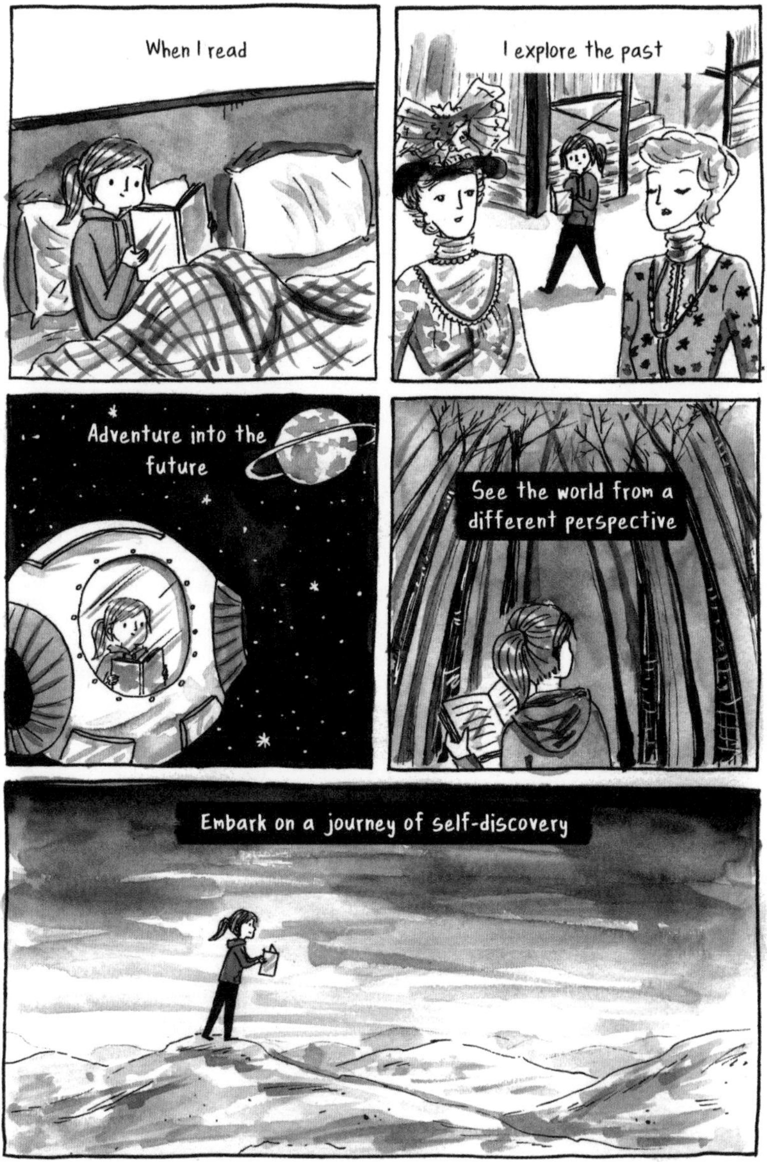
When I read
I explore the past
Adventure into the future
See the world from a different perspective
Embark on a journey of self-discovery

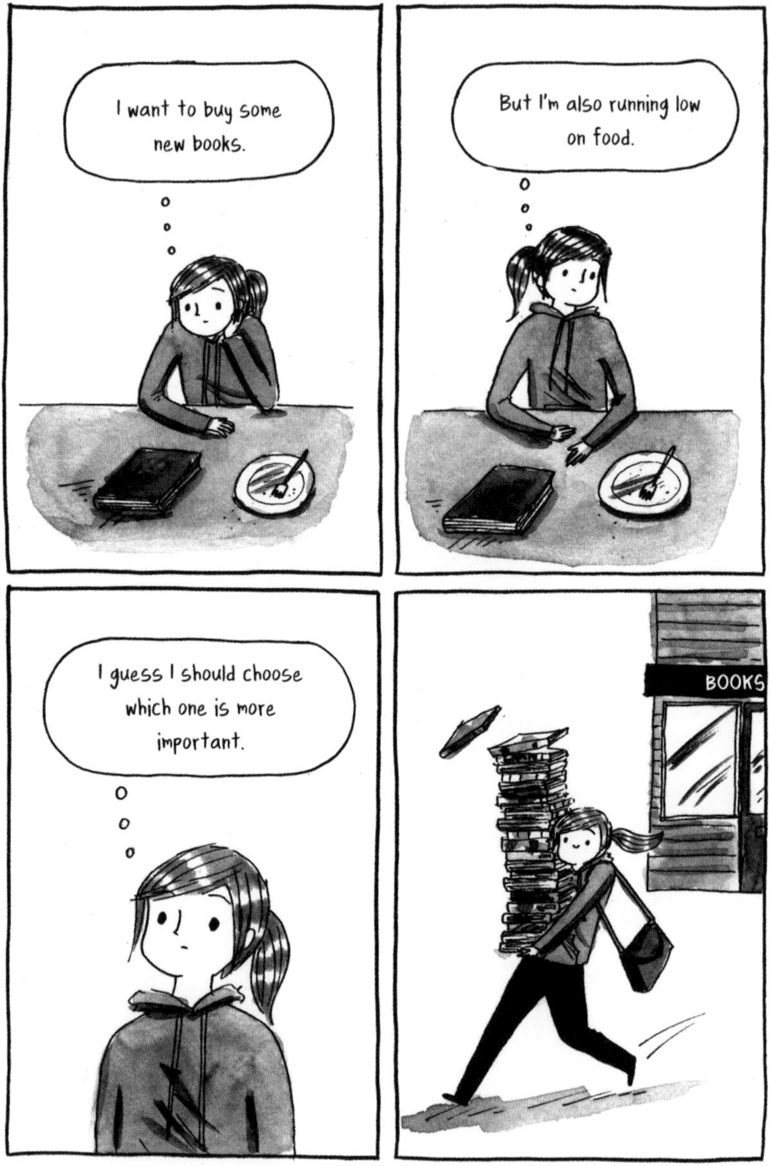
I want to buy some new books.
But I'm also running low on food.
I guess I should choose which one is more important.
BOOKS

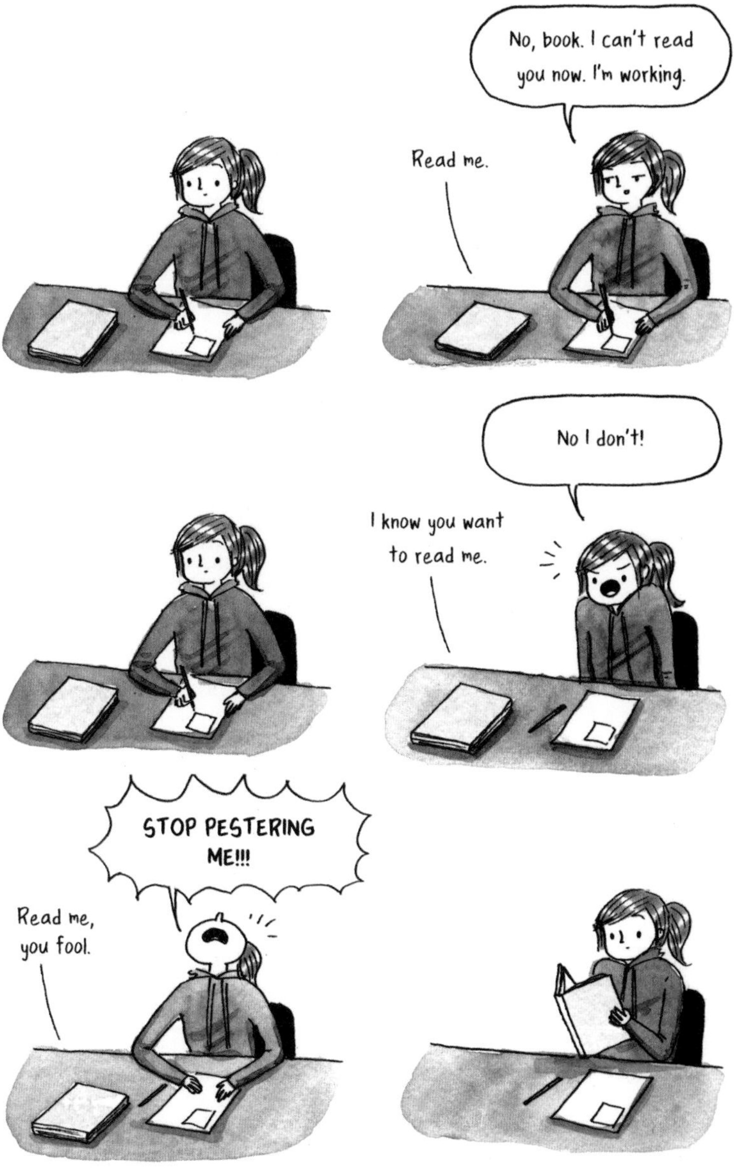
No, book. I can't read you now. I'm working.
Read me.
I know you want to read me.
No I don't!
STOP PESTERING ME!!!
Read me, you fool.

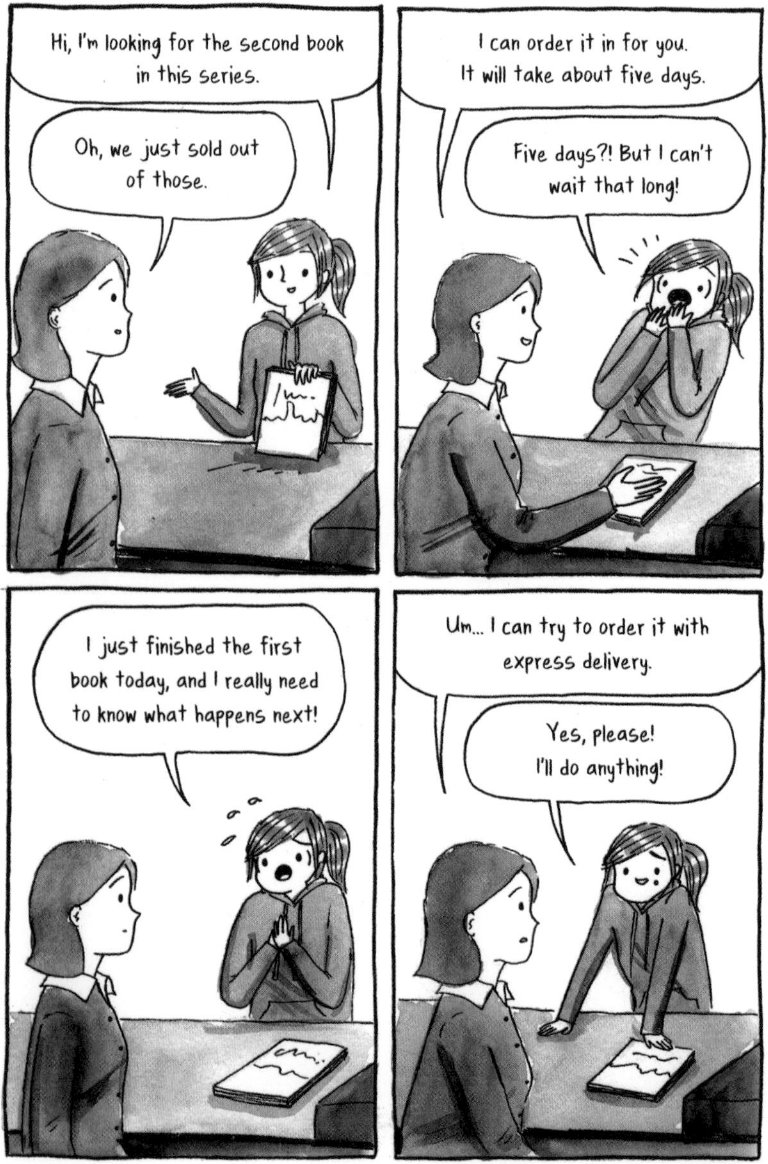
Hi, I'm looking for the second book in this series.
Oh, we just sold out of those.
I can order it in for you. It will take about five days.
Five days?! But I can't wait that long!
I just finished the first book today, and I really need to know what happens next!
Um... I can try to order it with express delivery.
Yes, please! I'll do anything!

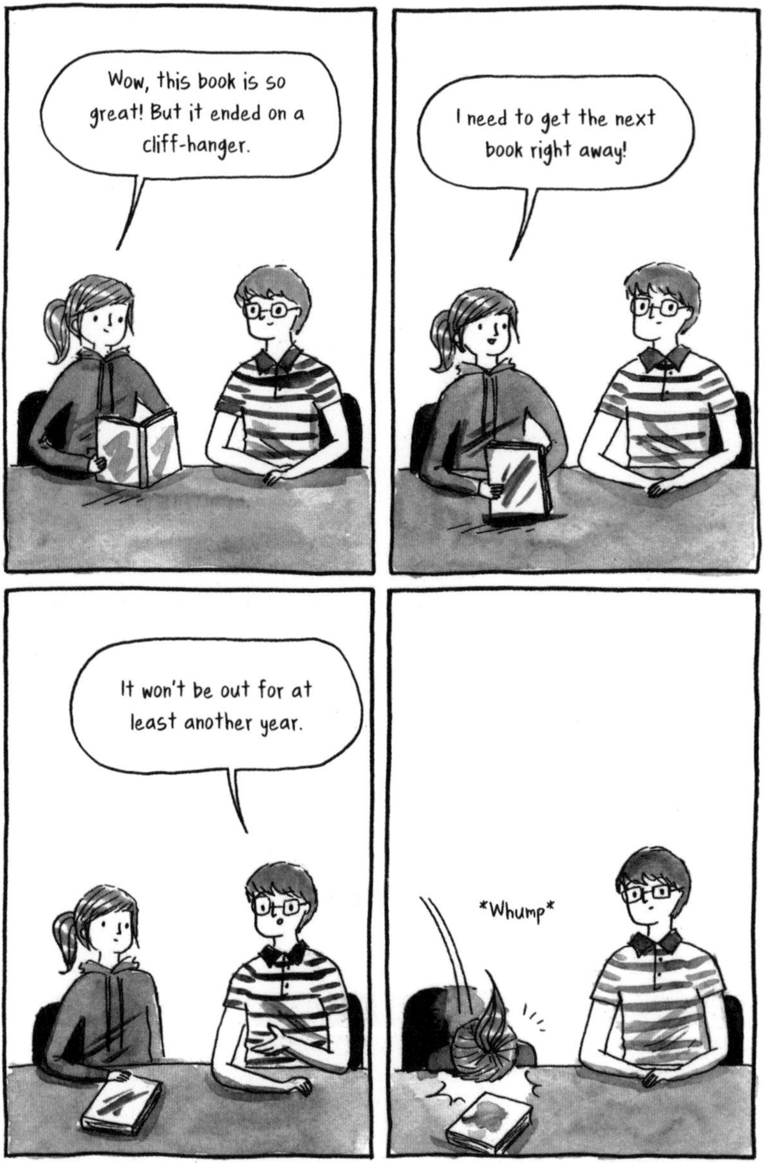
Wow, this book is so great! But it ended on a cliff-hanger.
I need to get the next book right away!
It won't be out for at least another year.
*Whump*

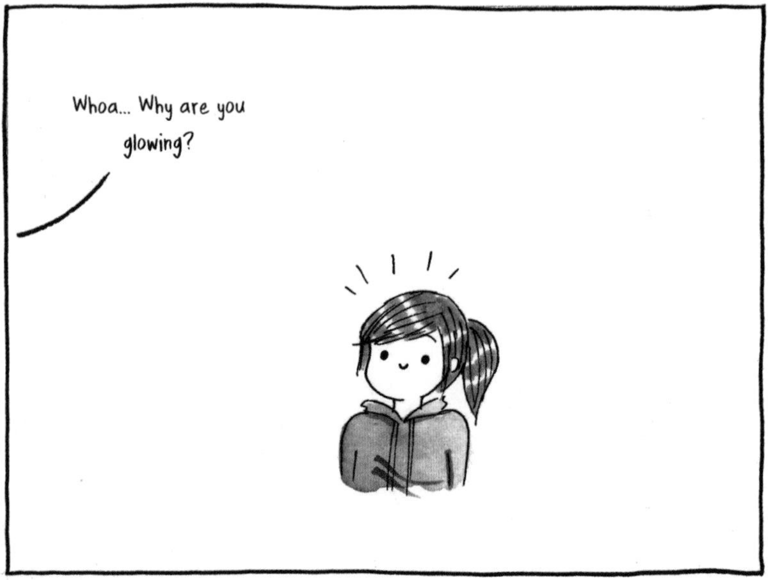
Whoa... Why are you glowing?

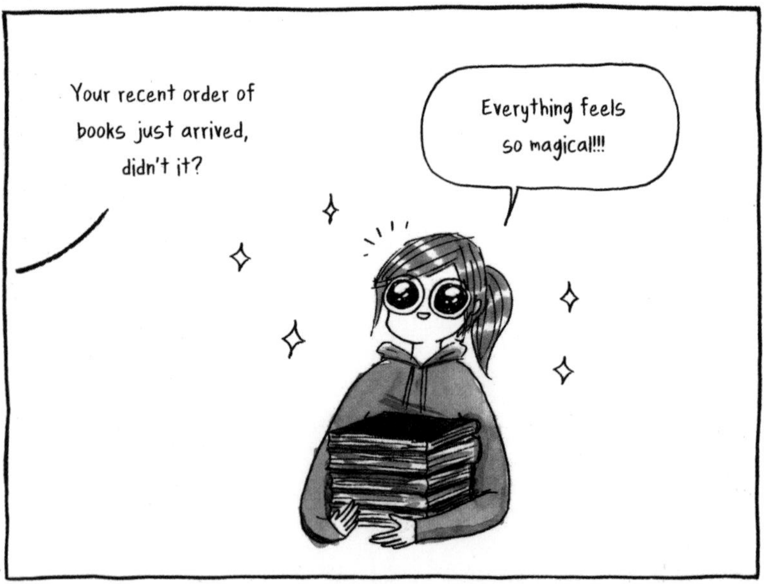
Your recent order of books just arrived, didn't it?
Everything feels so magical!!!

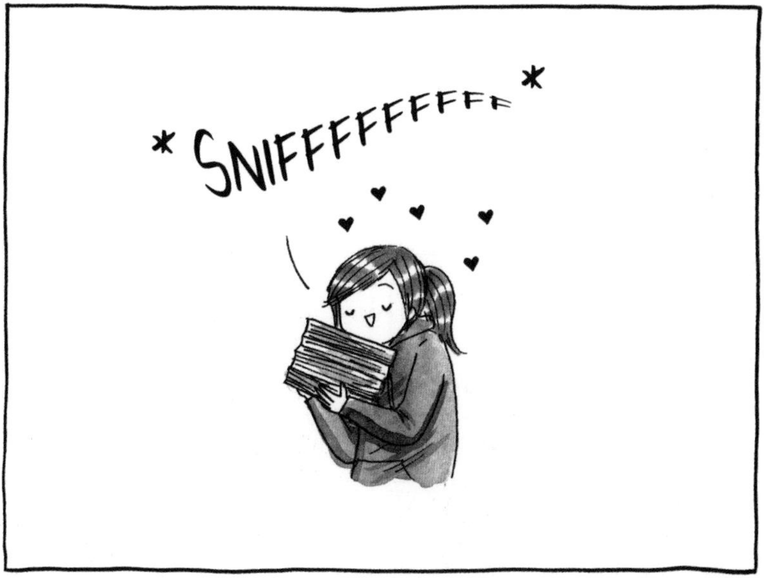
*SNIFFFFFFFFF*

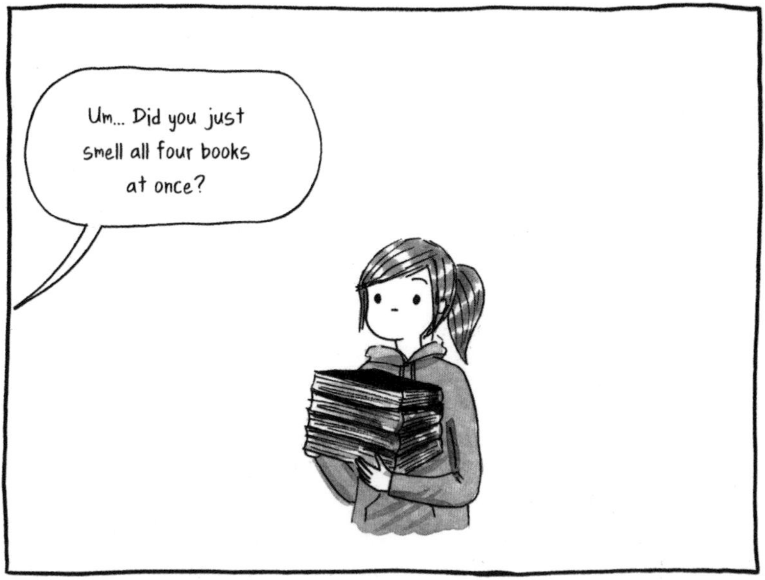
Um... Did you just smell all four books at once?

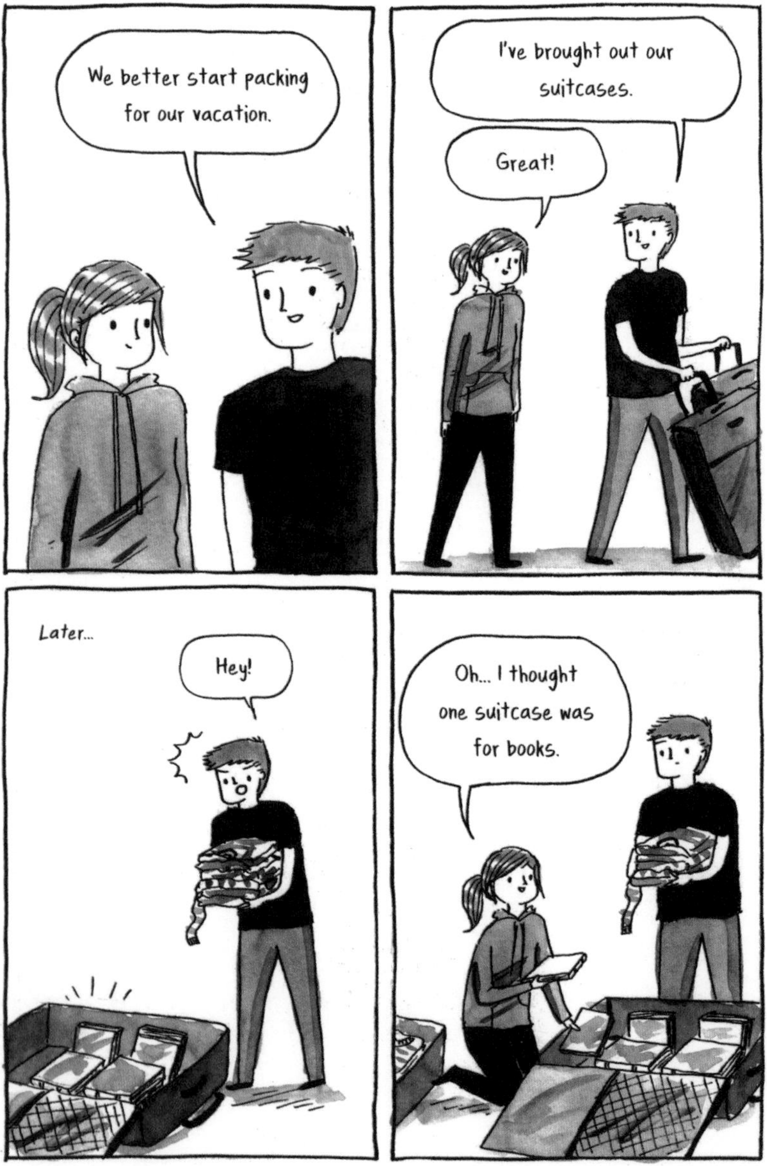
We better start packing for our vacation.
I've brought out our suitcases.
Great!
Later...
Hey!
Oh... I thought one suitcase was for books.

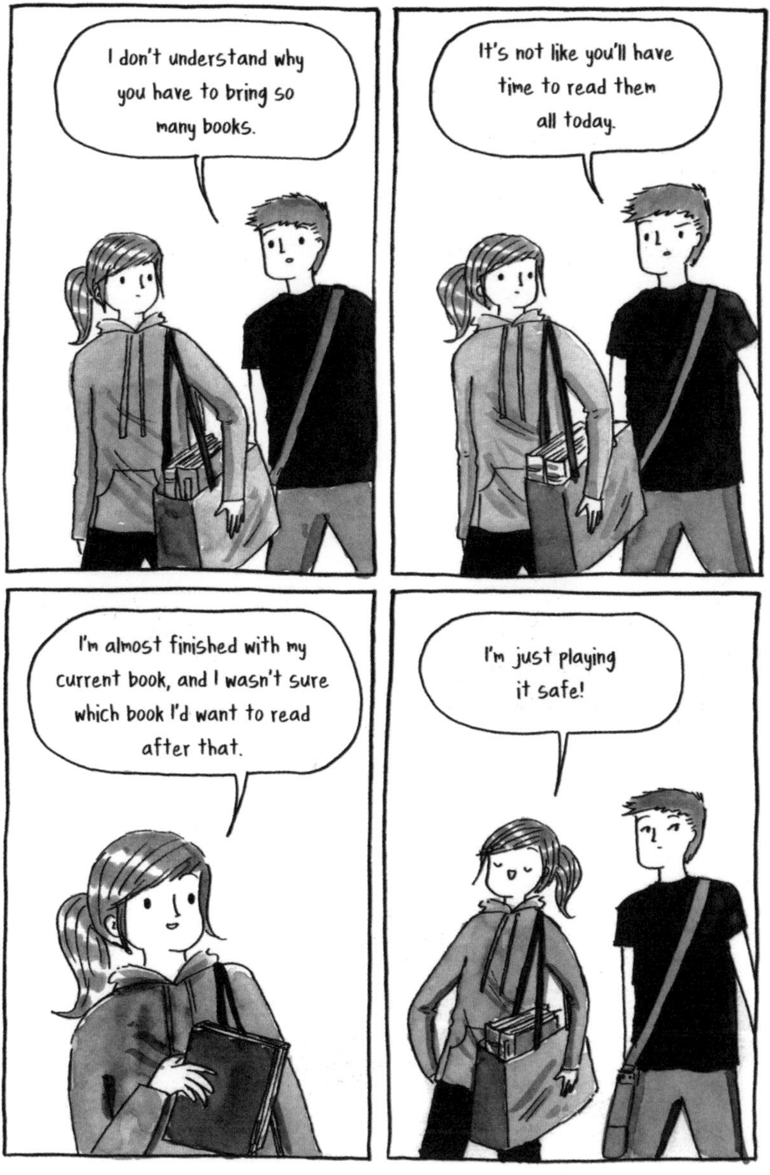
I don't understand why you have to bring so many books.
It's not like you'll have time to read them all today.
I'm almost finished with my current book, and I wasn't sure which book I'd want to read after that.
I'm just playing it safe!

# Some of the Best Places to Read

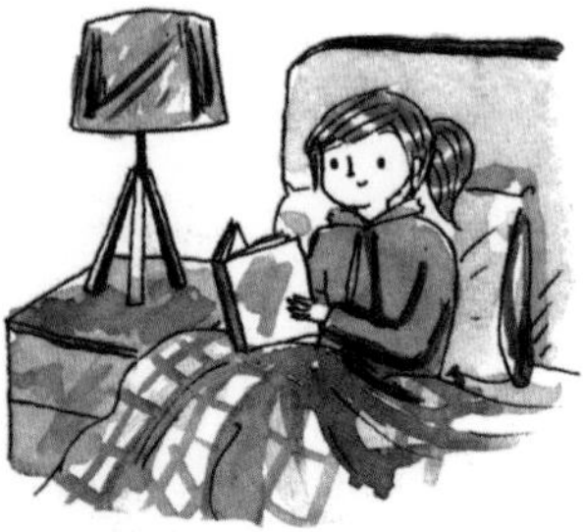

Cozy bed

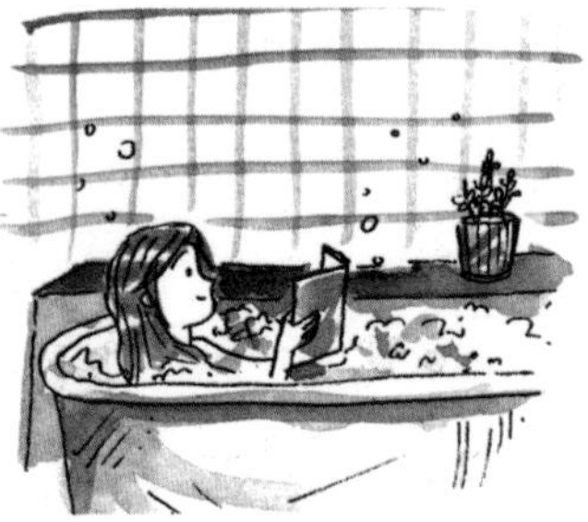

Bathtub

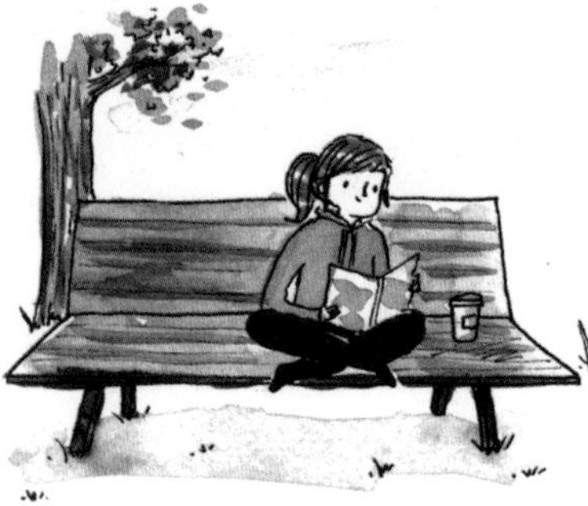

Park

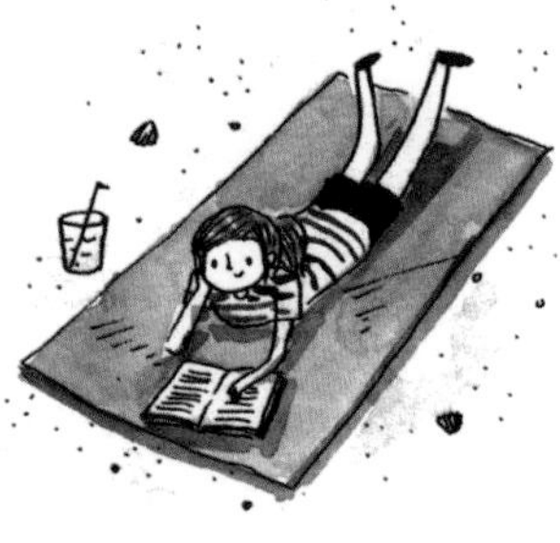

Beach

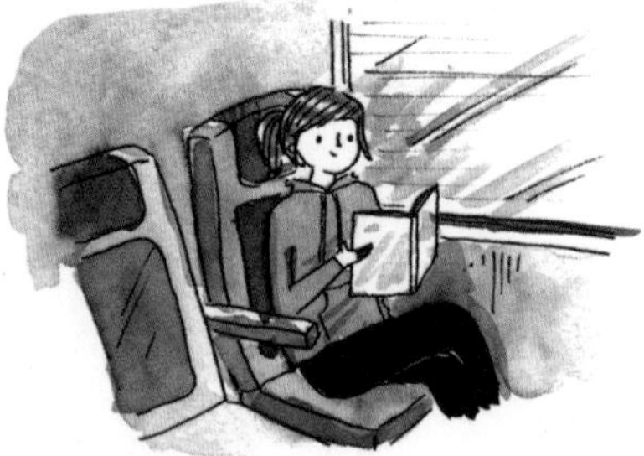

Public transportation

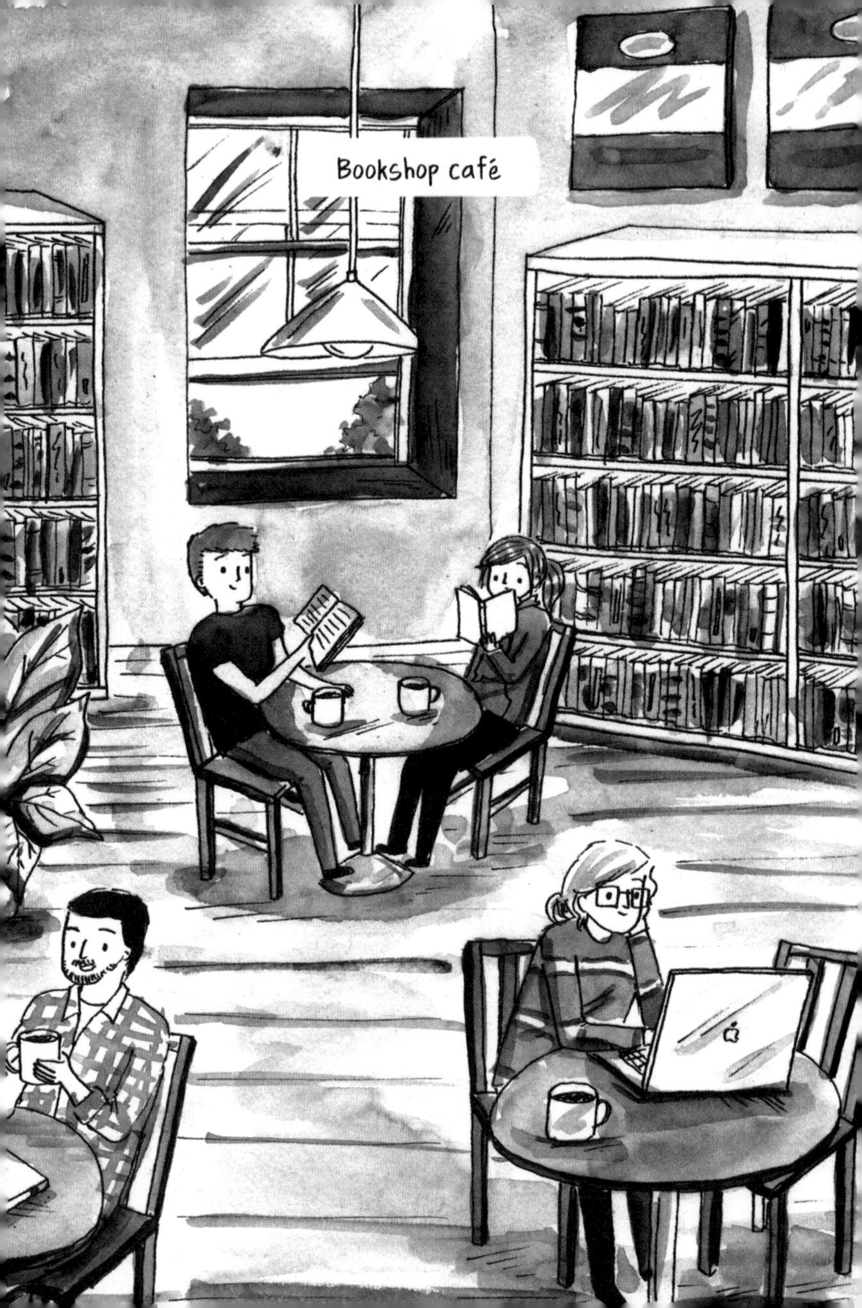
Bookshop café

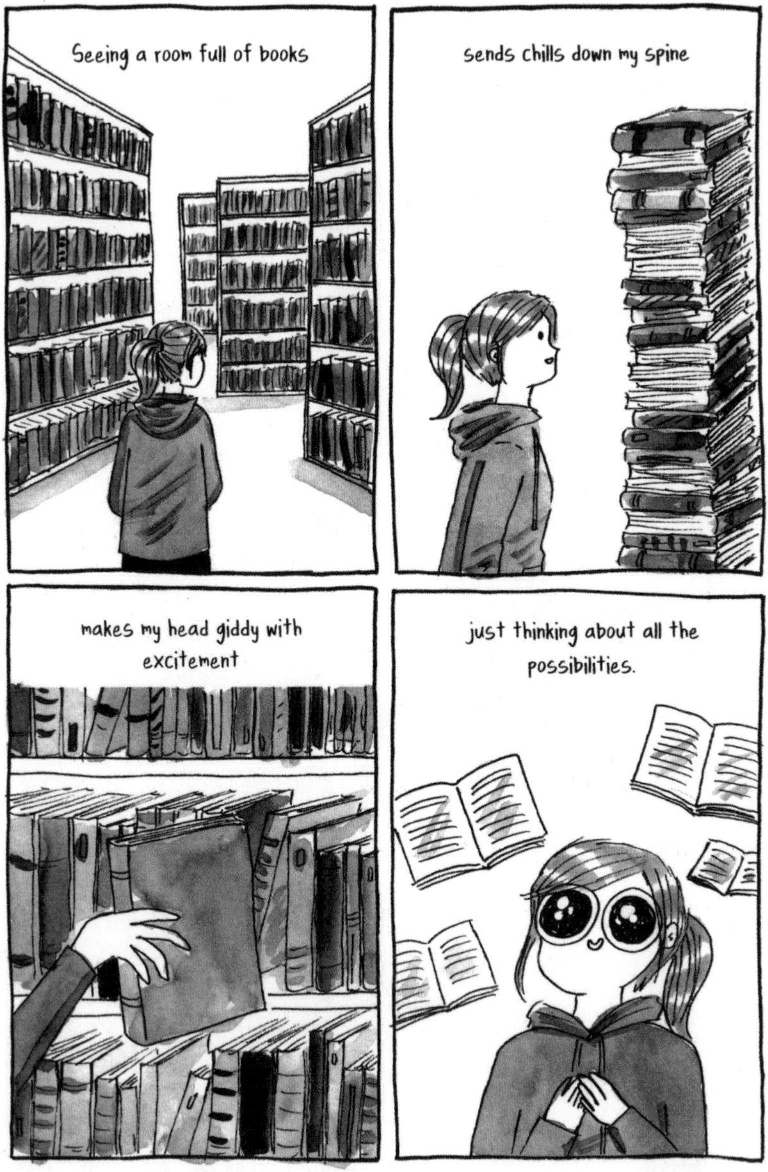
Seeing a room full of books
sends chills down my spine
makes my head giddy with excitement
just thinking about all the possibilities.

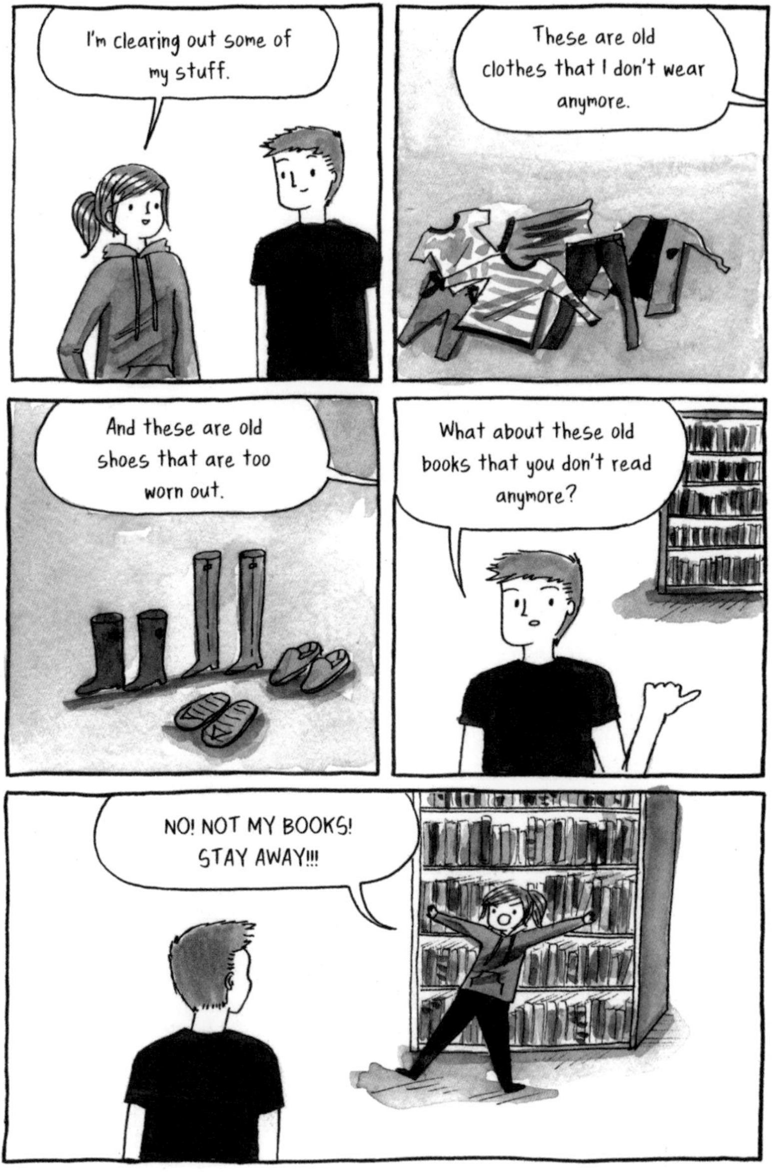
I'm clearing out some of my stuff.
These are old clothes that I don't wear anymore.
And these are old shoes that are too worn out.
What about these old books that you don't read anymore?
NO! NOT MY BOOKS! STAY AWAY!!!

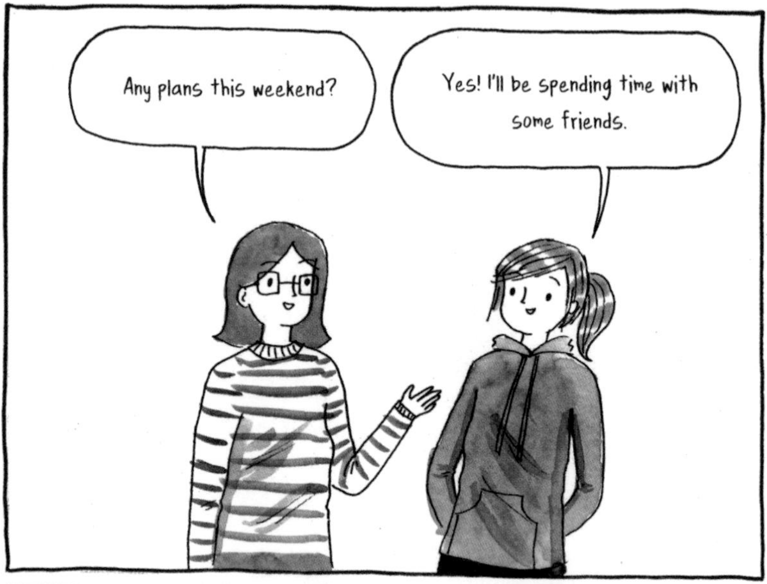
Any plans this weekend?
Yes! I'll be spending time with some friends.

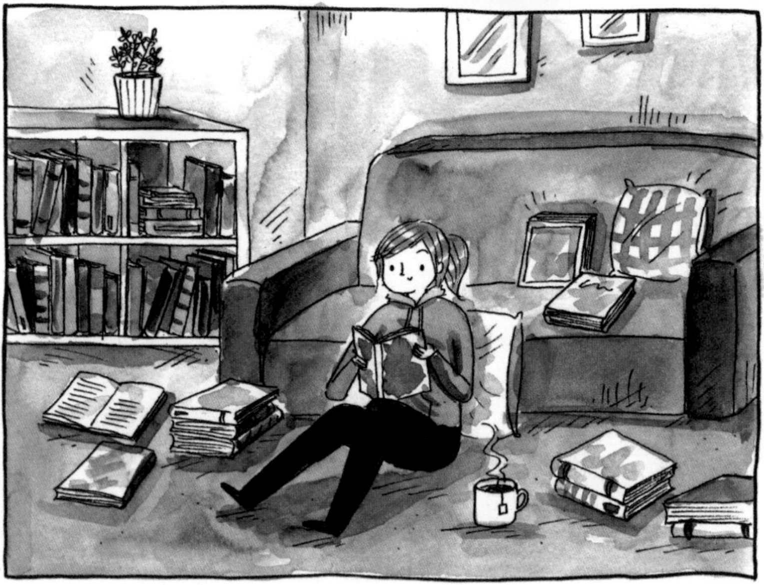

Books

Tea

= Perfect Weekend

# Why I Read

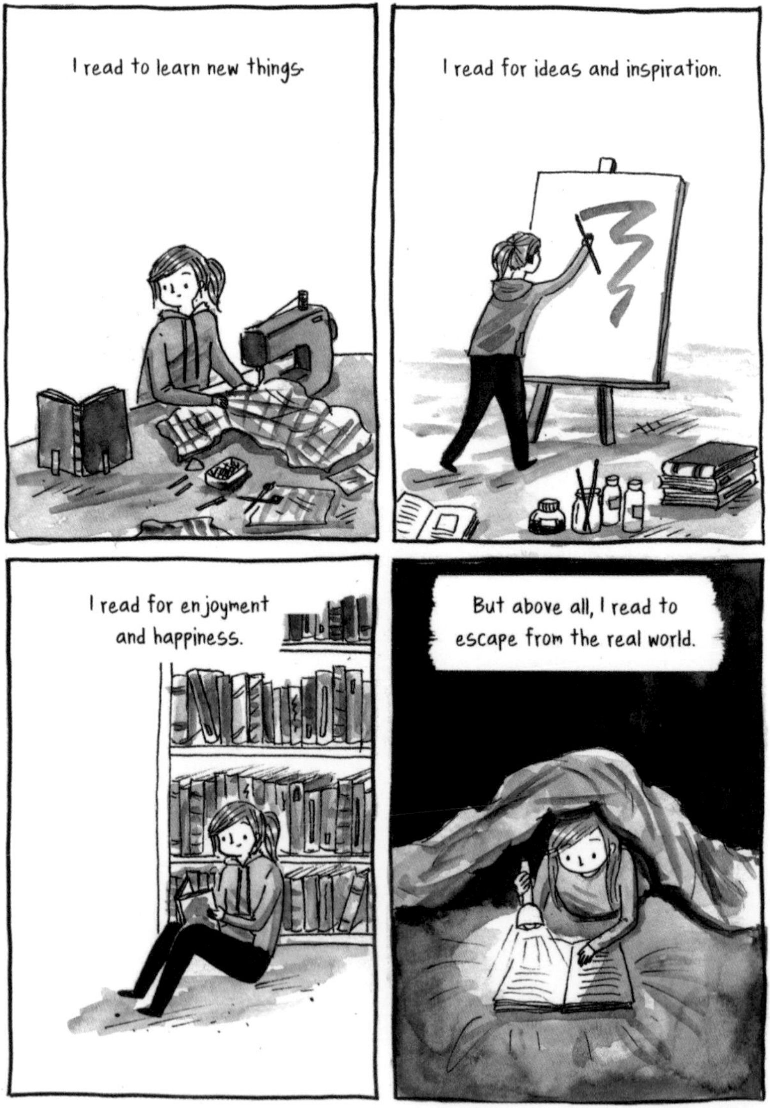
I read to learn new things.
I read for ideas and inspiration.
I read for enjoyment and happiness.
But above all, I read to escape from the real world.

# Things Books Have Taught Me

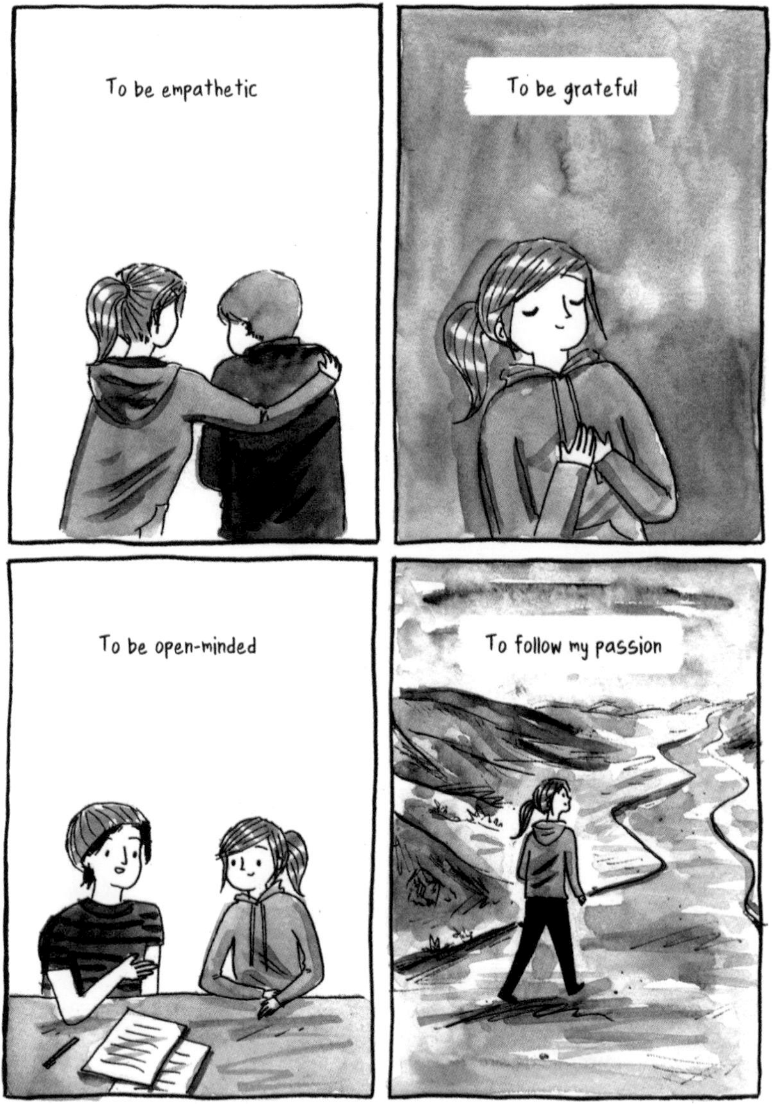
To be empathetic
To be grateful
To be open-minded
To follow my passion

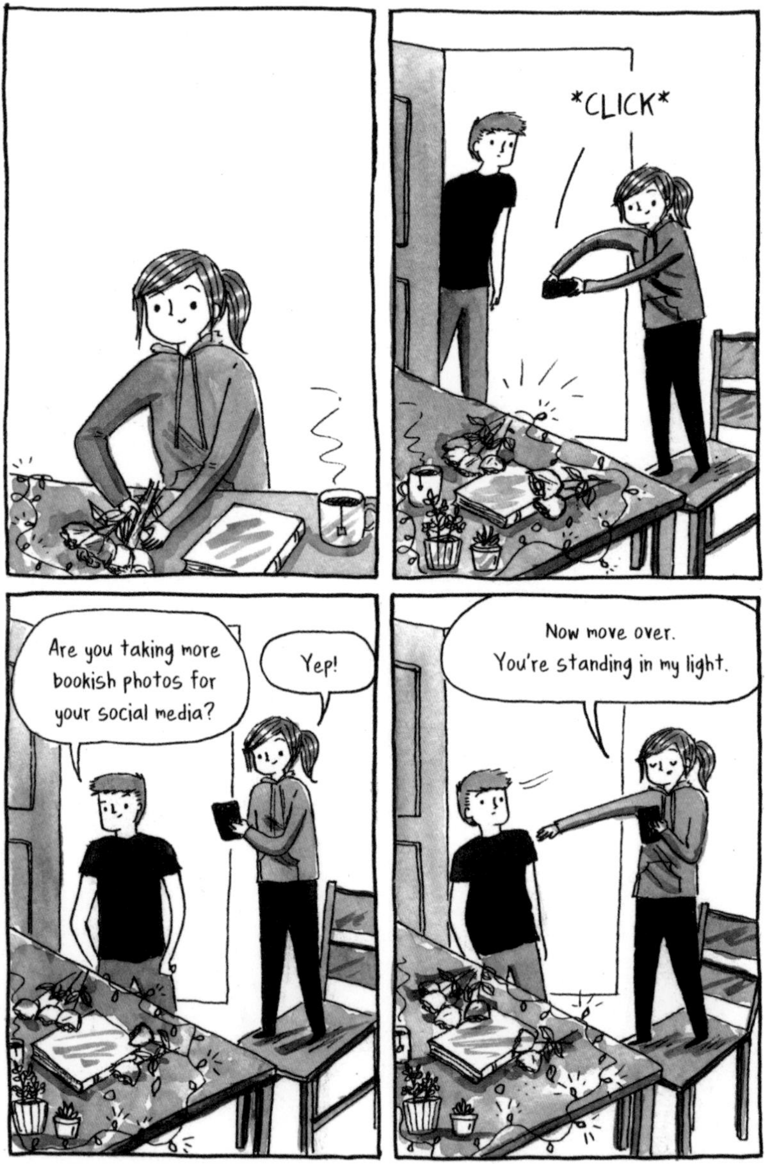
*CLICK*
Are you taking more bookish photos for your social media?
Yep!
Now move over. You're standing in my light.

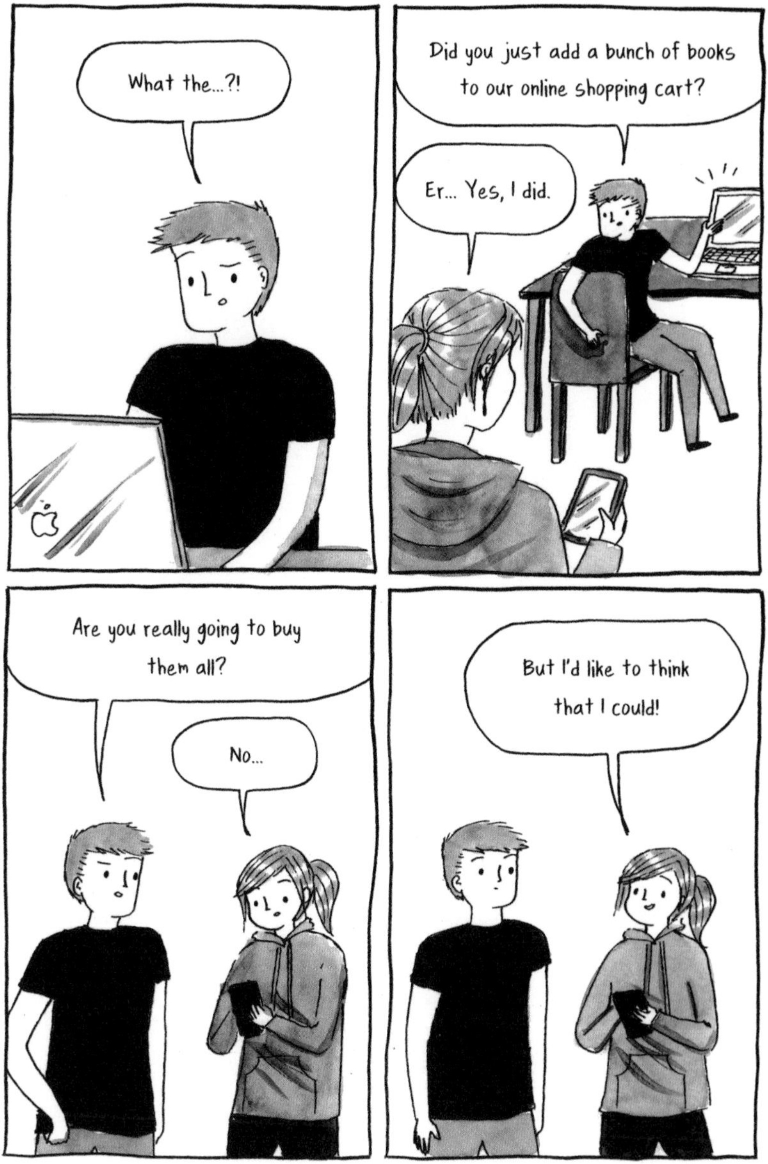
What the...?!
Did you just add a bunch of books to our online shopping cart?
Er... Yes, I did.
Are you really going to buy them all?
No...
But I'd like to think that I could!

# A Bookworm's Essentials

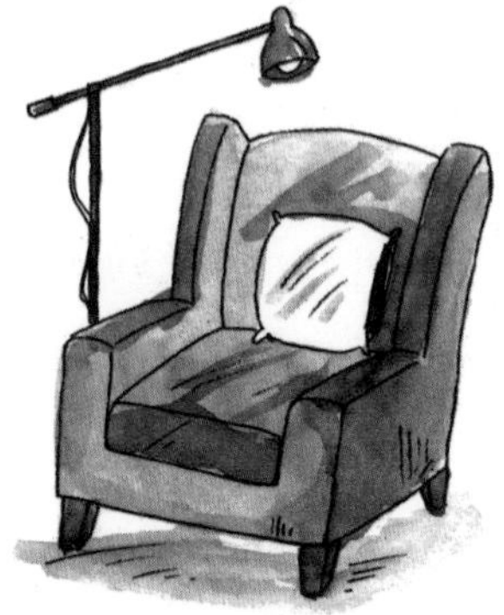

Comfortable reading chair

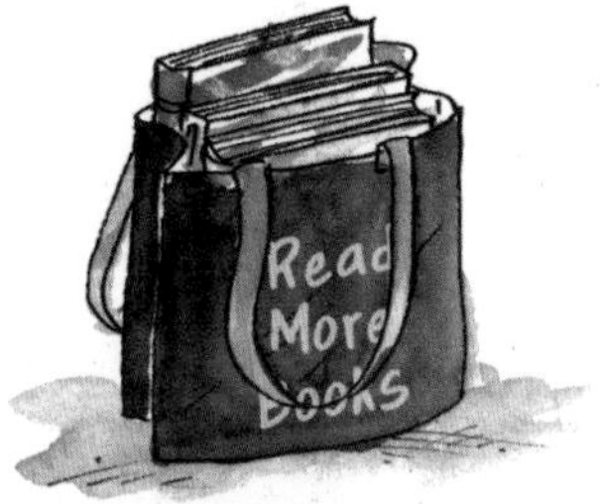
Read
More
Books

Bag big enough for books

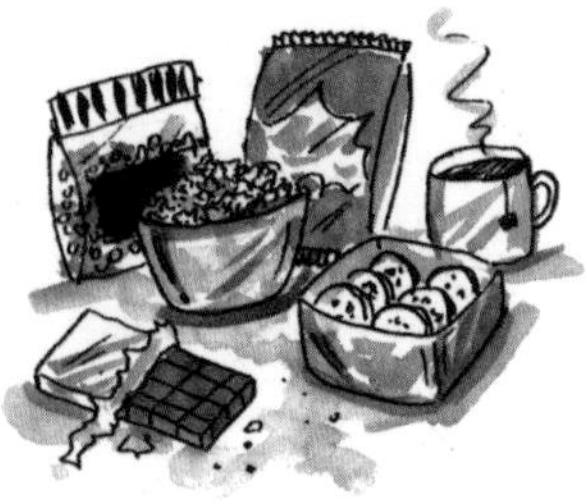

Adequate snacks for long periods of reading

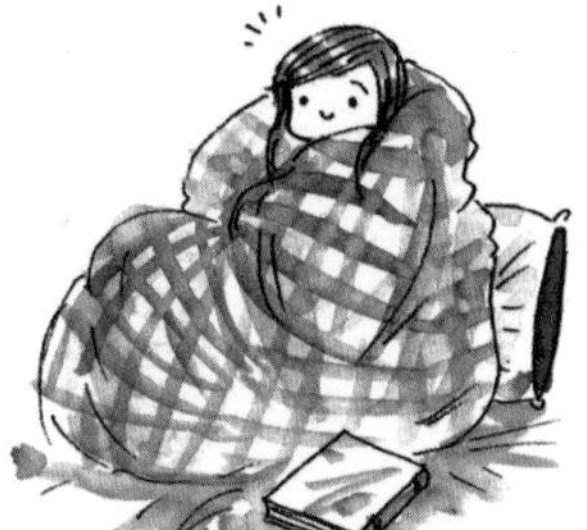

Warm, snuggly blanket

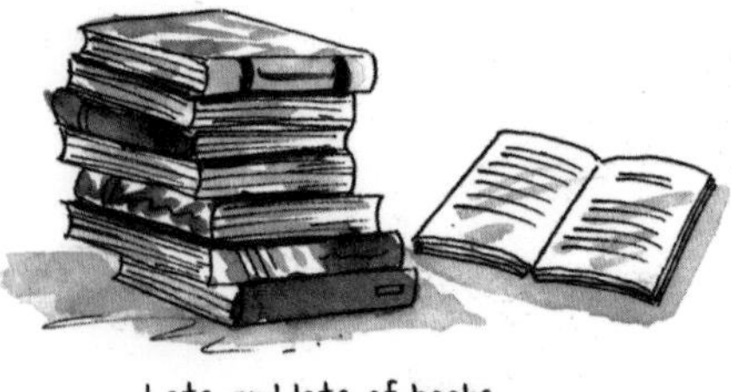

Lots and lots of books

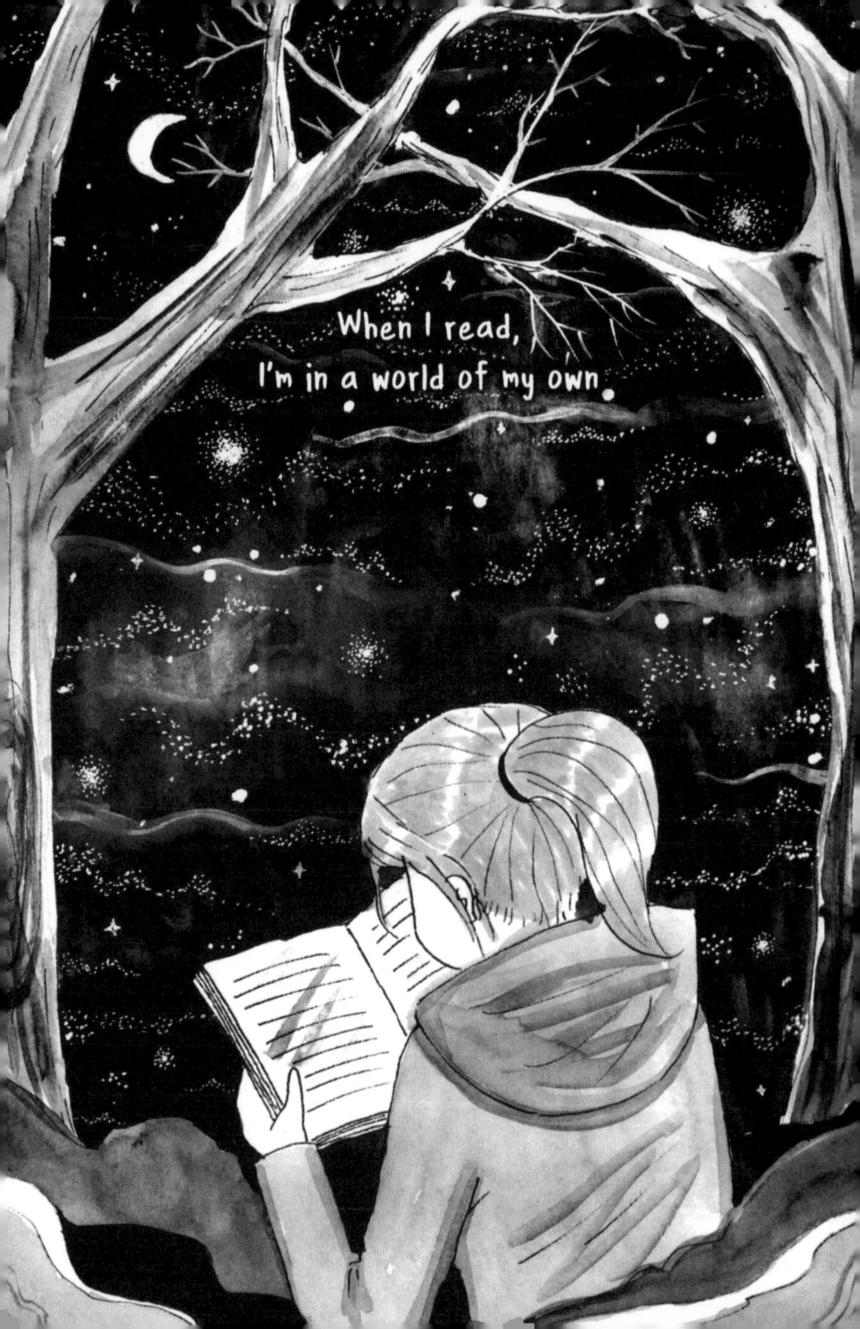
When I read,
I'm in a world of my own.

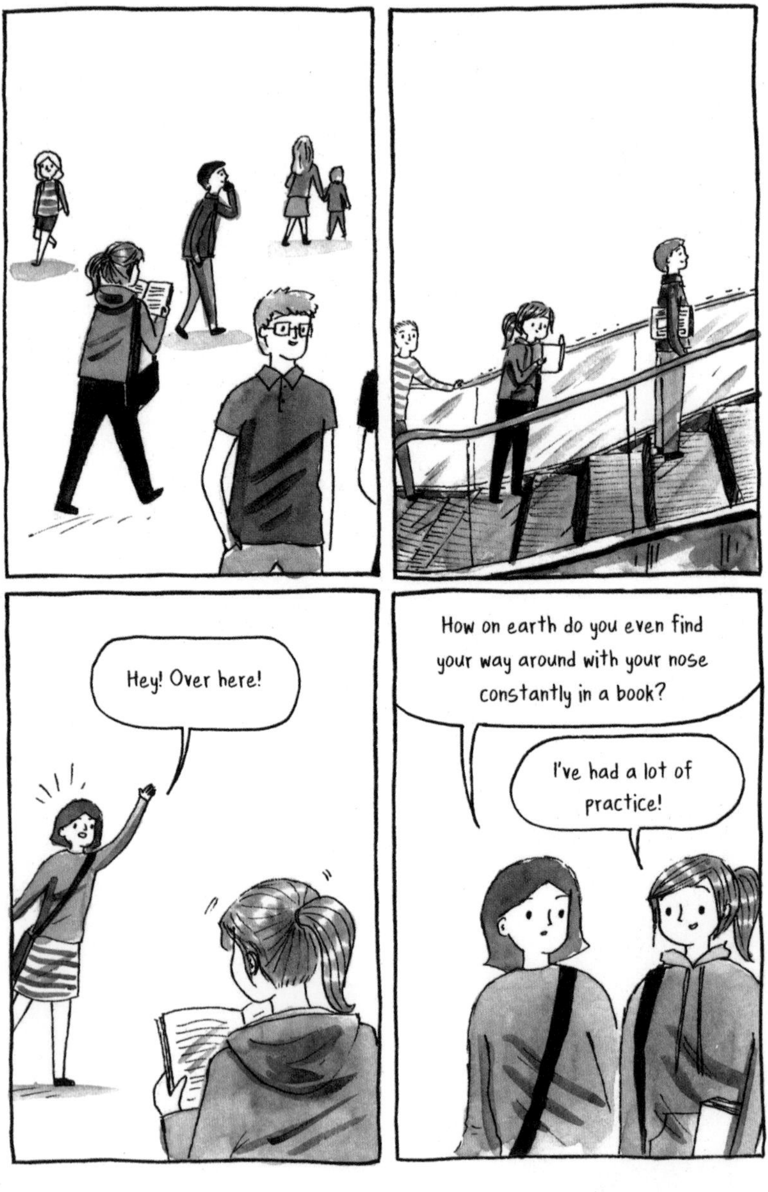
Hey! Over here!
How on earth do you even find your way around with your nose constantly in a book?
I've had a lot of practice!

Places Where I Browse for Books

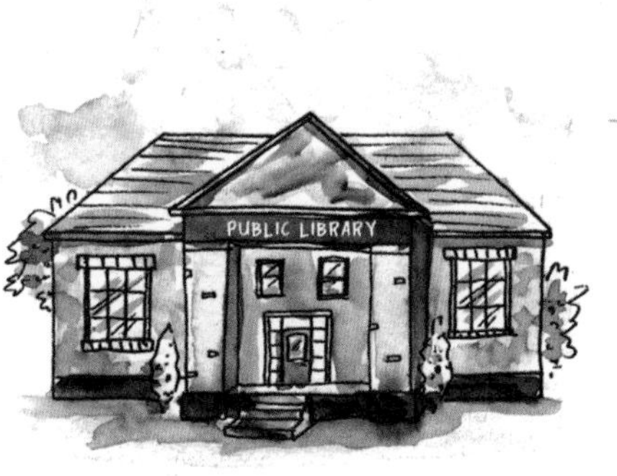
PUBLIC LIBRARY

Library

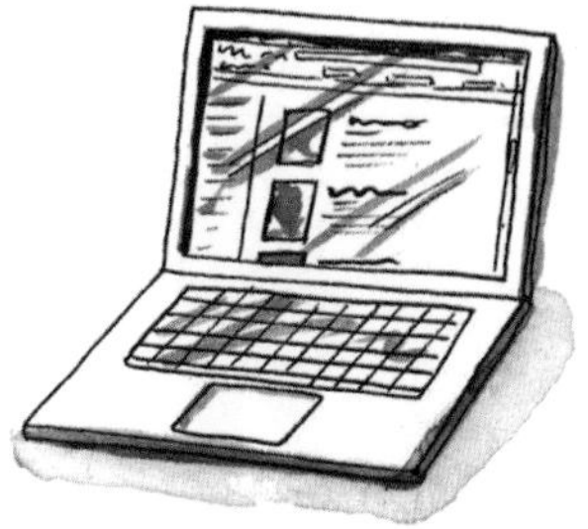

Online stores

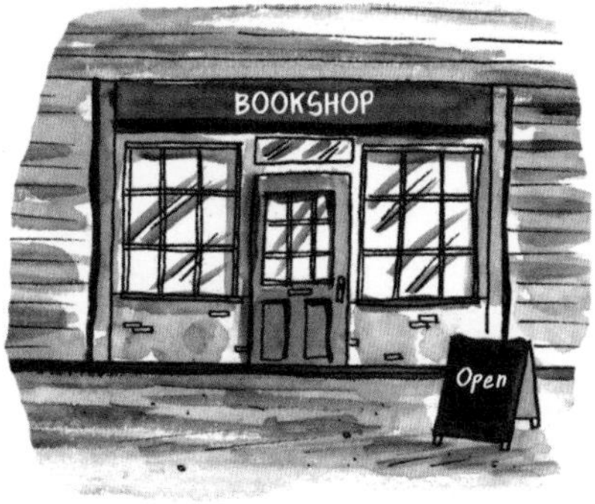
BOOKSHOP
Open

Local bookshop

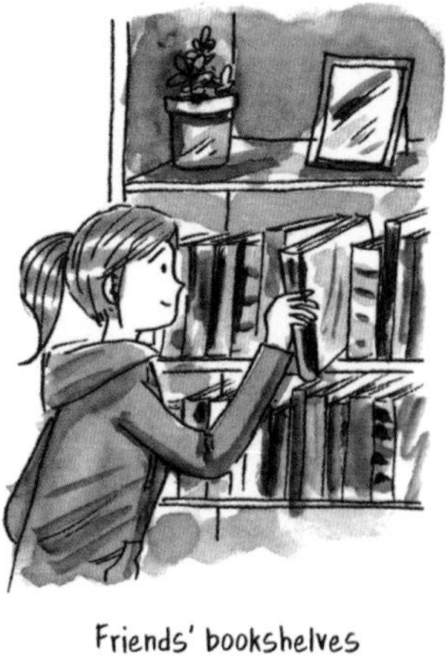

Friends' bookshelves

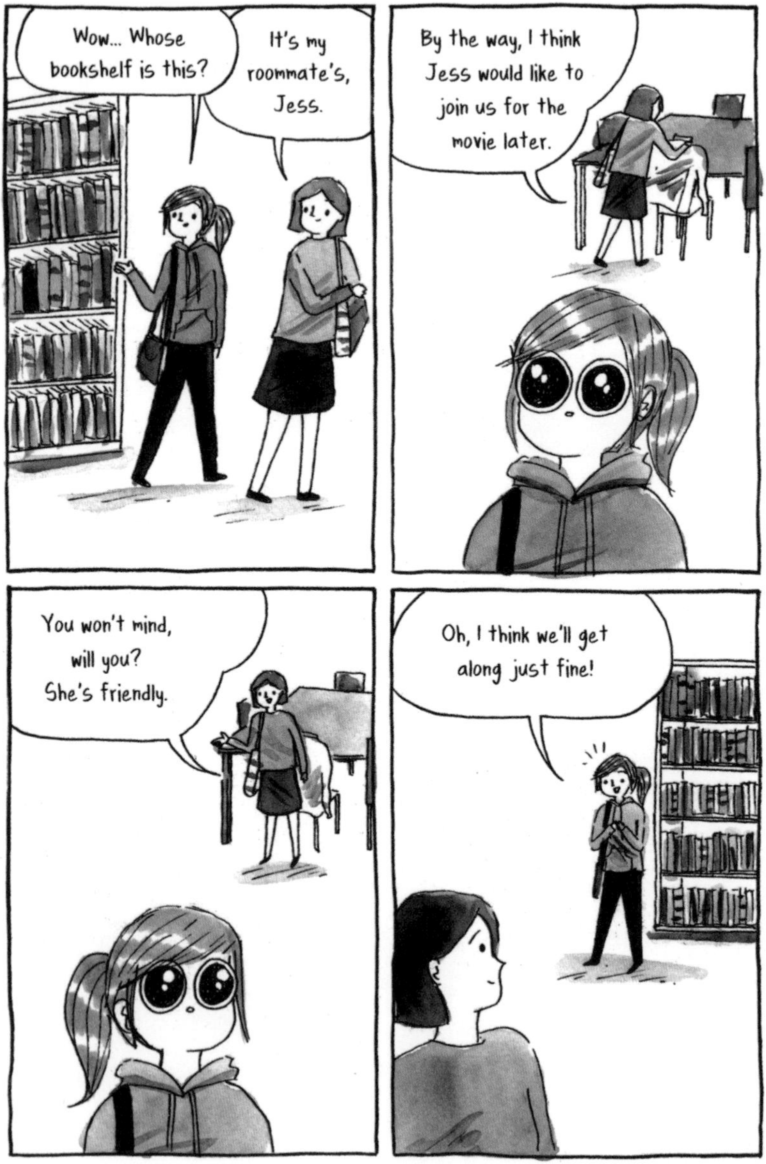
Wow... Whose bookshelf is this?
It's my roommate's, Jess.
By the way, I think Jess would like to join us for the movie later.
You won't mind, will you? She's friendly.
Oh, I think we'll get along just fine!

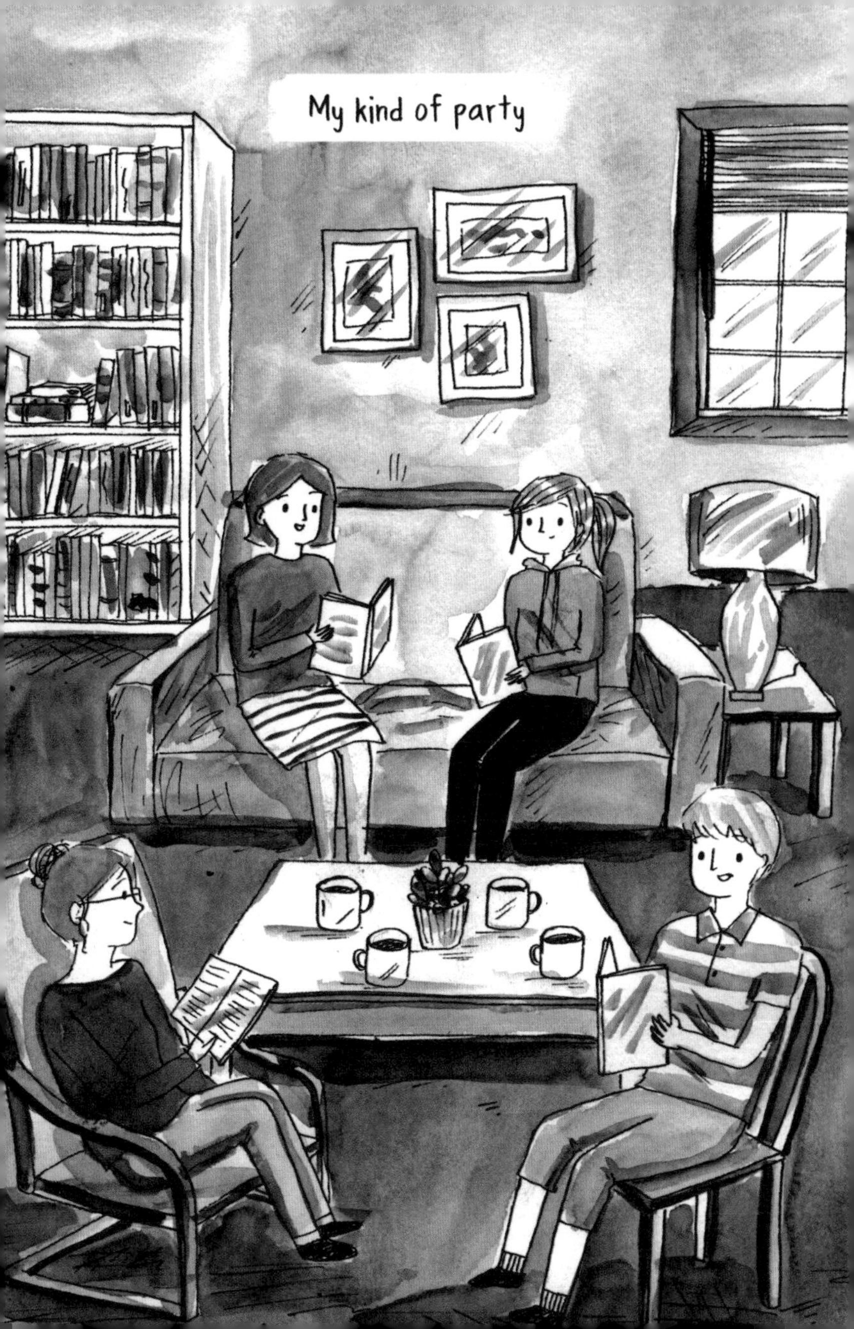
My kind of party

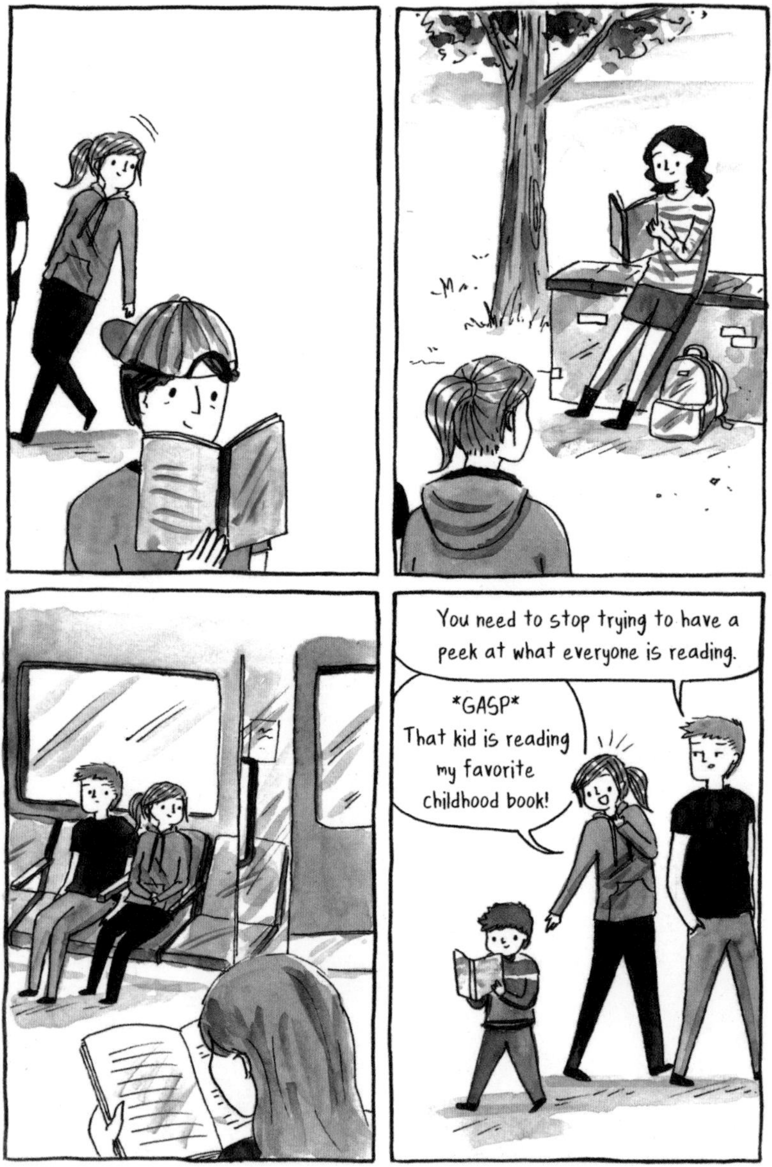
*GASP*
That kid is reading my favorite childhood book!
You need to stop trying to have a peek at what everyone is reading.

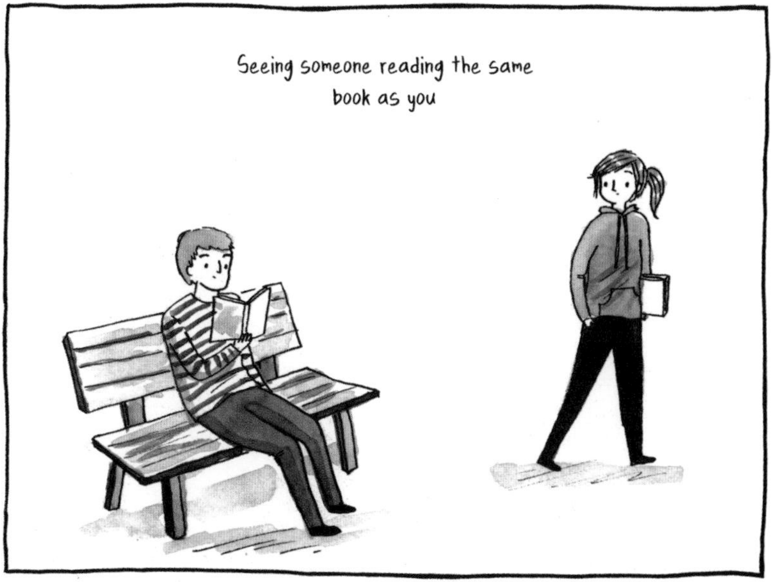
Seeing someone reading the same book as you

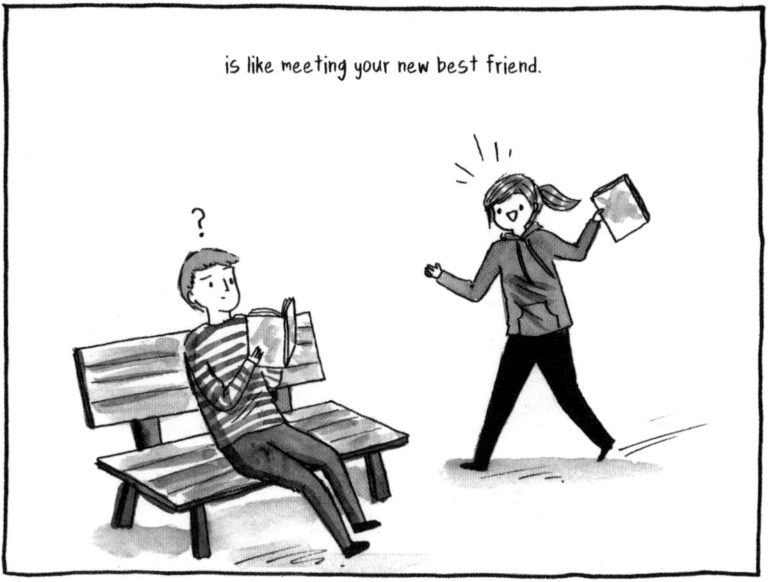
is like meeting your new best friend.
?

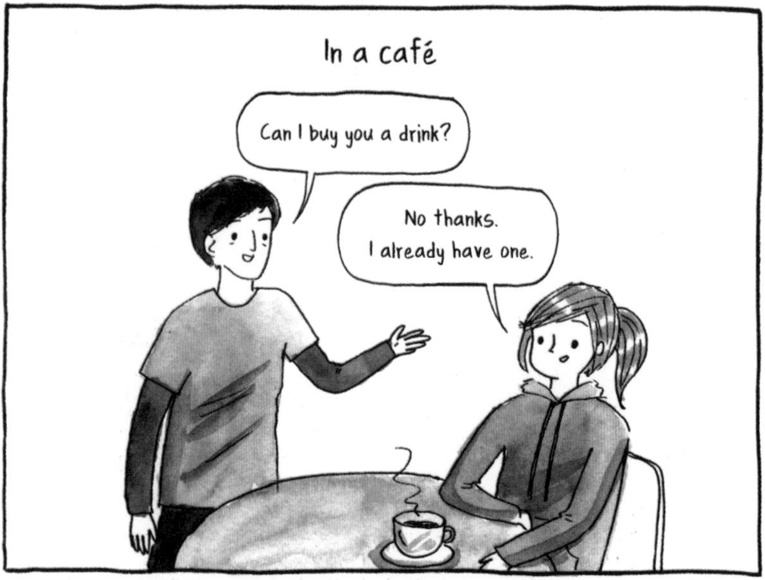
In a café
Can I buy you a drink?
No thanks.
I already have one.

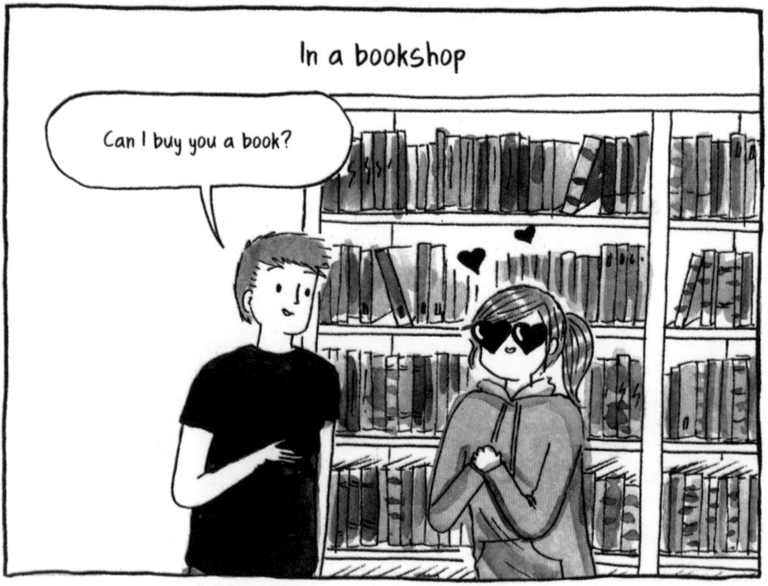
In a bookshop
Can I buy you a book?

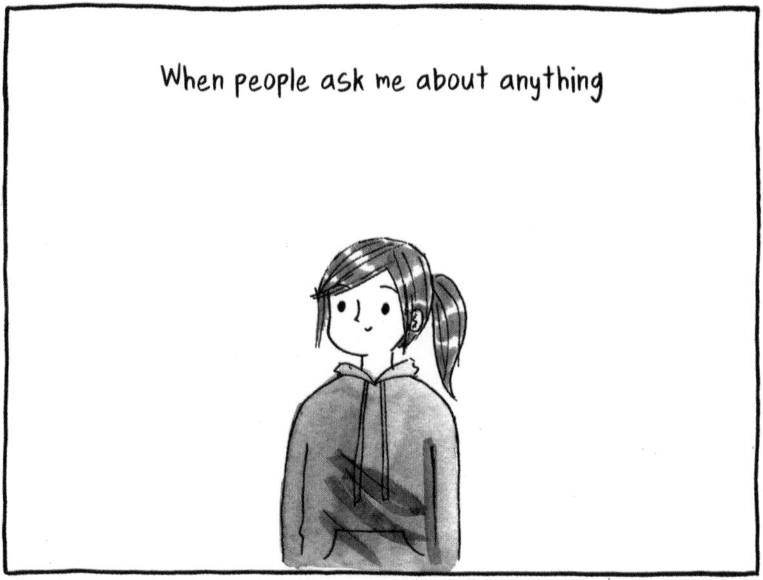
When people ask me about anything

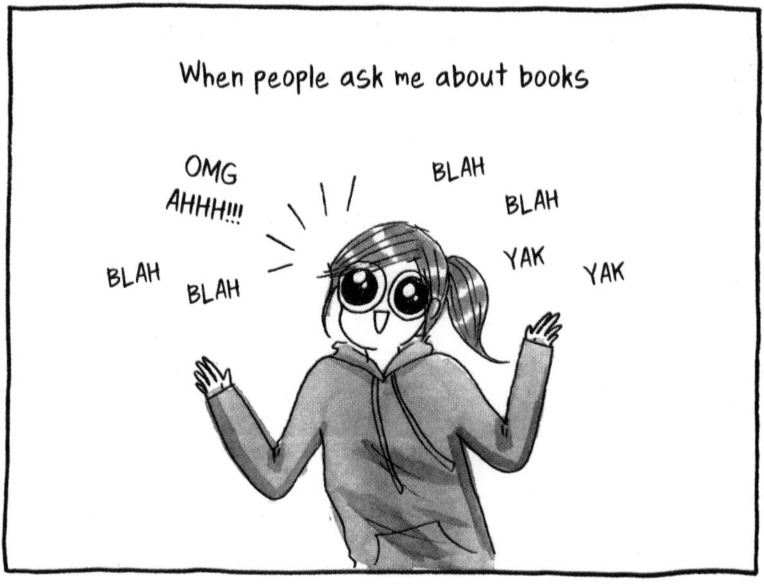
When people ask me about books
OMG AHHH!!!
BLAH
BLAH
BLAH
BLAH
YAK
YAK

# Happiness for Bookworms

Finding the perfect spot
in a café

A book sale

Taking out a fresh stack
of library books

Talking about books
they've read

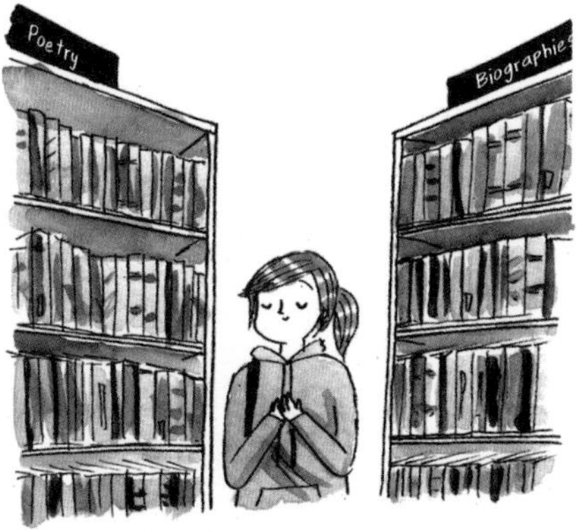
Poetry
Biographie

The intoxicating smell of a bookshop

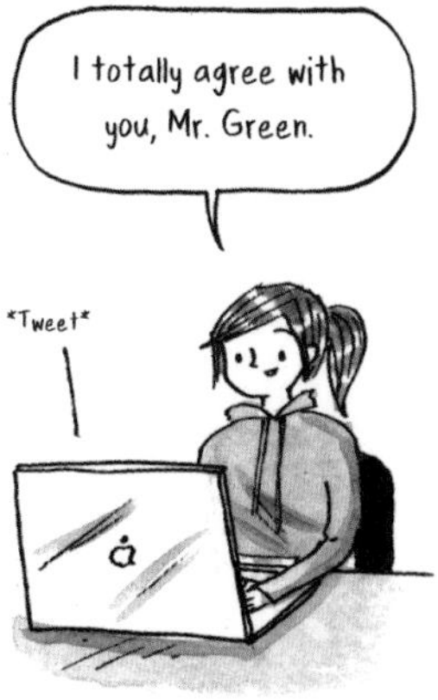
I totally agree with you, Mr. Green.
*Tweet*

Following your favorite authors on social media and acting as if they're your friends

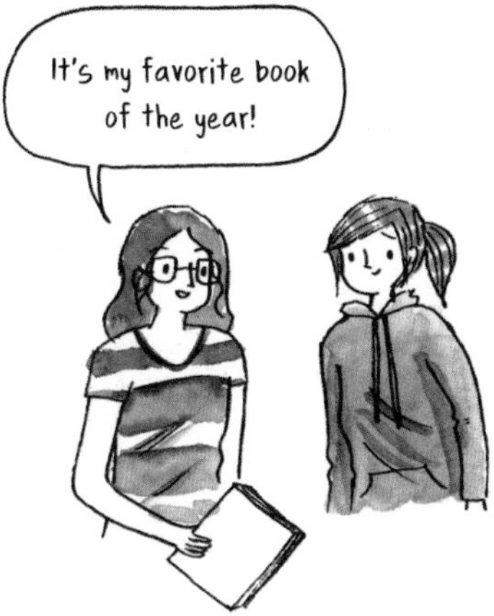
It's my favorite book of the year!

Someone saying they loved a book you recommended

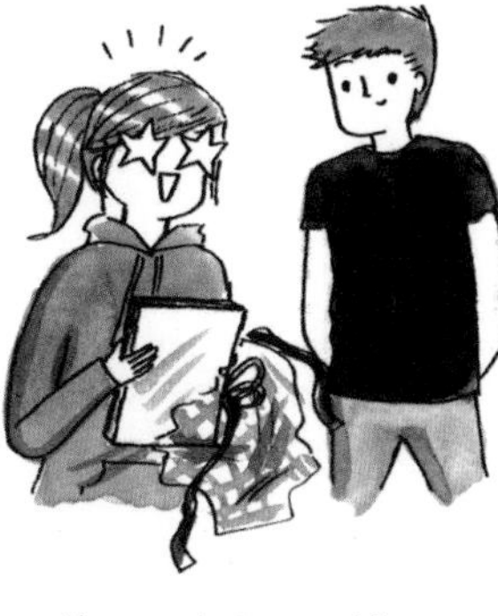

Unexpectedly receiving a gift, and it's the book you always wanted

# Why Books Are the Best Gifts

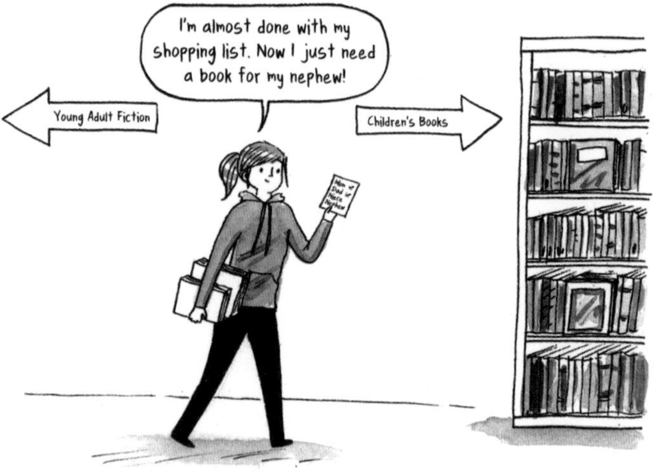
I'm almost done with my shopping list. Now I just need a book for my nephew!
Young Adult Fiction
Children's Books

There is a book for everyone.

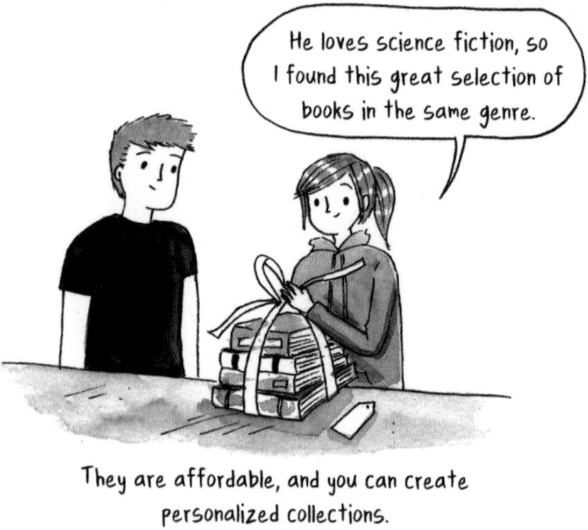
He loves science fiction, so I found this great selection of books in the same genre.

They are affordable, and you can create personalized collections.

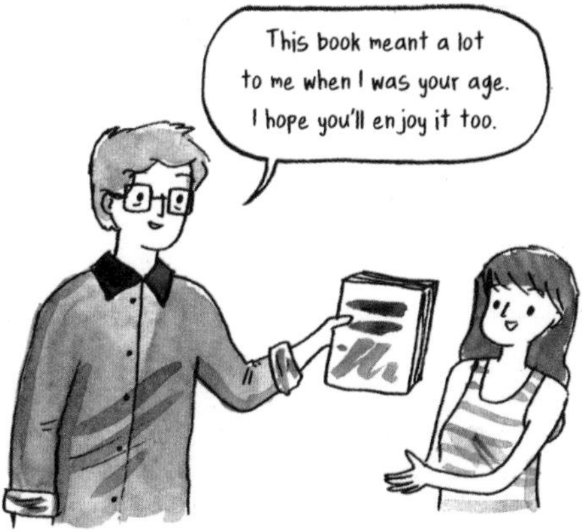
This book meant a lot to me when I was your age. I hope you'll enjoy it too.

Books last a long time. They can be shared or passed on to others to enjoy.

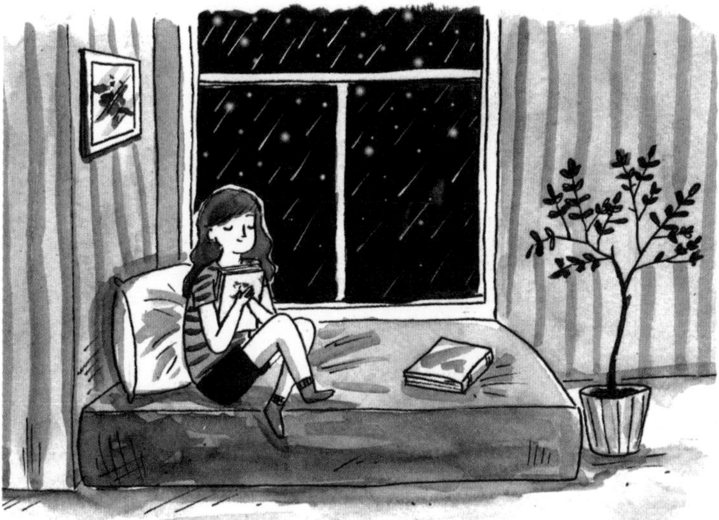

The right book will have stories that stay with the reader forever.

## Where You Can Find Bookshops

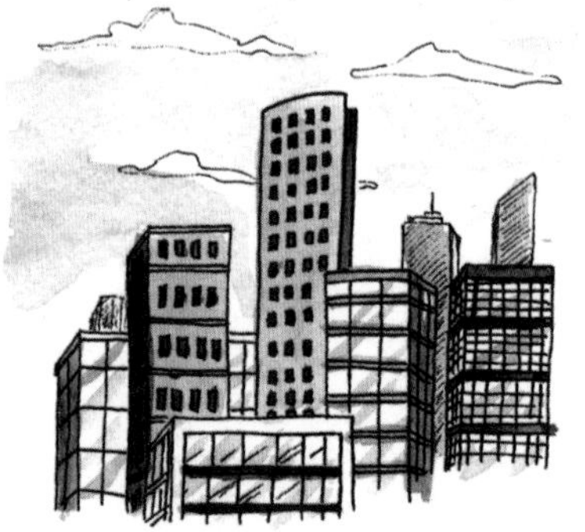

City center

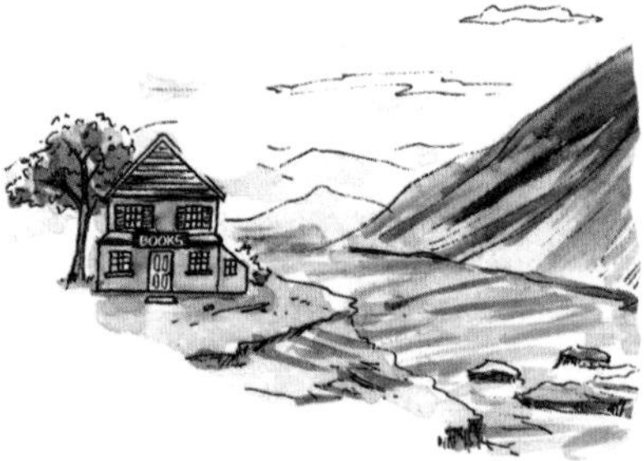
BOOKS

Quiet, remote areas

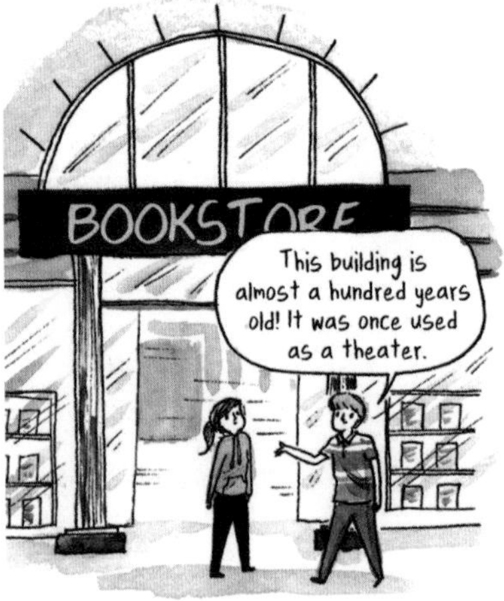
BOOKSTORE
This building is almost a hundred years old! It was once used as a theater.

Converted old buildings

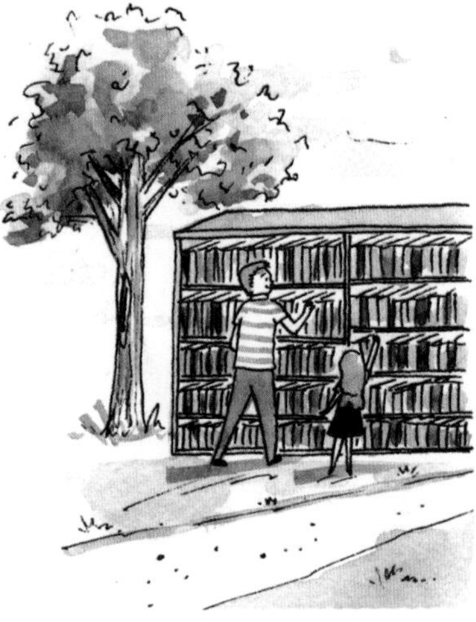

Outdoors

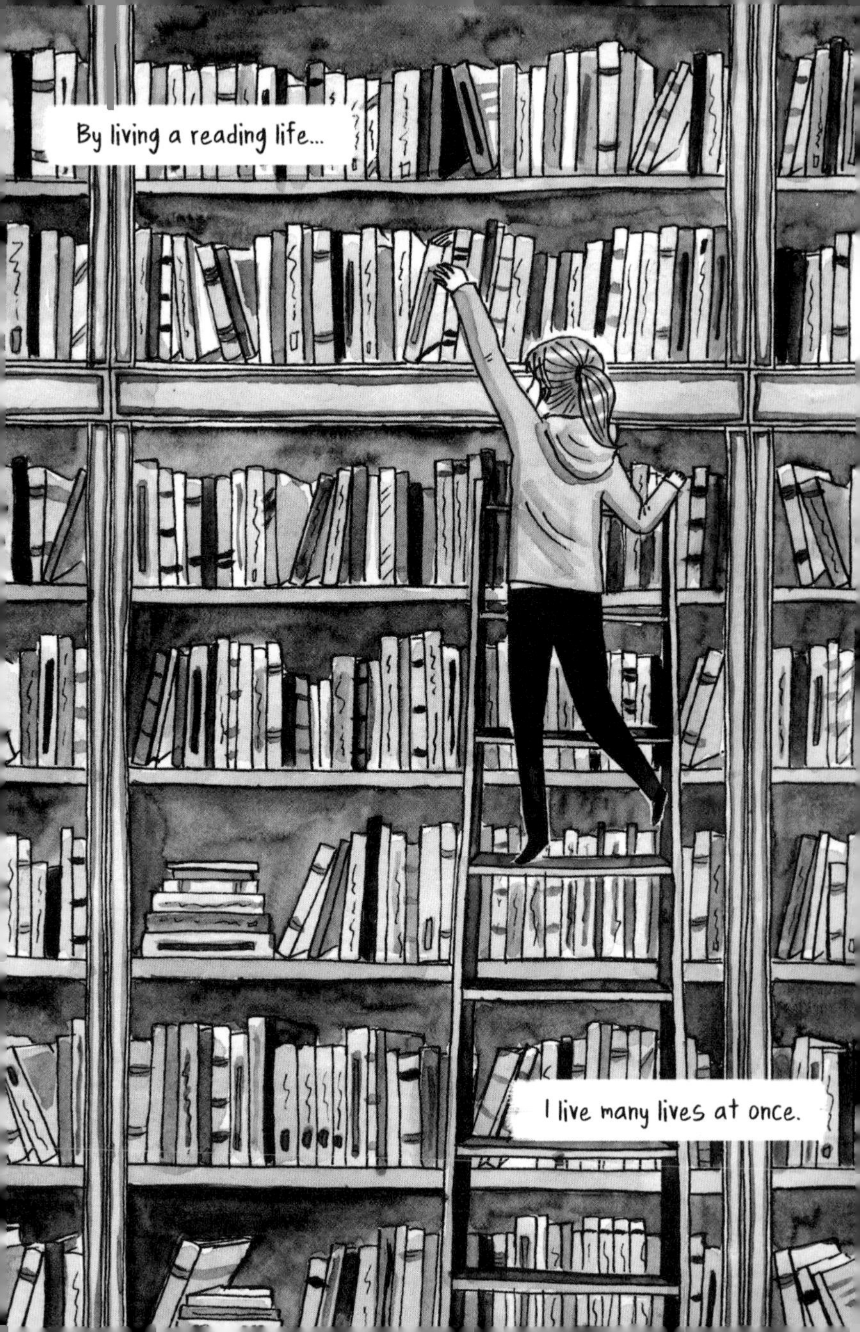
By living a reading life...
I live many lives at once.

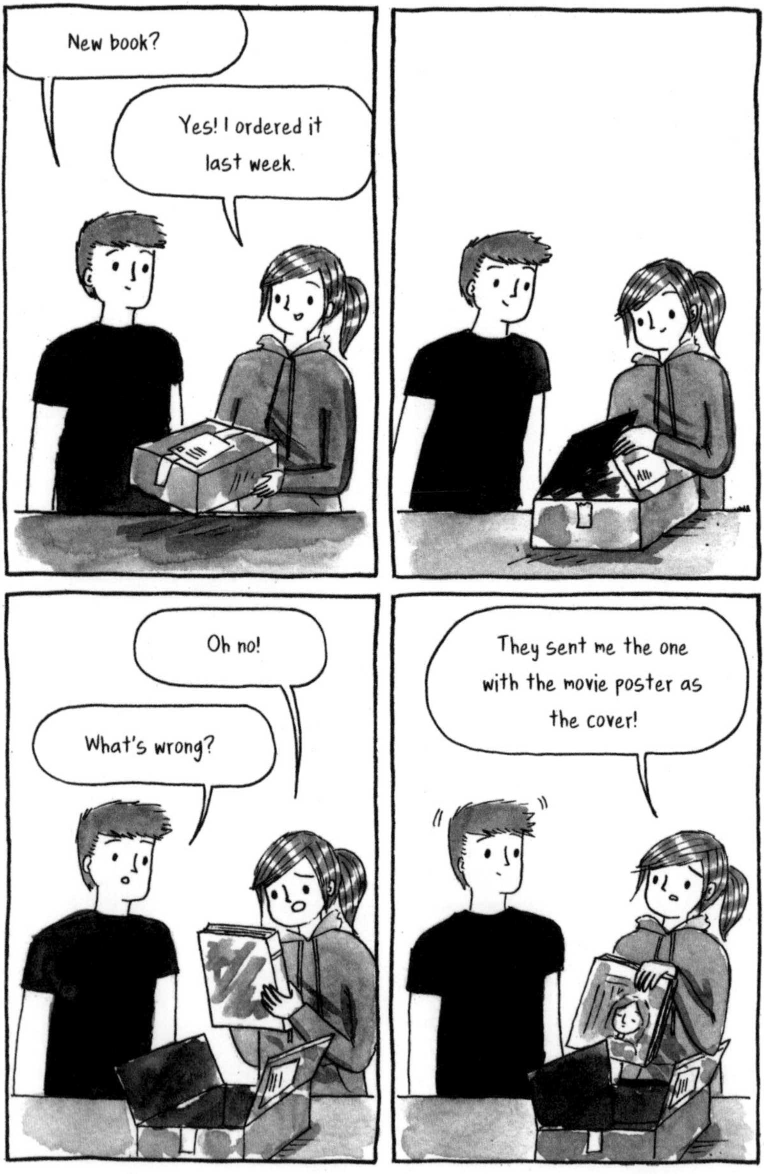
New book?
Yes! I ordered it last week.
Oh no!
What's wrong?
They sent me the one with the movie poster as the cover!

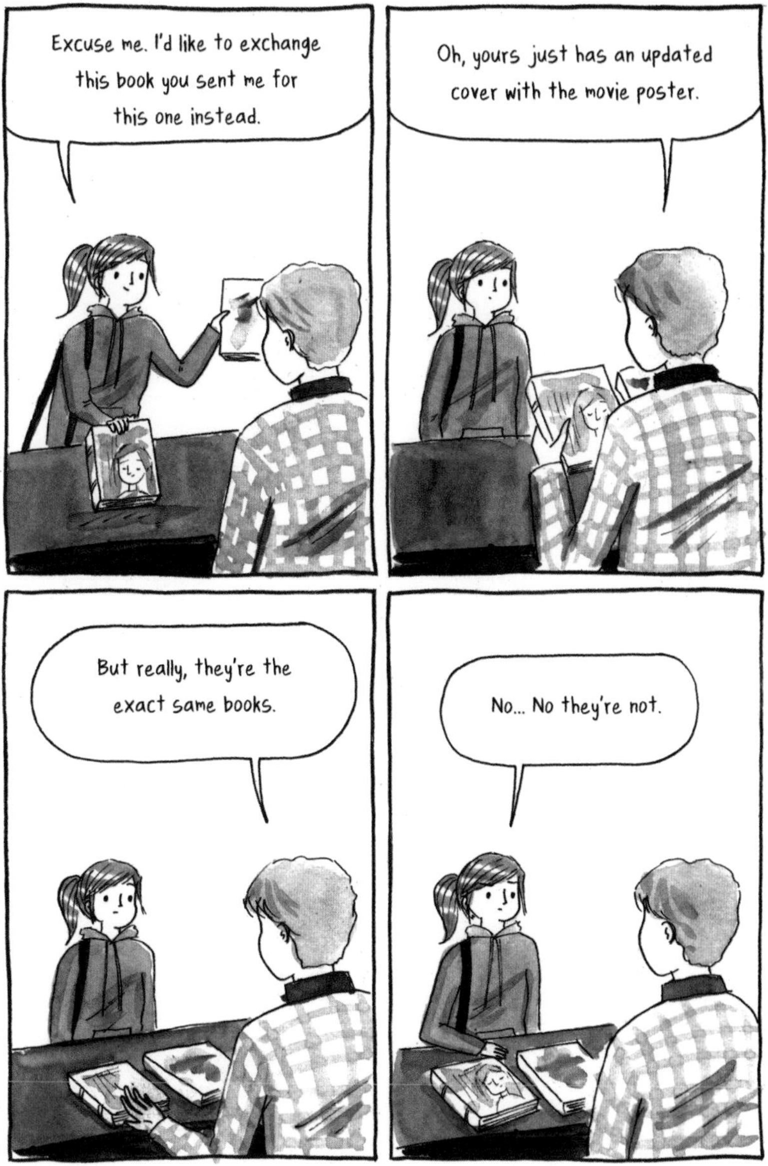
Excuse me. I'd like to exchange this book you sent me for this one instead.
Oh, yours just has an updated cover with the movie poster.
But really, they're the exact same books.
No... No they're not.

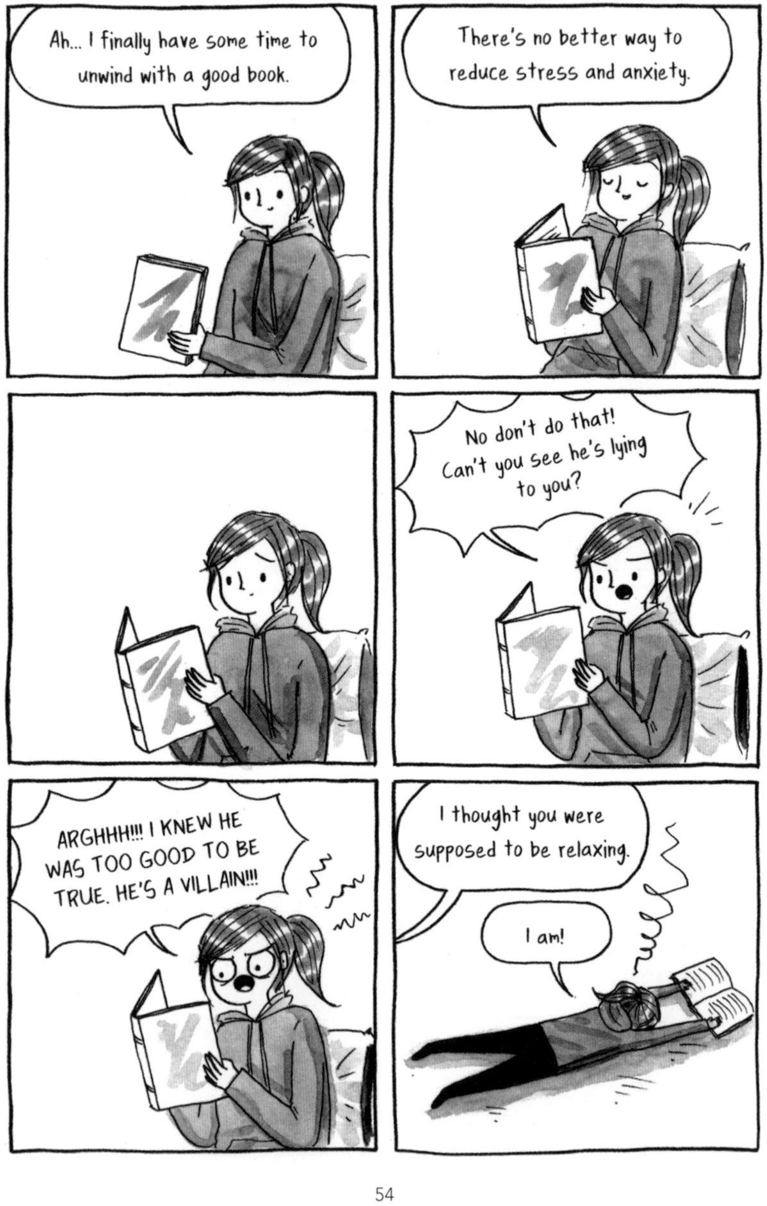
Ah... I finally have some time to unwind with a good book.
There's no better way to reduce stress and anxiety.
No don't do that! Can't you see he's lying to you?
ARGHHH!!! I KNEW HE WAS TOO GOOD TO BE TRUE. HE'S A VILLAIN!!!
I thought you were supposed to be relaxing.
I am!

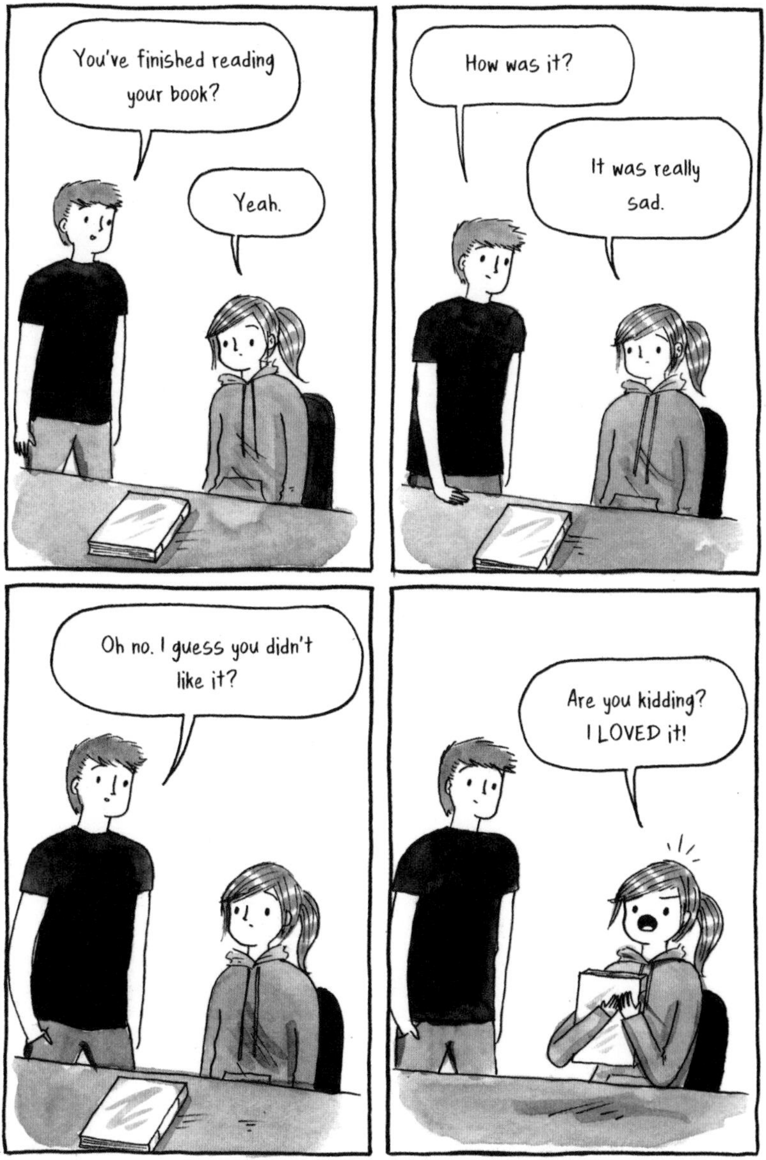
You've finished reading your book?
Yeah.
How was it?
It was really sad.
Oh no. I guess you didn't like it?
Are you kidding? I LOVED it!

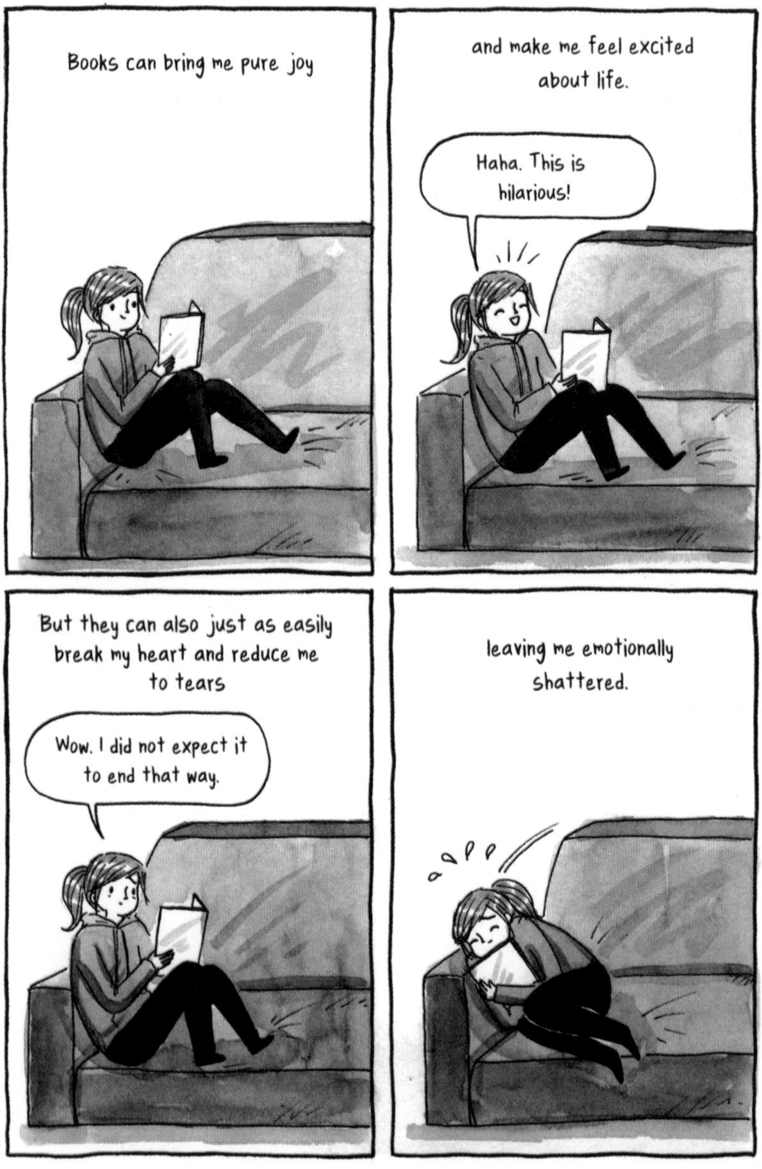
Books can bring me pure joy
and make me feel excited about life.
Haha. This is hilarious!
But they can also just as easily break my heart and reduce me to tears
Wow. I did not expect it to end that way.
leaving me emotionally shattered.

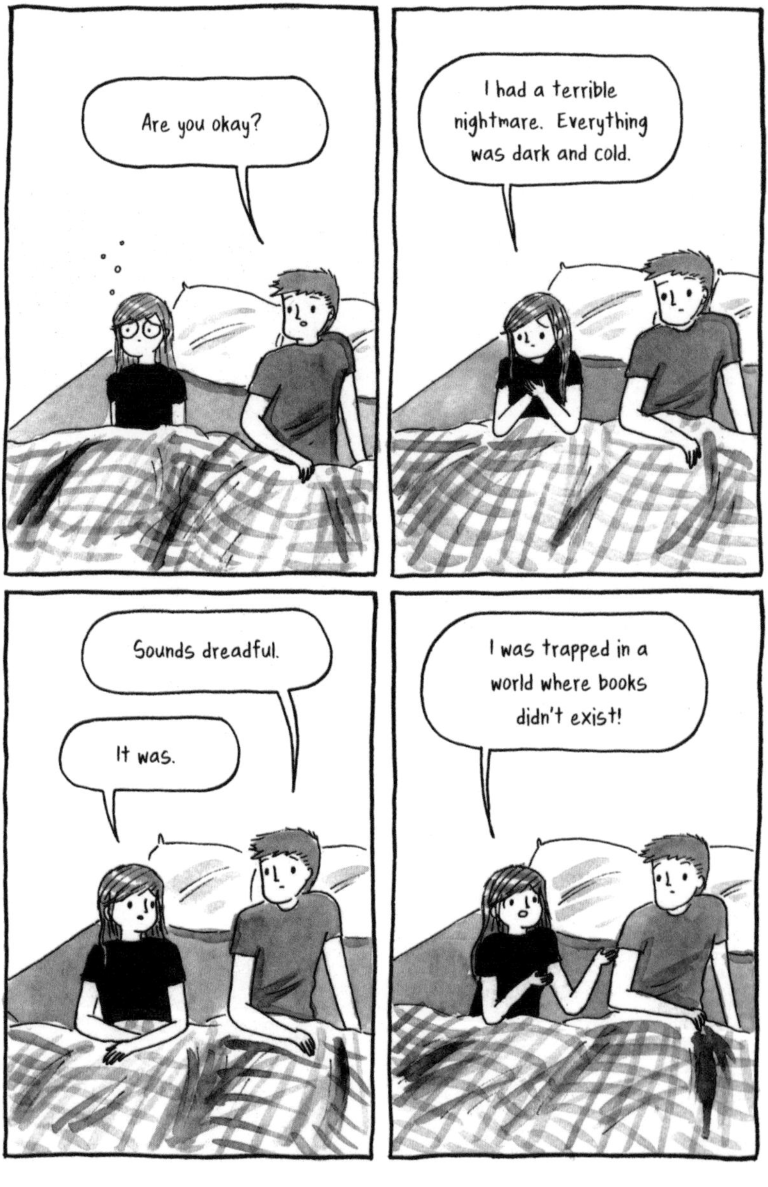
Are you okay?
I had a terrible nightmare. Everything was dark and cold.
Sounds dreadful.
It was.
I was trapped in a world where books didn't exist!

# Bookworm Fears

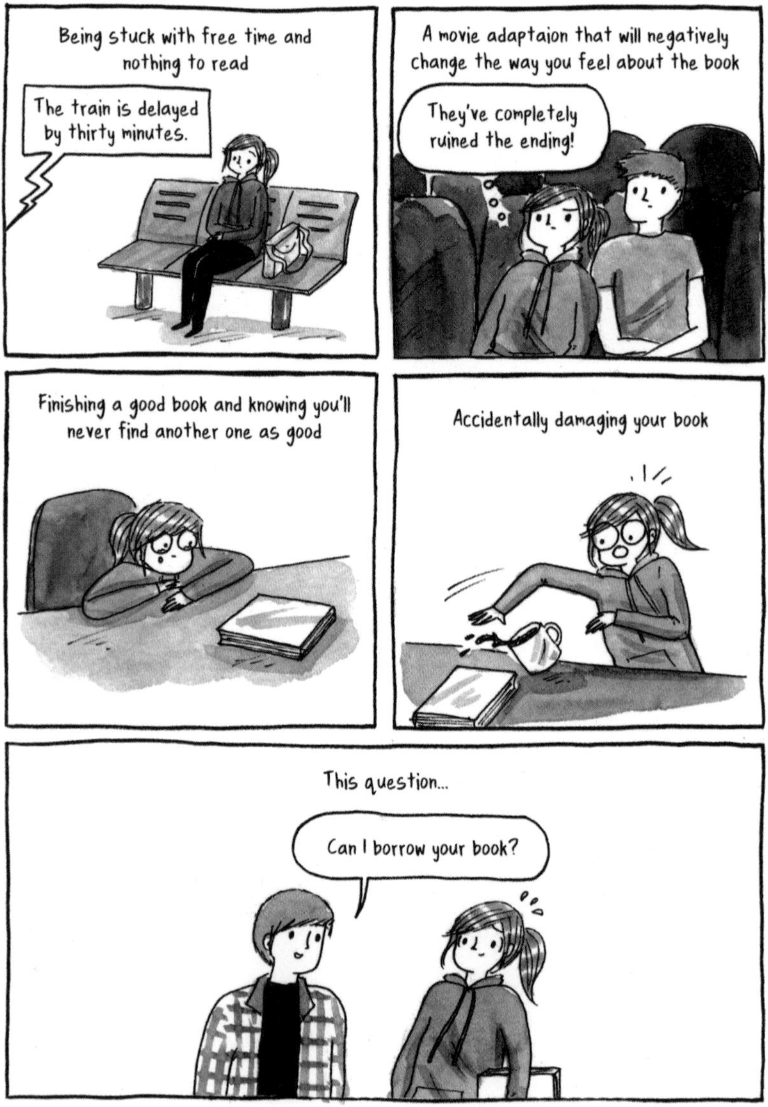

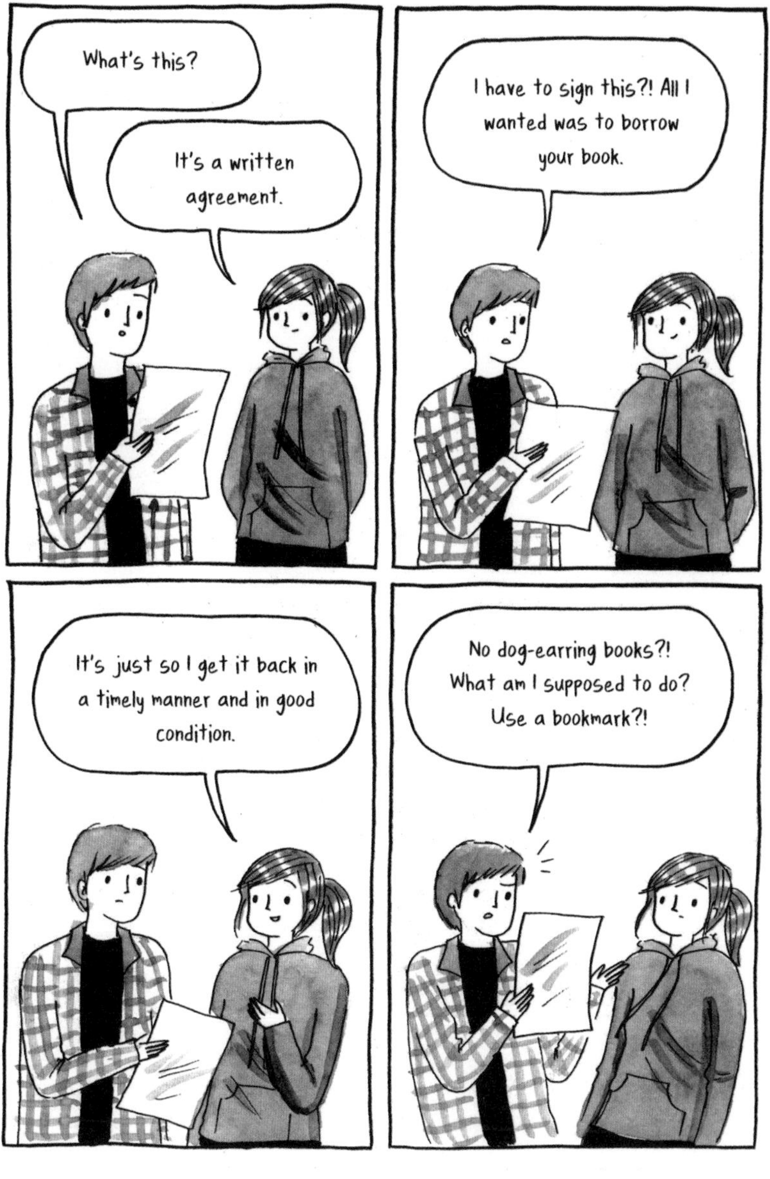
What's this?
It's a written agreement.
I have to sign this?! All I wanted was to borrow your book.
It's just so I get it back in a timely manner and in good condition.
No dog-earring books?! What am I supposed to do? Use a bookmark?!

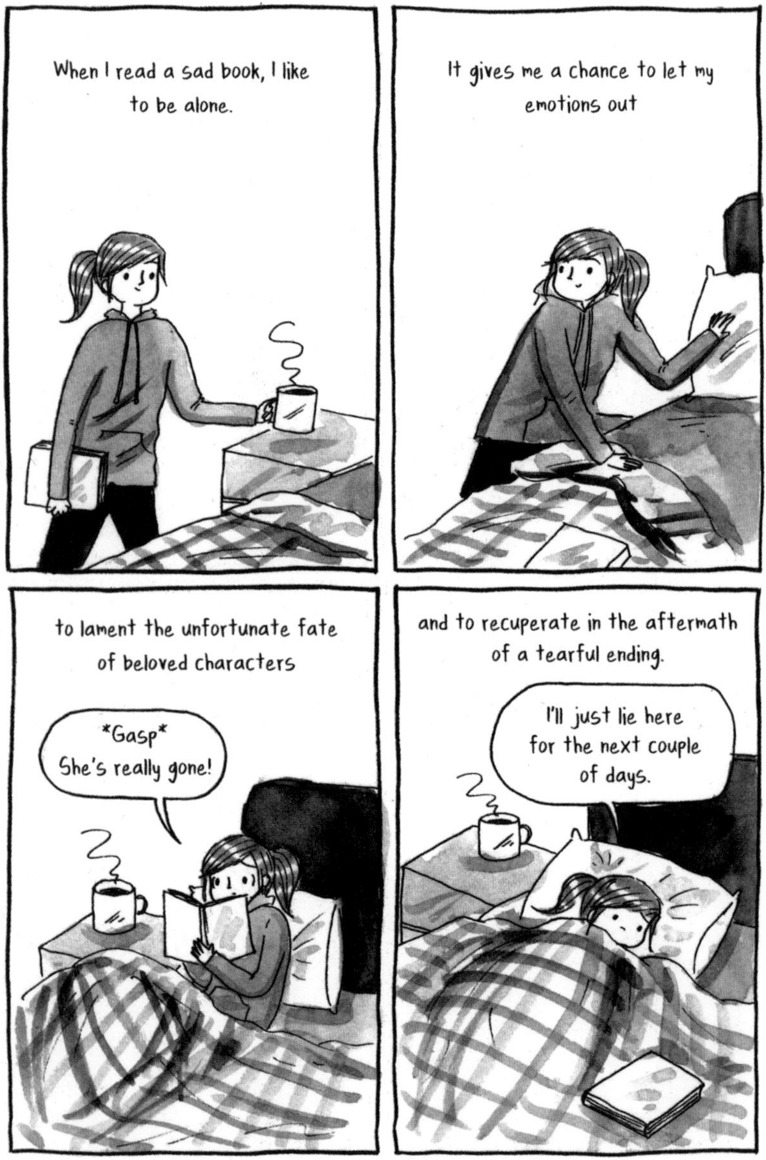
When I read a sad book, I like to be alone.
It gives me a chance to let my emotions out
to lament the unfortunate fate of beloved characters
*Gasp* She's really gone!
and to recuperate in the aftermath of a tearful ending.
I'll just lie here for the next couple of days.

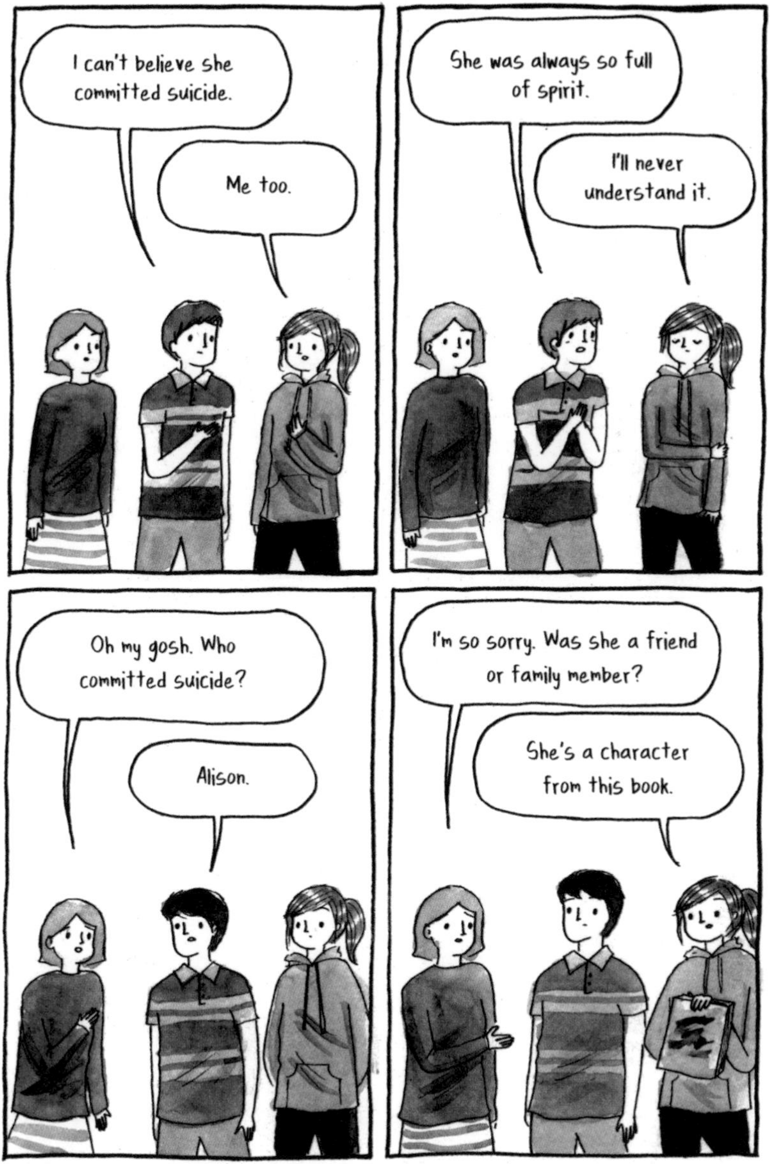
I can't believe she committed suicide.
Me too.
She was always so full of spirit.
I'll never understand it.
Oh my gosh. Who committed suicide?
Alison.
I'm so sorry. Was she a friend or family member?
She's a character from this book.

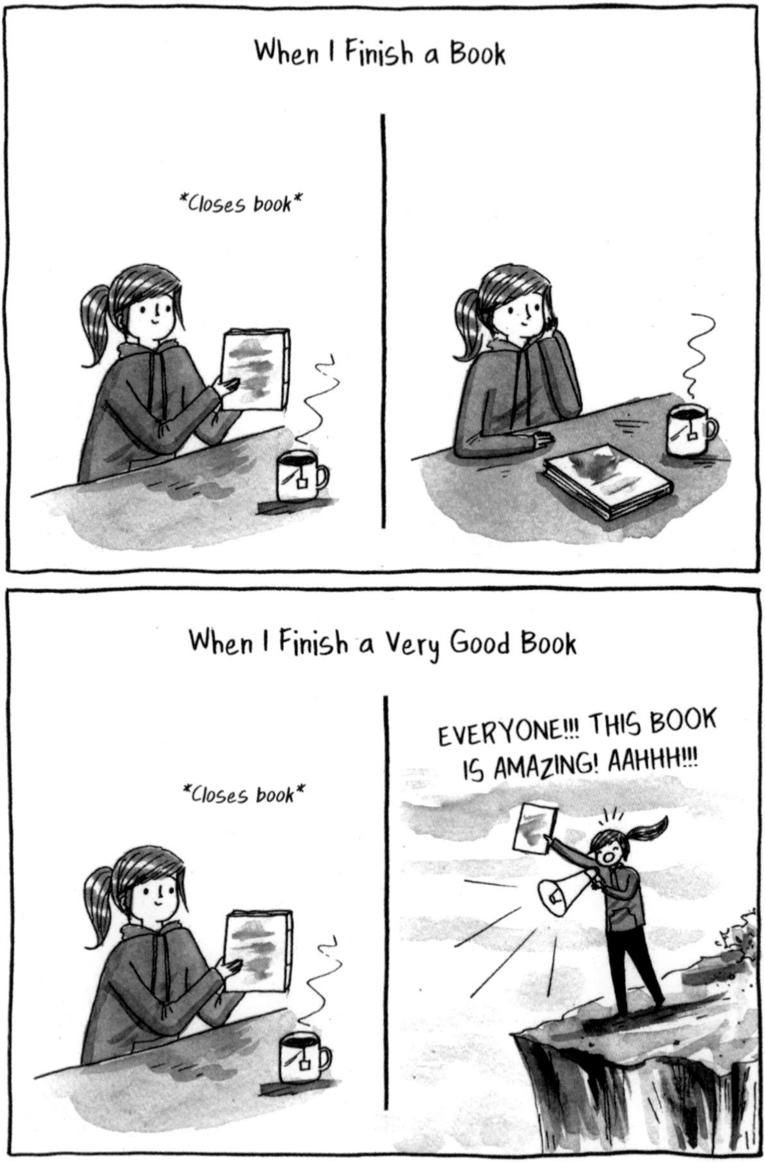
When I Finish a Book
*Closes book*
When I Finish a Very Good Book
*Closes book*
EVERYONE!!! THIS BOOK IS AMAZING! AAHHH!!!

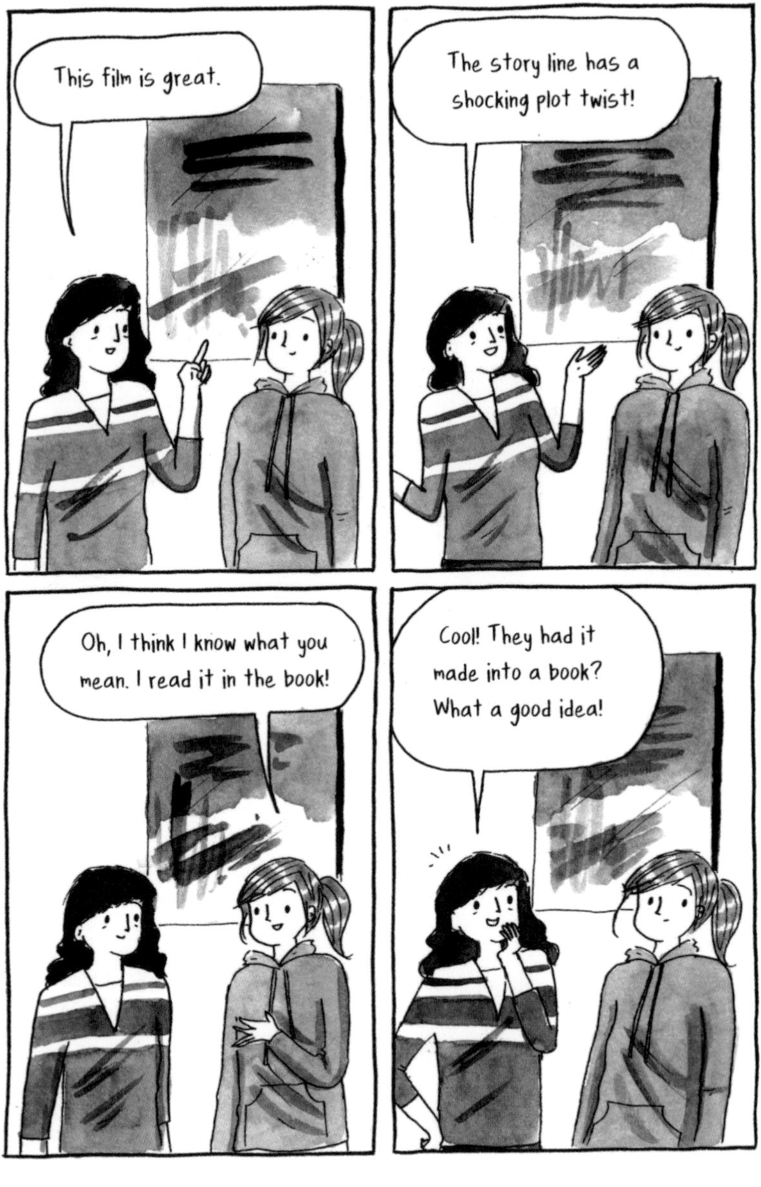
This film is great.
The story line has a shocking plot twist!
Oh, I think I know what you mean. I read it in the book!
Cool! They had it made into a book? What a good idea!

## E-Books Vs. Paper Books

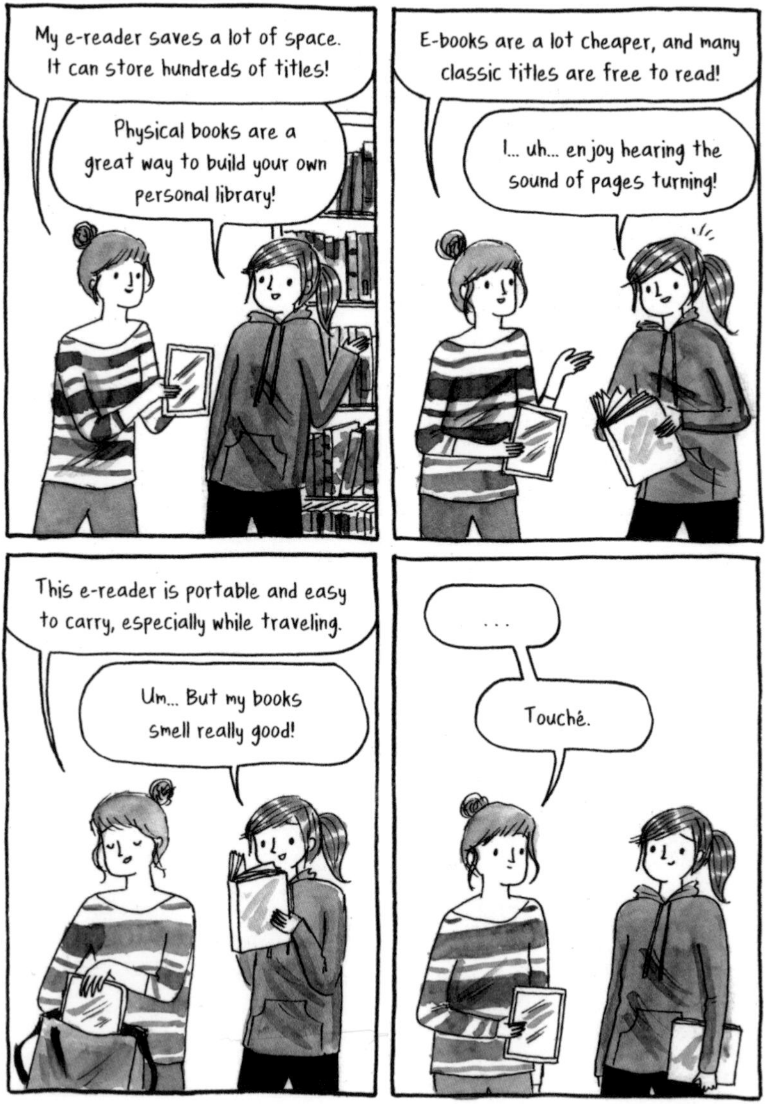
My e-reader saves a lot of space. It can store hundreds of titles!
Physical books are a great way to build your own personal library!
E-books are a lot cheaper, and many classic titles are free to read!
I... uh... enjoy hearing the sound of pages turning!
This e-reader is portable and easy to carry, especially while traveling.
Um... But my books smell really good!
. . .
Touché.

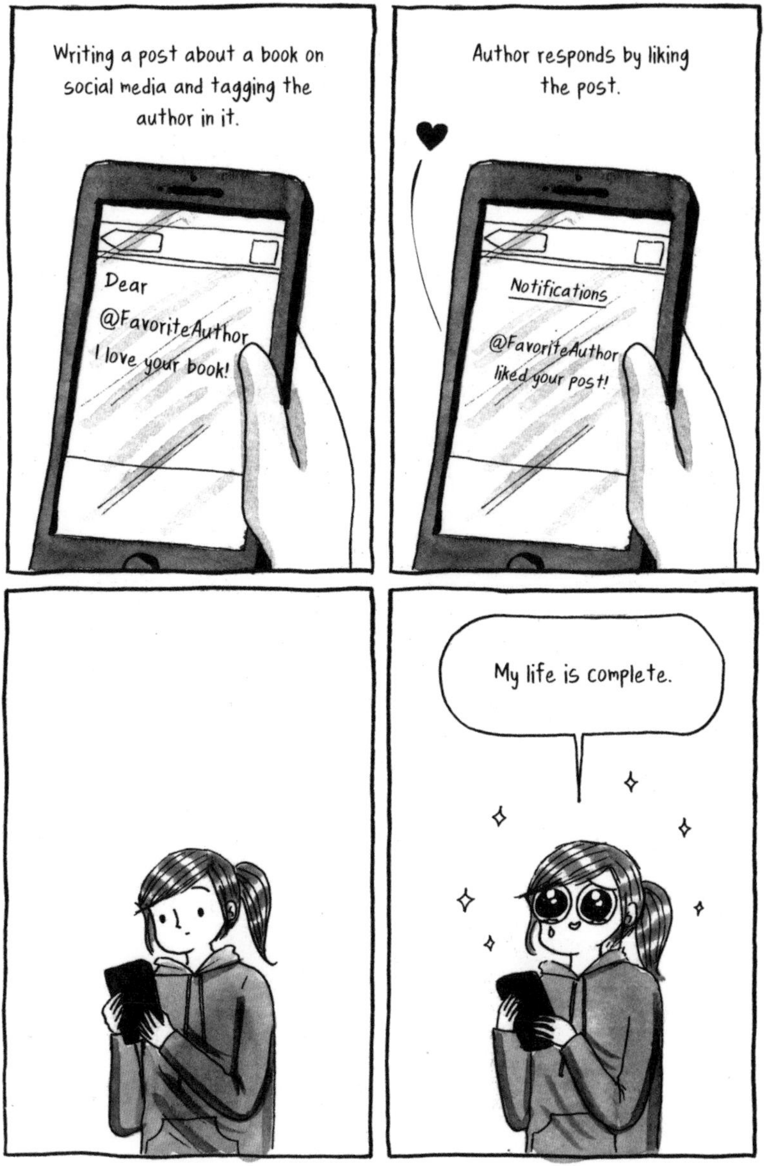
Writing a post about a book on social media and tagging the author in it.
Dear
@FavoriteAuthor
I love your book!
Author responds by liking the post.
Notifications
@FavoriteAuthor
liked your post!
My life is complete.

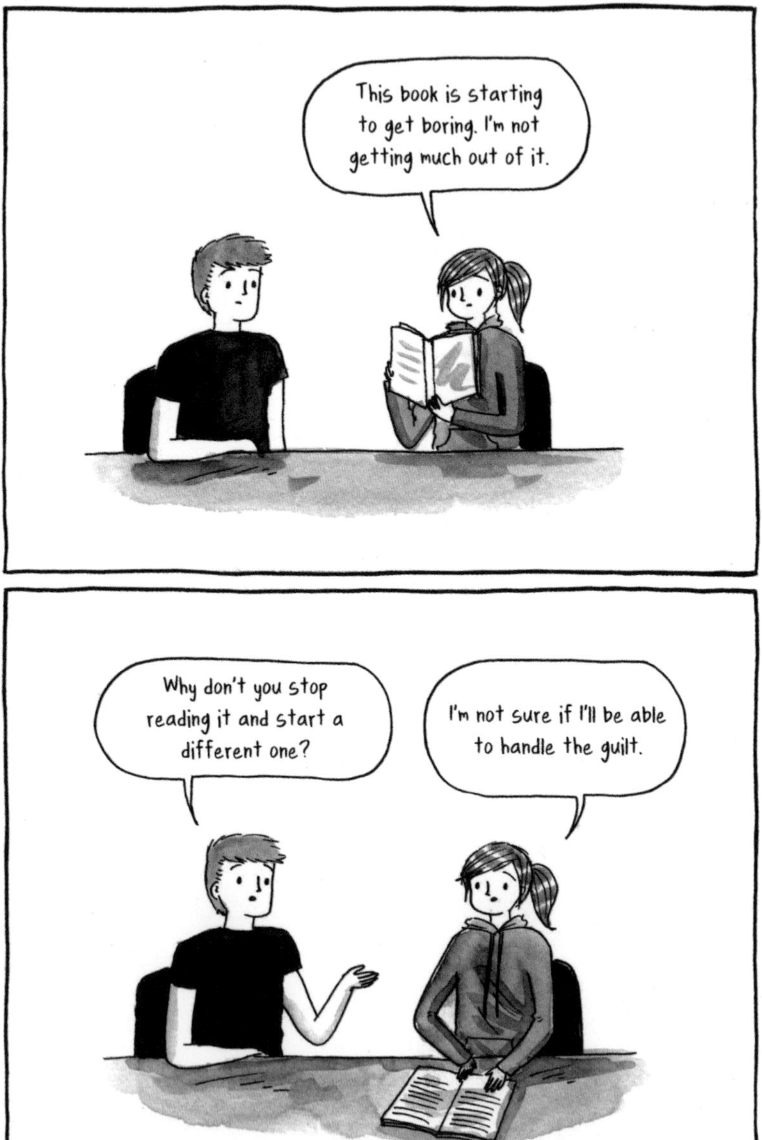
This book is starting to get boring. I'm not getting much out of it.
Why don't you stop reading it and start a different one?
I'm not sure if I'll be able to handle the guilt.

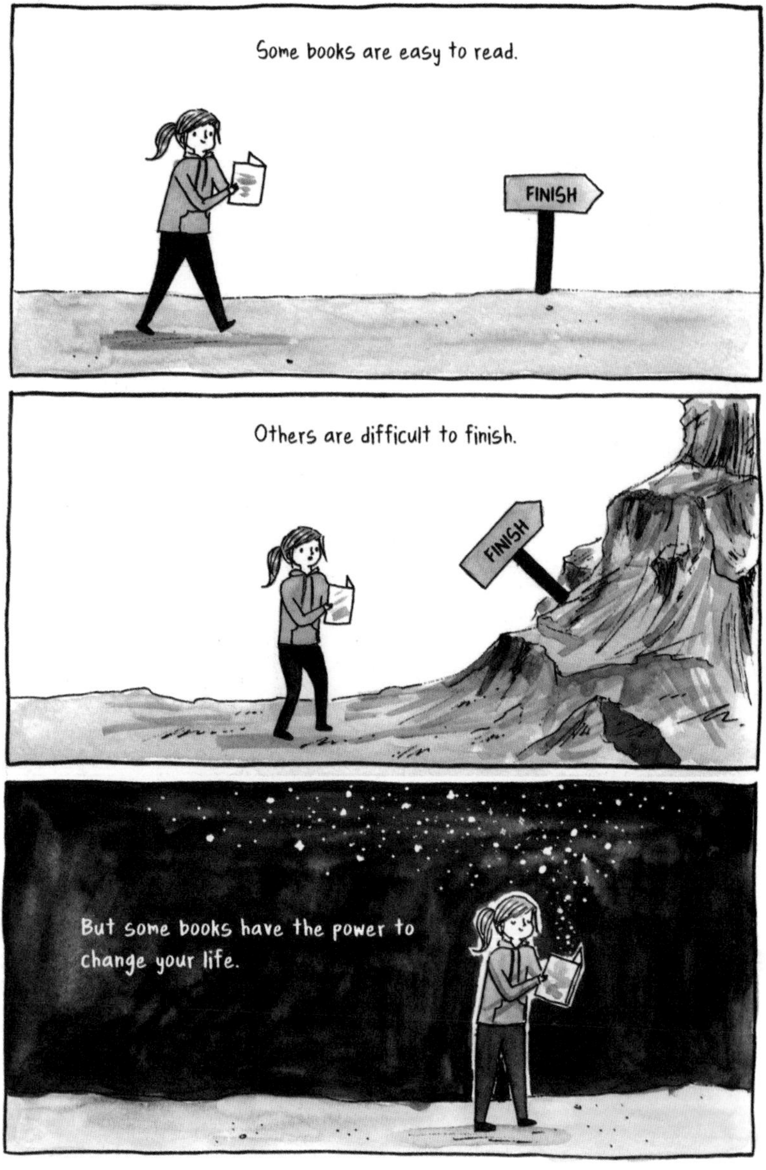

Some books are easy to read.
FINISH
Others are difficult to finish.
FINISH
But some books have the power to change your life.

## Some Amazing Books

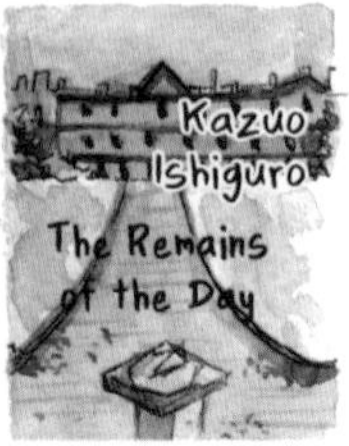
Kazuo Ishiguro
The Remains of the Day

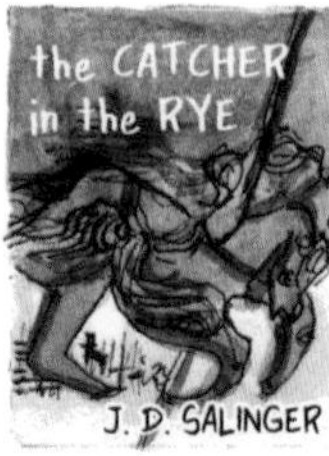
the CATCHER in the RYE
J. D. SALINGER

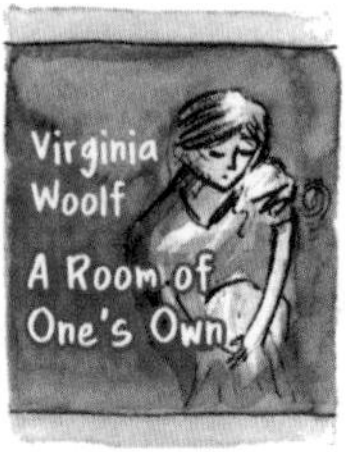
Virginia Woolf
A Room of One's Own

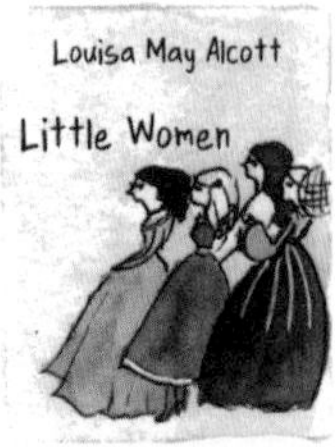
Louisa May Alcott
Little Women

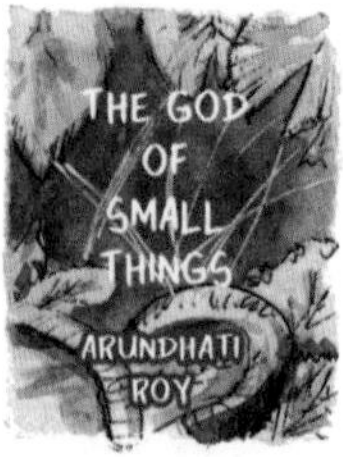
THE GOD OF SMALL THINGS
ARUNDHATI ROY

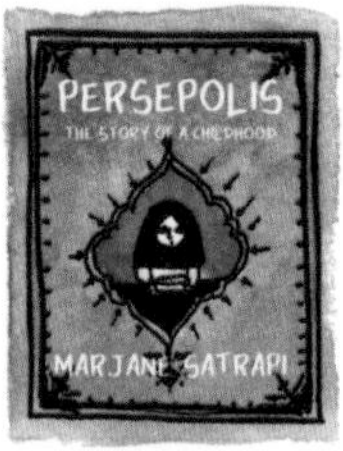
PERSEPOLIS
THE STORY OF A CHILDHOOD
MARJANE SATRAPI

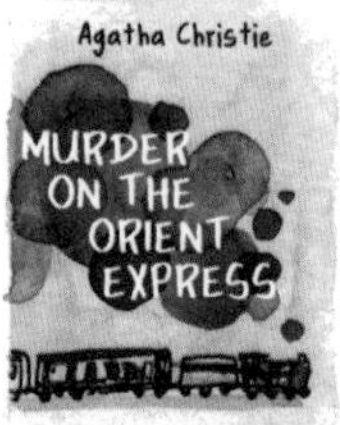
Agatha Christie
MURDER ON THE ORIENT EXPRESS

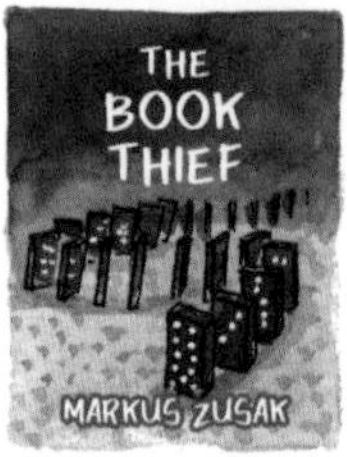
THE BOOK THIEF
MARKUS ZUSAK

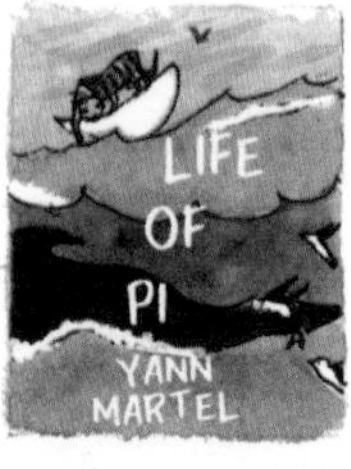
LIFE OF PI
YANN MARTEL

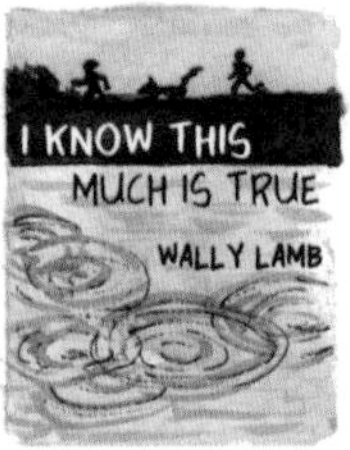
I KNOW THIS MUCH IS TRUE
WALLY LAMB

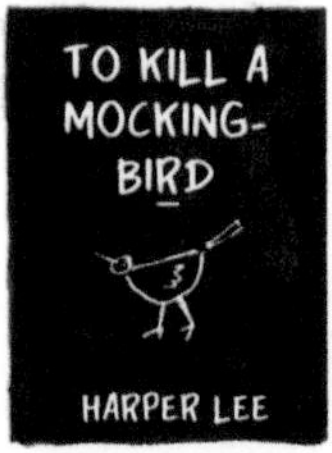
TO KILL A MOCKING-BIRD
HARPER LEE

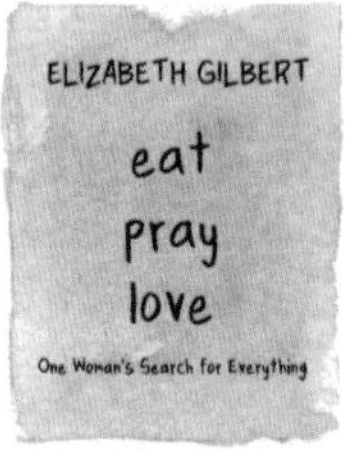
ELIZABETH GILBERT
eat pray love
One Woman's Search for Everything

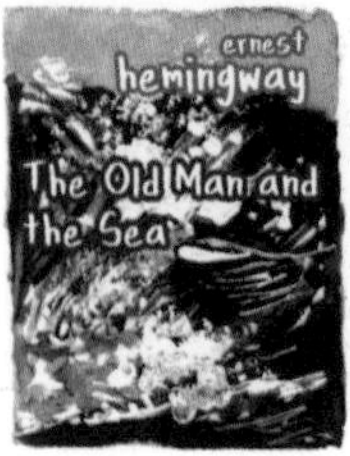
ernest hemingway
The Old Man and the Sea

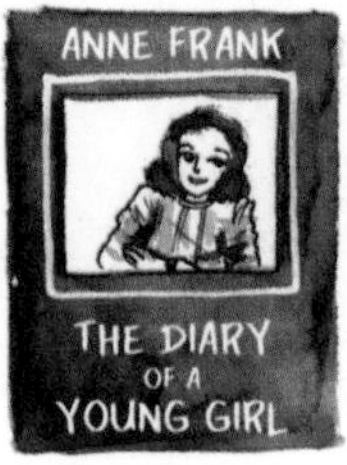
ANNE FRANK
THE DIARY OF A YOUNG GIRL

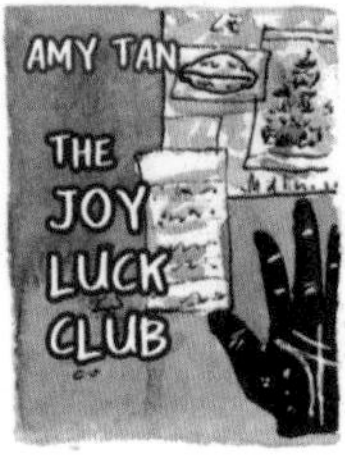
AMY TAN
THE JOY LUCK CLUB

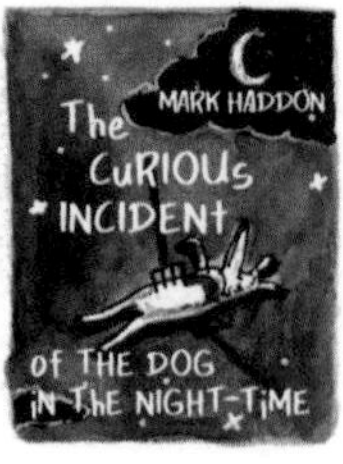
MARK HADDON
The CuRIOUs INCIDENT of THE DOG IN THE NIGHT-TIME

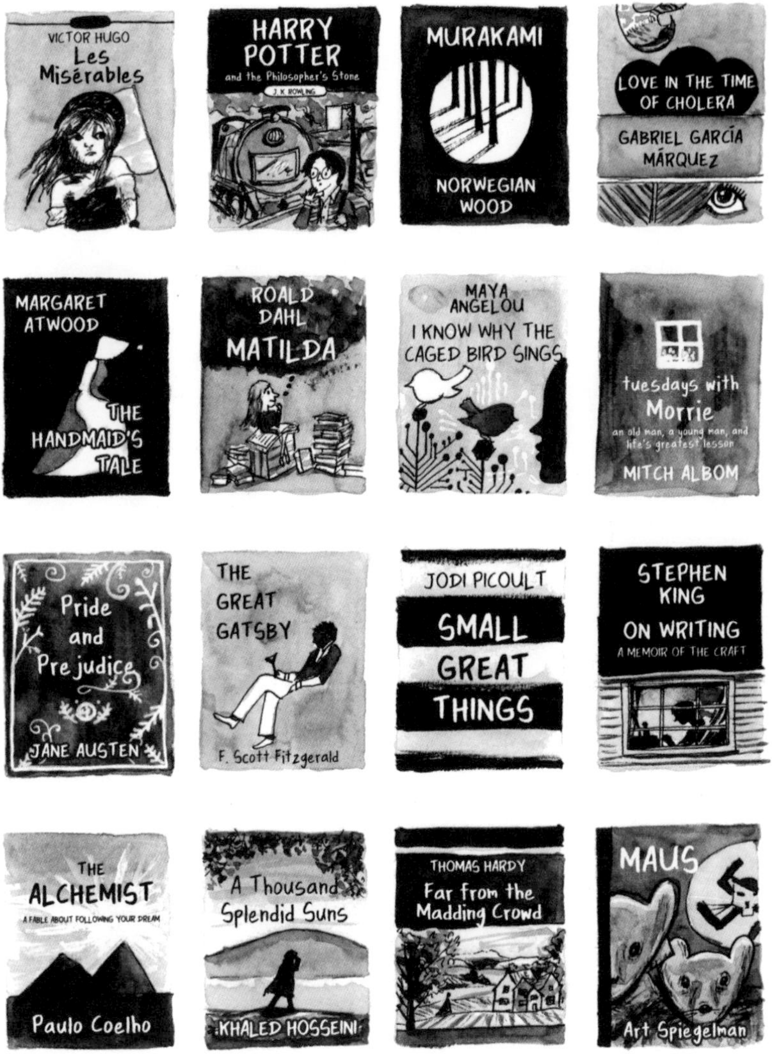
VICTOR HUGO
Les Misérables
HARRY POTTER
and the Philosopher's Stone
J.K ROWLING
MURAKAMI
NORWEGIAN WOOD
LOVE IN THE TIME OF CHOLERA
GABRIEL GARCÍA MÁRQUEZ
MARGARET ATWOOD
THE HANDMAID'S TALE
ROALD DAHL
MATILDA
MAYA ANGELOU
I KNOW WHY THE CAGED BIRD SINGS
tuesdays with Morrie
an old man, a young man, and life's greatest lesson
MITCH ALBOM
Pride and Prejudice
JANE AUSTEN
THE GREAT GATSBY
F. Scott Fitzgerald
JODI PICOULT
SMALL GREAT THINGS
STEPHEN KING
ON WRITING
A MEMOIR OF THE CRAFT
THE ALCHEMIST
A FABLE ABOUT FOLLOWING YOUR DREAM
Paulo Coelho
A Thousand Splendid Suns
KHALED HOSSEINI
THOMAS HARDY
Far from the Madding Crowd
MAUS
Art Spiegelman

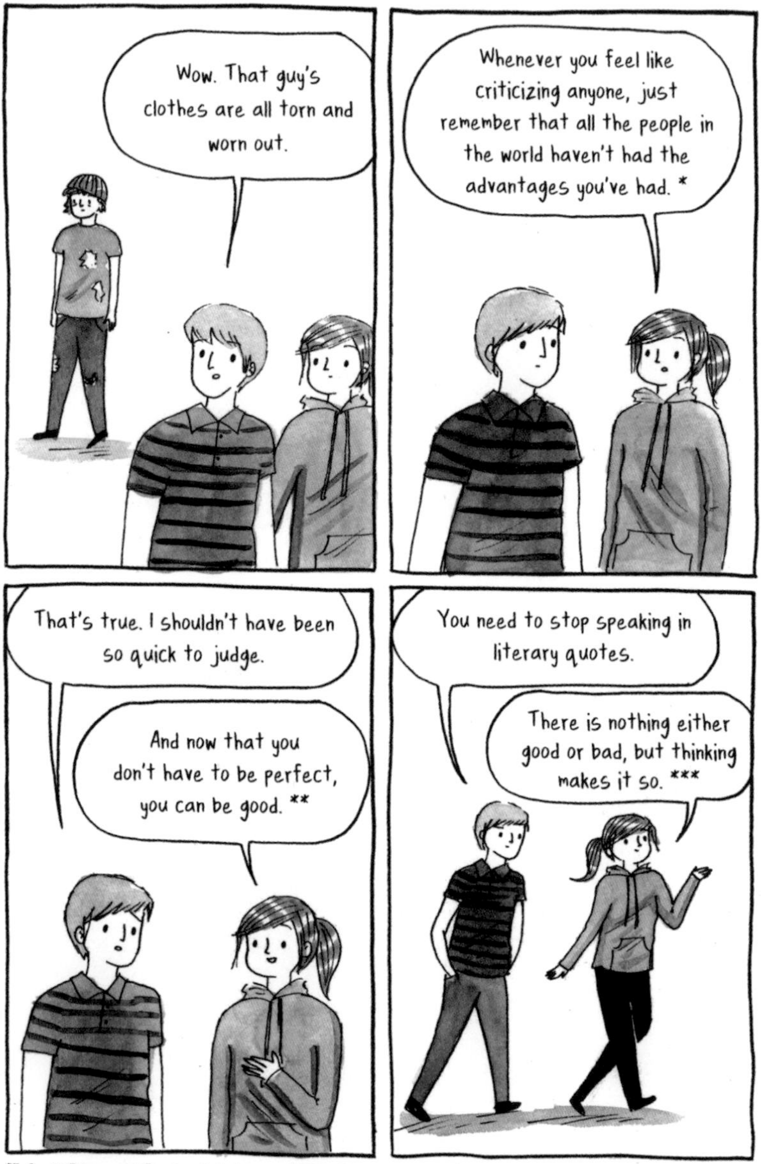
Wow. That guy's clothes are all torn and worn out.
Whenever you feel like criticizing anyone, just remember that all the people in the world haven't had the advantages you've had. *
That's true. I shouldn't have been so quick to judge.
And now that you don't have to be perfect, you can be good. **
You need to stop speaking in literary quotes.
There is nothing either good or bad, but thinking makes it so. ***

*F. Scott Fitzgerald, The Great Gatsby **John Steinbeck, East of Eden ***William Shakespeare, Hamlet

## Memoirs I Could Write

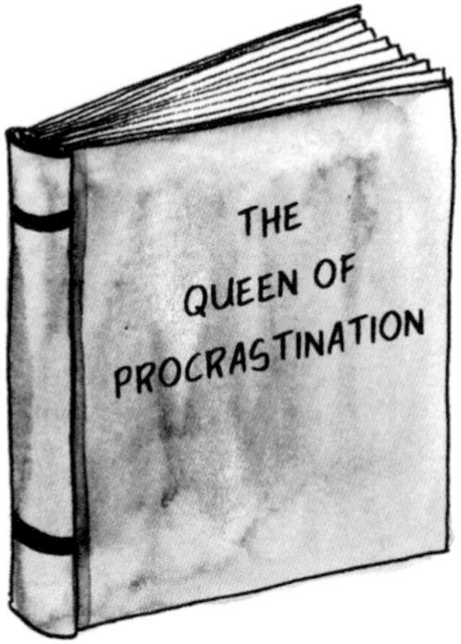
THE
QUEEN OF
PROCRASTINATION

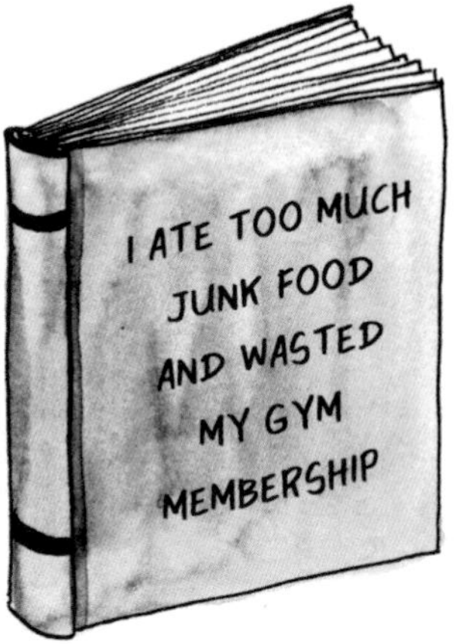
I ATE TOO MUCH
JUNK FOOD
AND WASTED
MY GYM
MEMBERSHIP

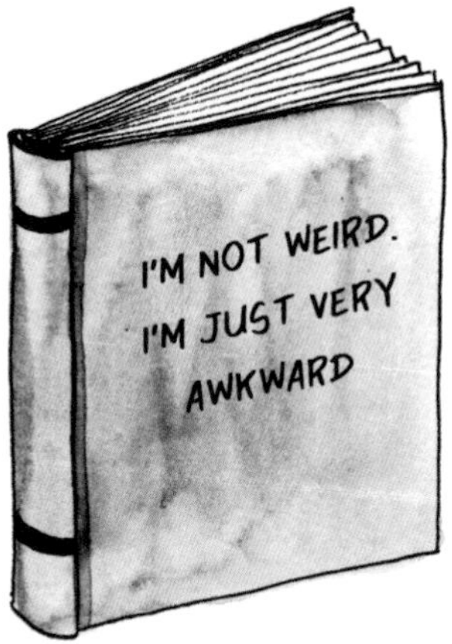
I'M NOT WEIRD.
I'M JUST VERY
AWKWARD

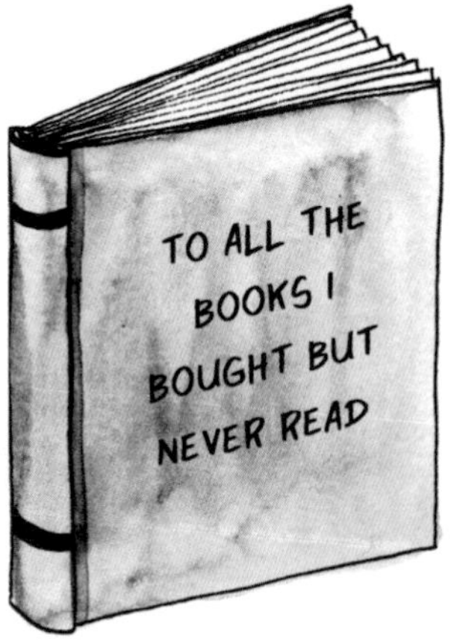
TO ALL THE
BOOKS I
BOUGHT BUT
NEVER READ

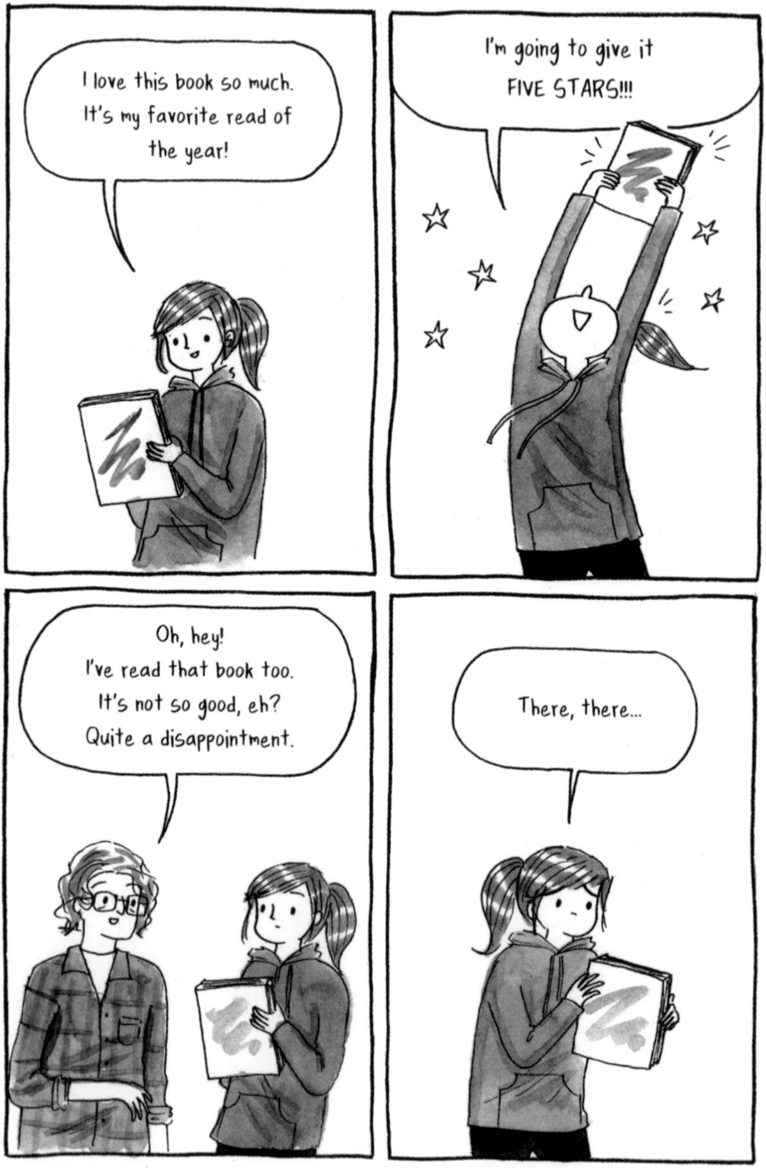
I love this book so much. It's my favorite read of the year!
I'm going to give it FIVE STARS!!!
Oh, hey! I've read that book too. It's not so good, eh? Quite a disappointment.
There, there...

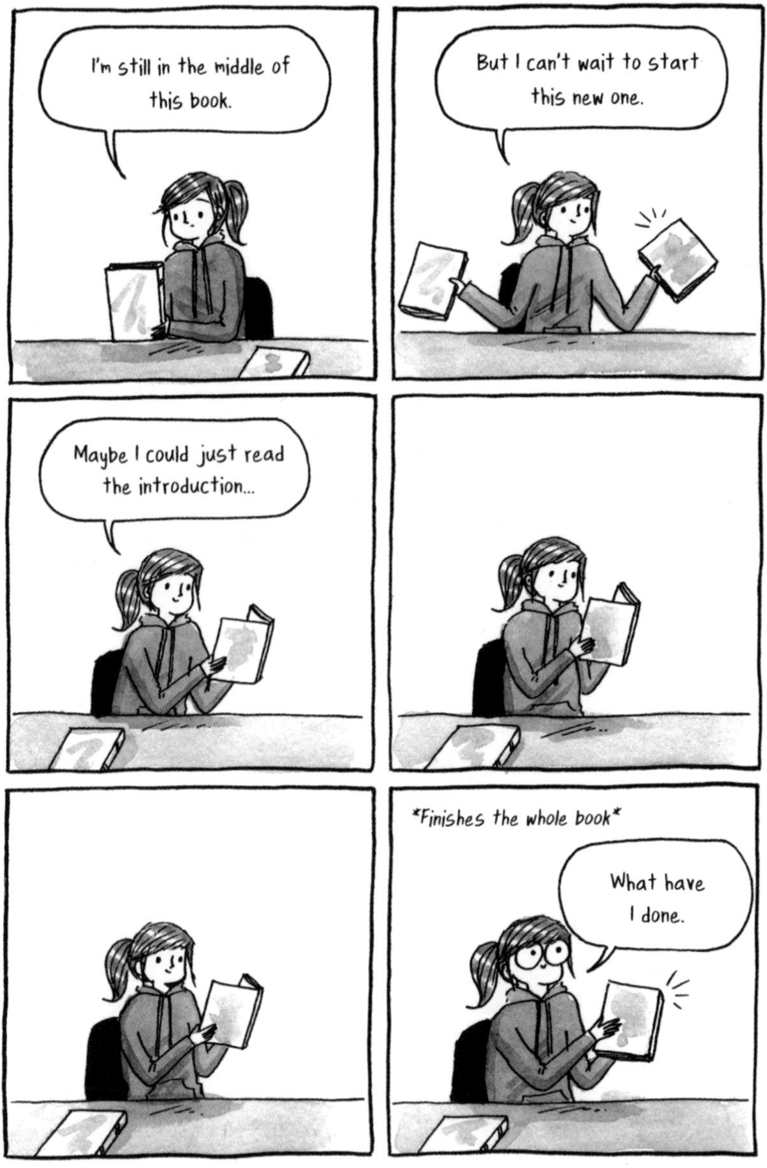
I'm still in the middle of this book.
But I can't wait to start this new one.
Maybe I could just read the introduction...
*Finishes the whole book*
What have I done.

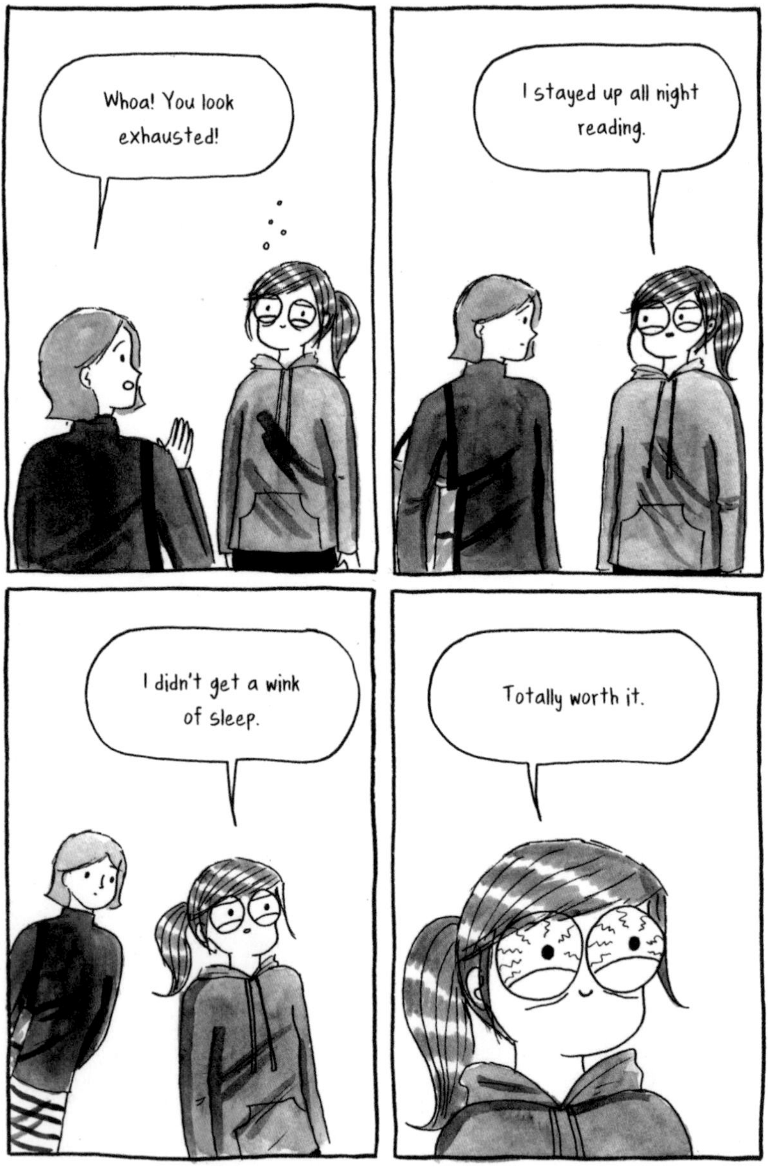
Whoa! You look exhausted!
I stayed up all night reading.
I didn't get a wink of sleep.
Totally worth it.

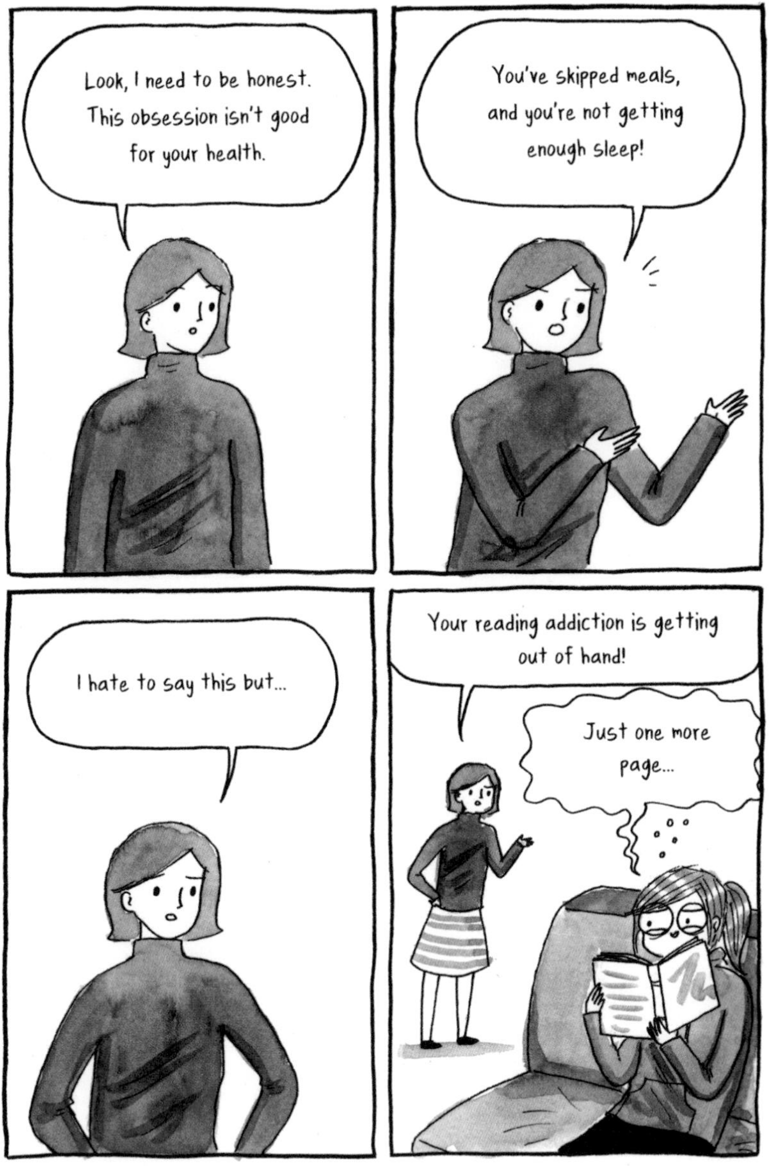
Look, I need to be honest. This obsession isn't good for your health.
You've skipped meals, and you're not getting enough sleep!
I hate to say this but...
Your reading addiction is getting out of hand!
Just one more page...

# How to Get More Reading Done

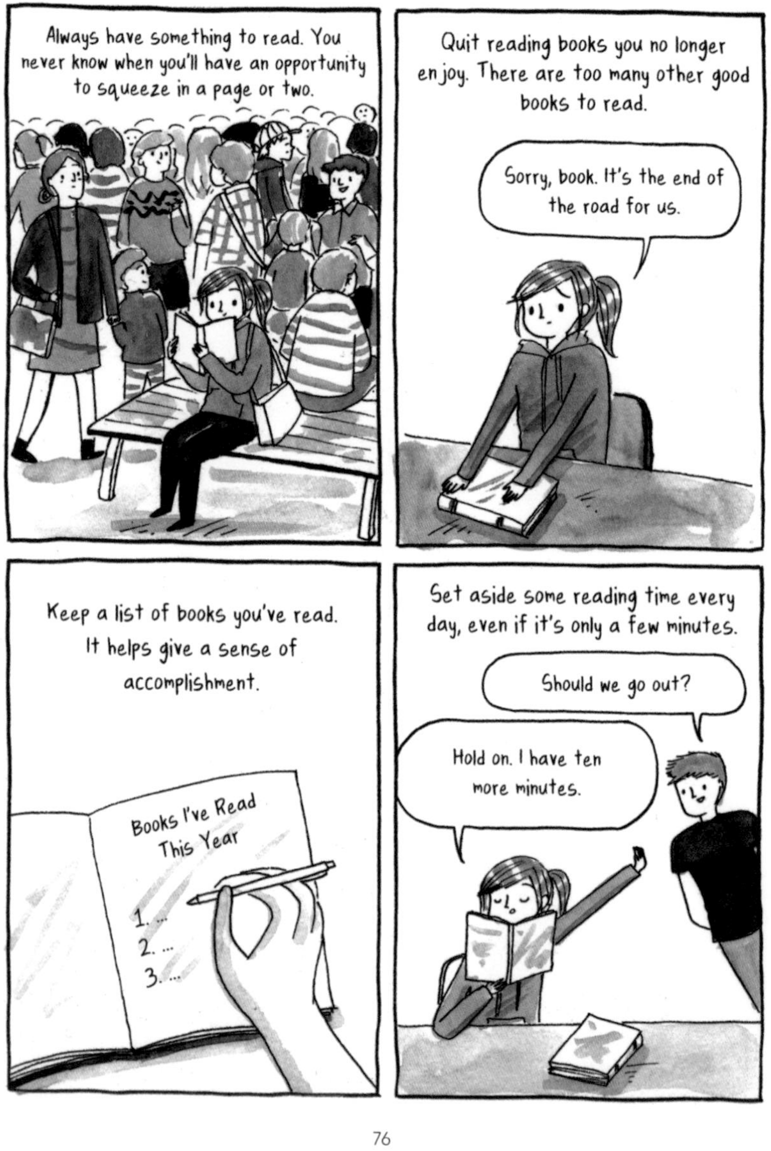
Always have something to read. You never know when you'll have an opportunity to squeeze in a page or two.
Quit reading books you no longer enjoy. There are too many other good books to read.
Sorry, book. It's the end of the road for us.
Keep a list of books you've read. It helps give a sense of accomplishment.
Books I've Read This Year
1. ...
2. ...
3. ...
Set aside some reading time every day, even if it's only a few minutes.
Should we go out?
Hold on. I have ten more minutes.

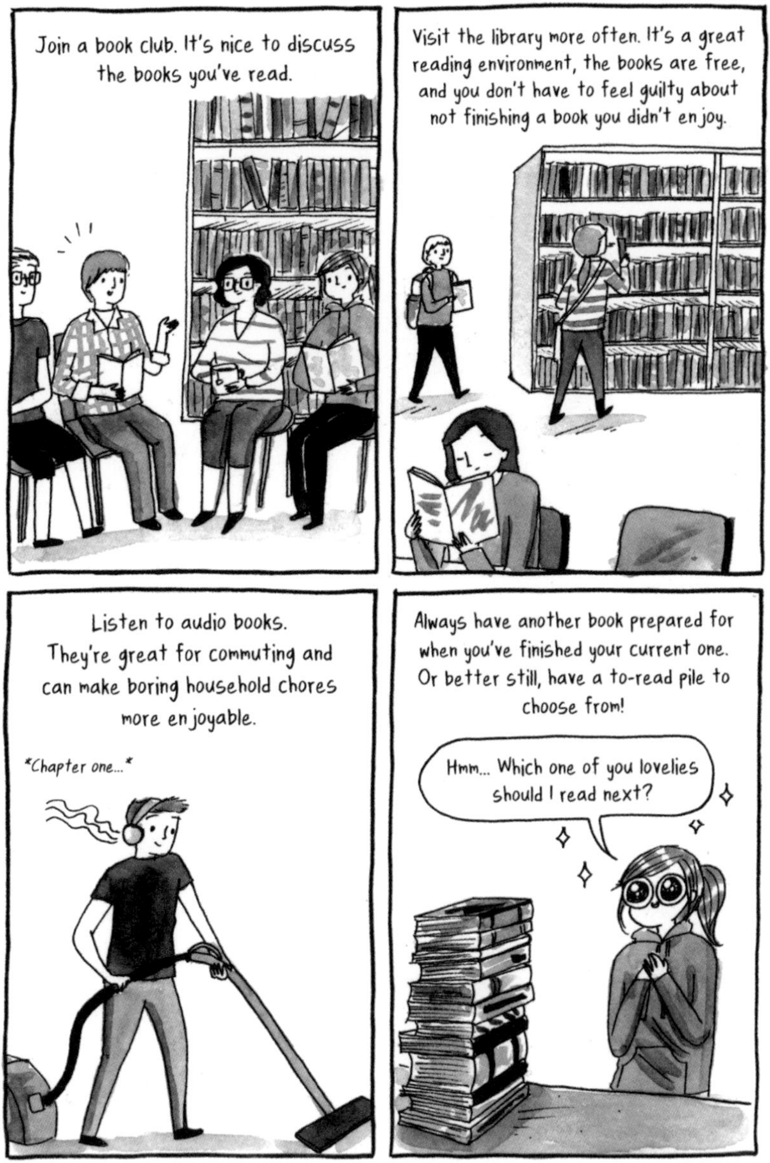
Join a book club. It's nice to discuss the books you've read.
Visit the library more often. It's a great reading environment, the books are free, and you don't have to feel guilty about not finishing a book you didn't enjoy.
Listen to audio books. They're great for commuting and can make boring household chores more enjoyable.
*Chapter one...*
Always have another book prepared for when you've finished your current one. Or better still, have a to-read pile to choose from!
Hmm... Which one of you lovelies should I read next?

# Why I Love Old Secondhand Books

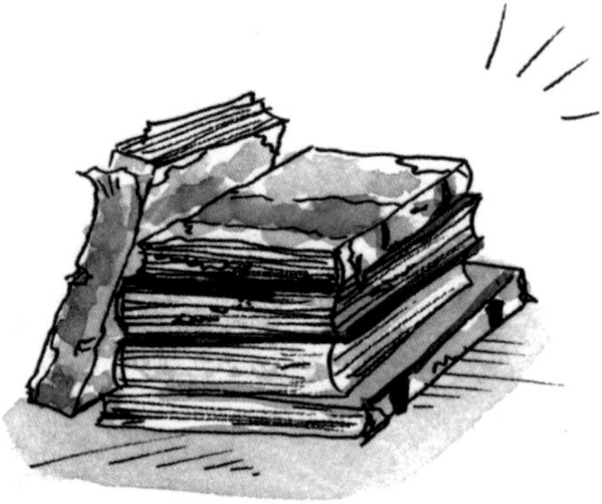

Many of them contain stories that have been long forgotten and are waiting to be discovered.

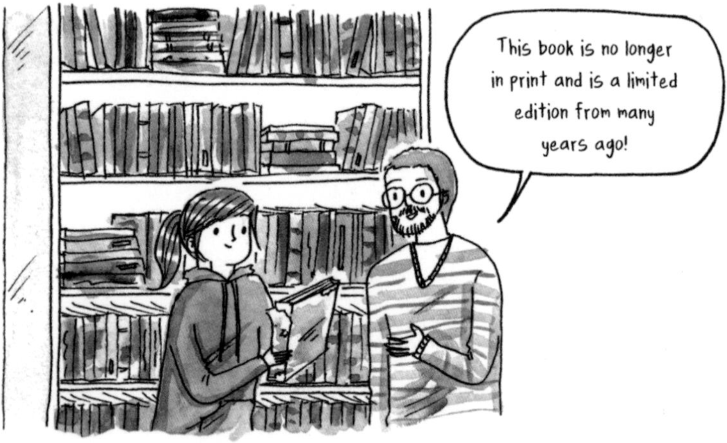
This book is no longer in print and is a limited edition from many years ago!

It's unlikely you'll ever see the same book anywhere else.

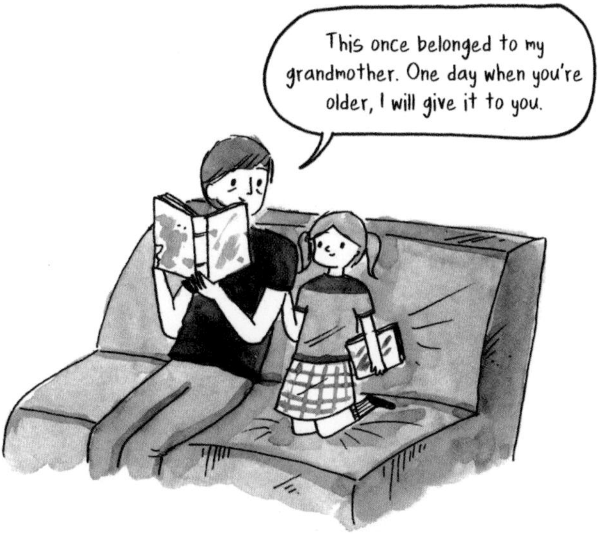
This once belonged to my grandmother. One day when you're older, I will give it to you.

Their disheveled spines and worn-out pages show that they were once loved and well read.

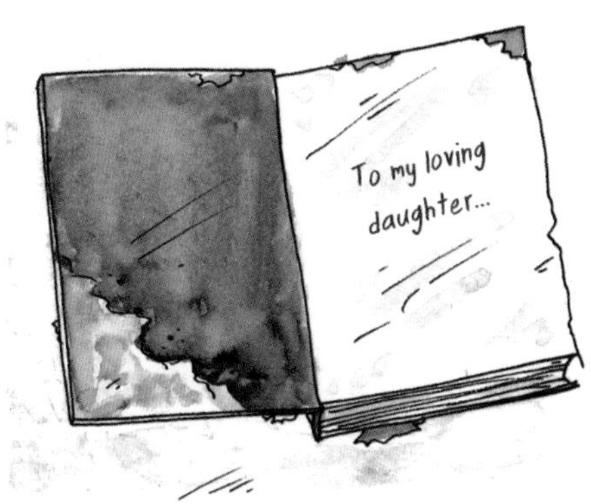
To my loving daughter...

Some have interesting inscriptions. You wonder who the book belonged to, and it feels like a mystery in itself.

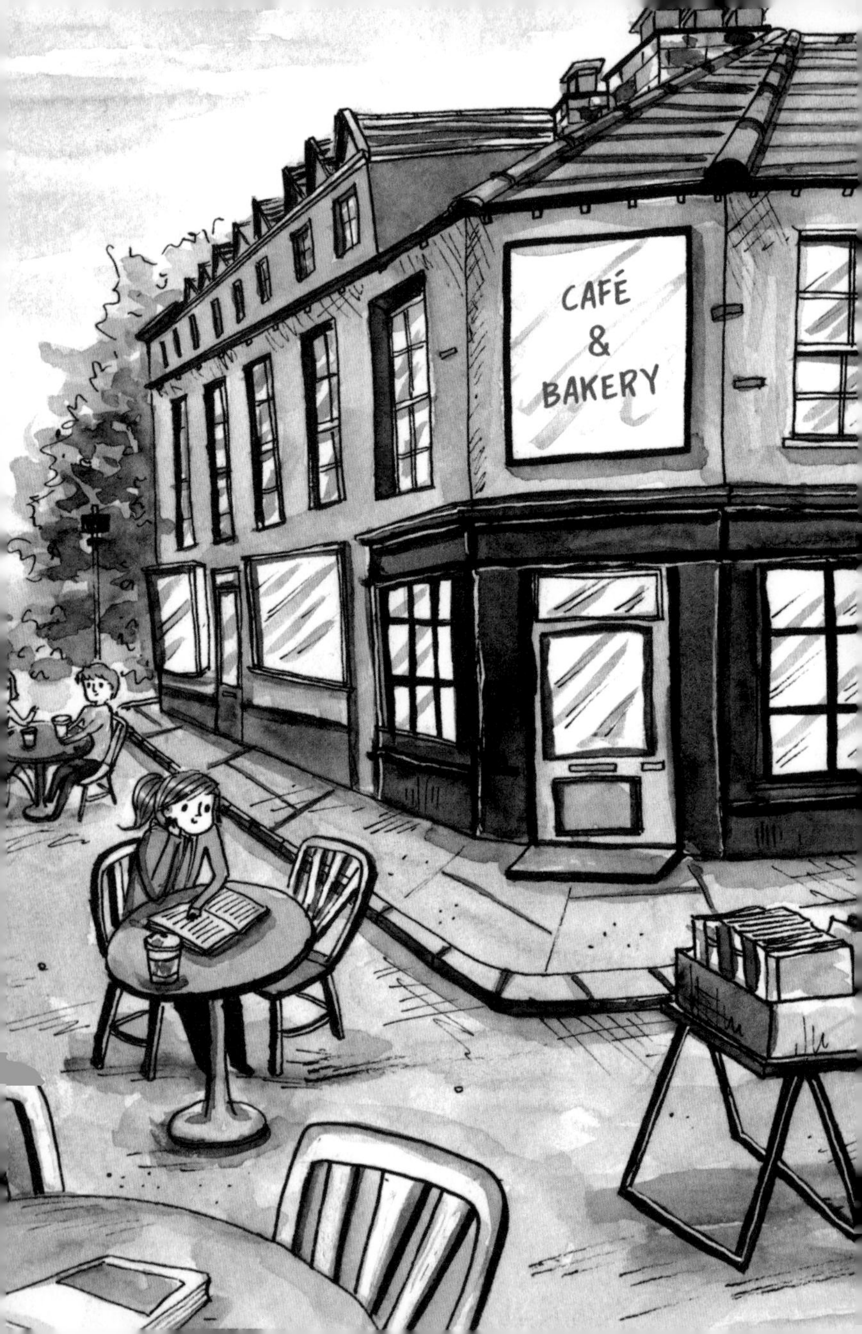
CAFÉ
&
BAKERY

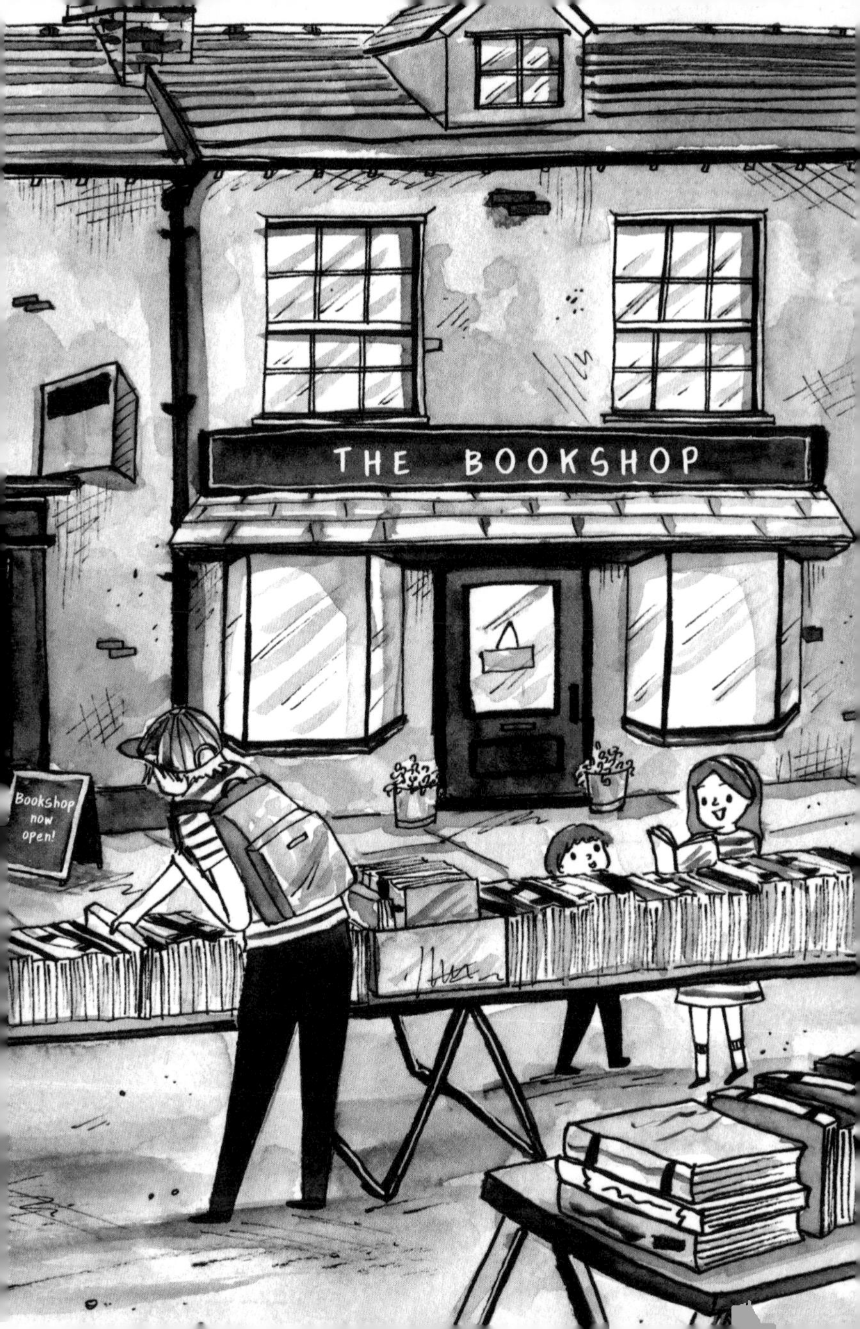
THE BOOKSHOP
Bookshop now open!

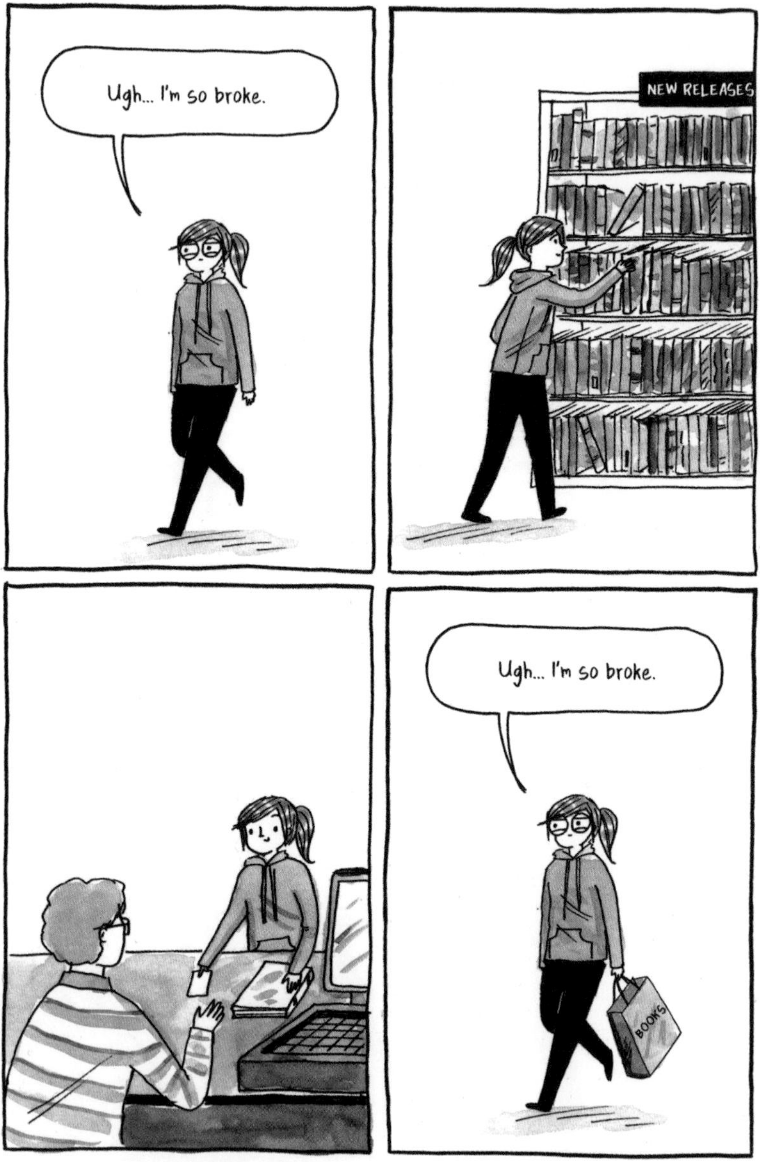
Ugh... I'm so broke.
NEW RELEASES
Ugh... I'm so broke.
BOOKS

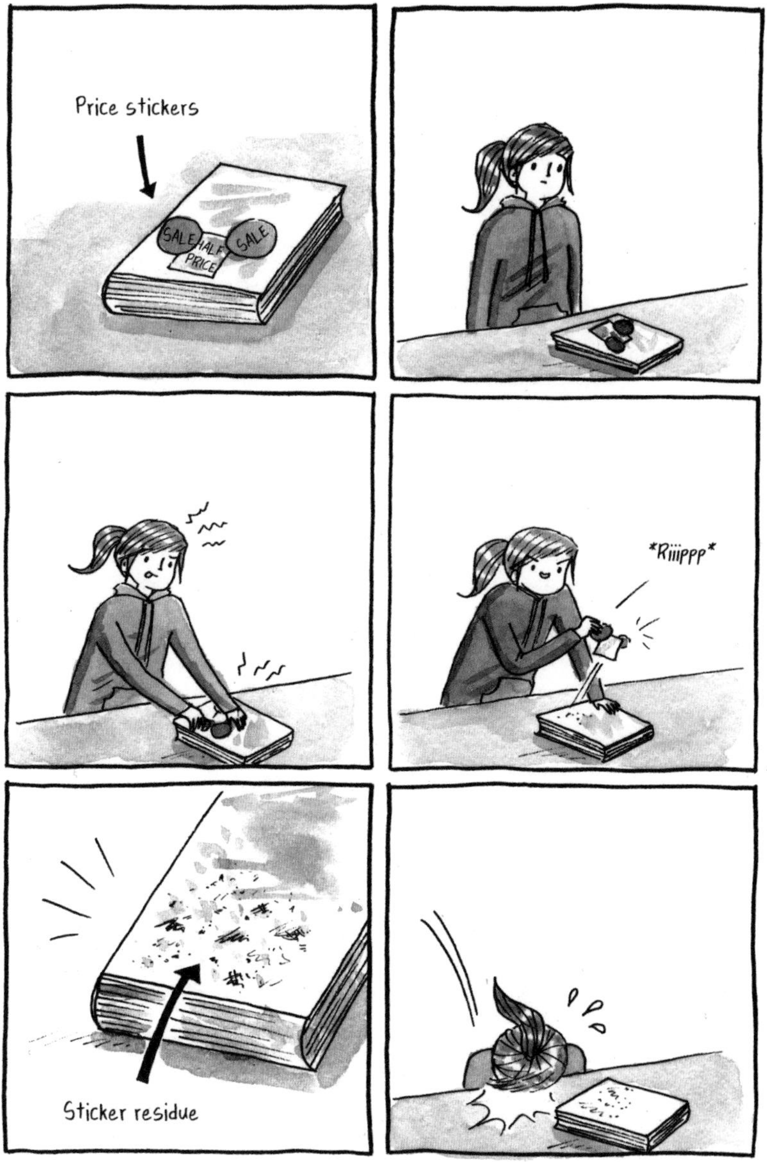
Price stickers
SALE
HALF PRICE
SALE
*Riiippp*
Sticker residue

# Other Things Books Can Be Used For

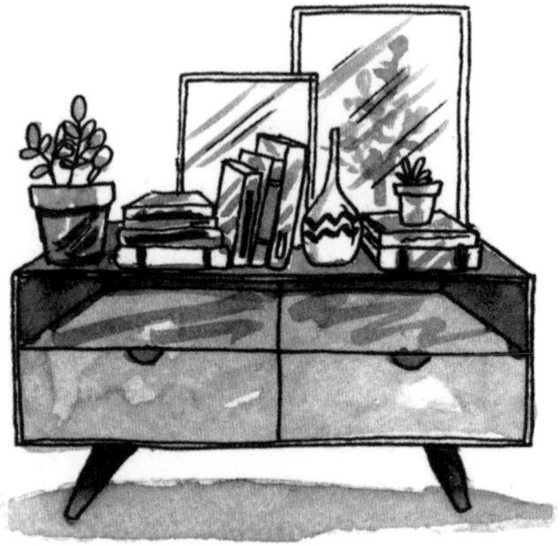

Decoration

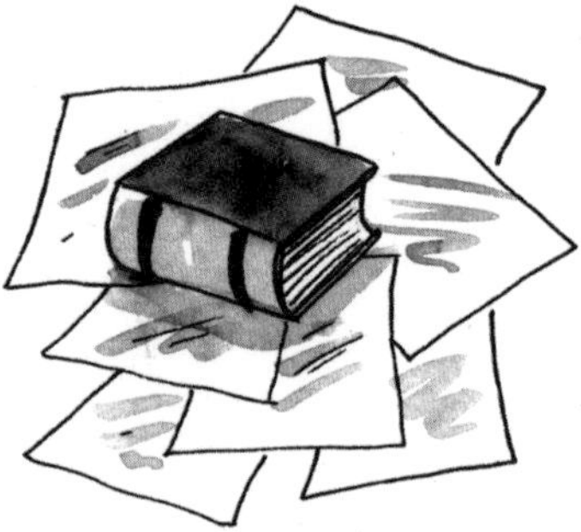

Paperweight

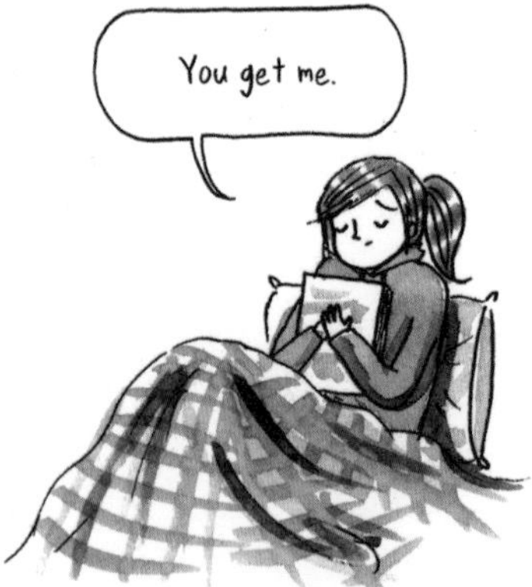
You get me.

Security blanket

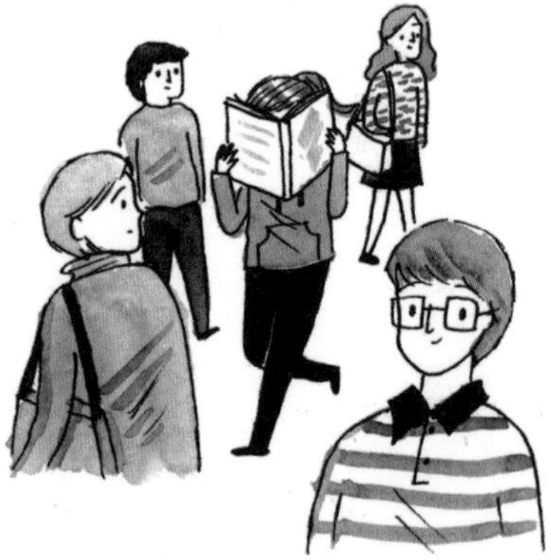

A way to avoid small talk with strangers

When People Interrupt Me While I'm Reading

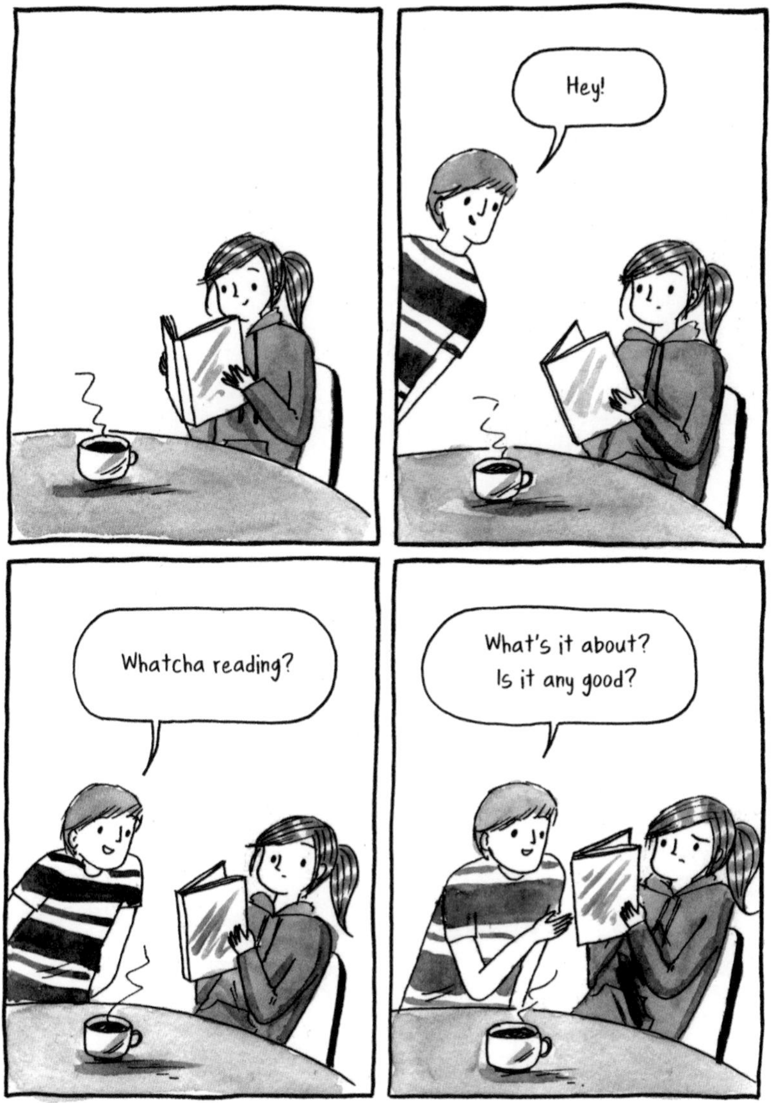
Hey!
Whatcha reading?
What's it about?
Is it any good?

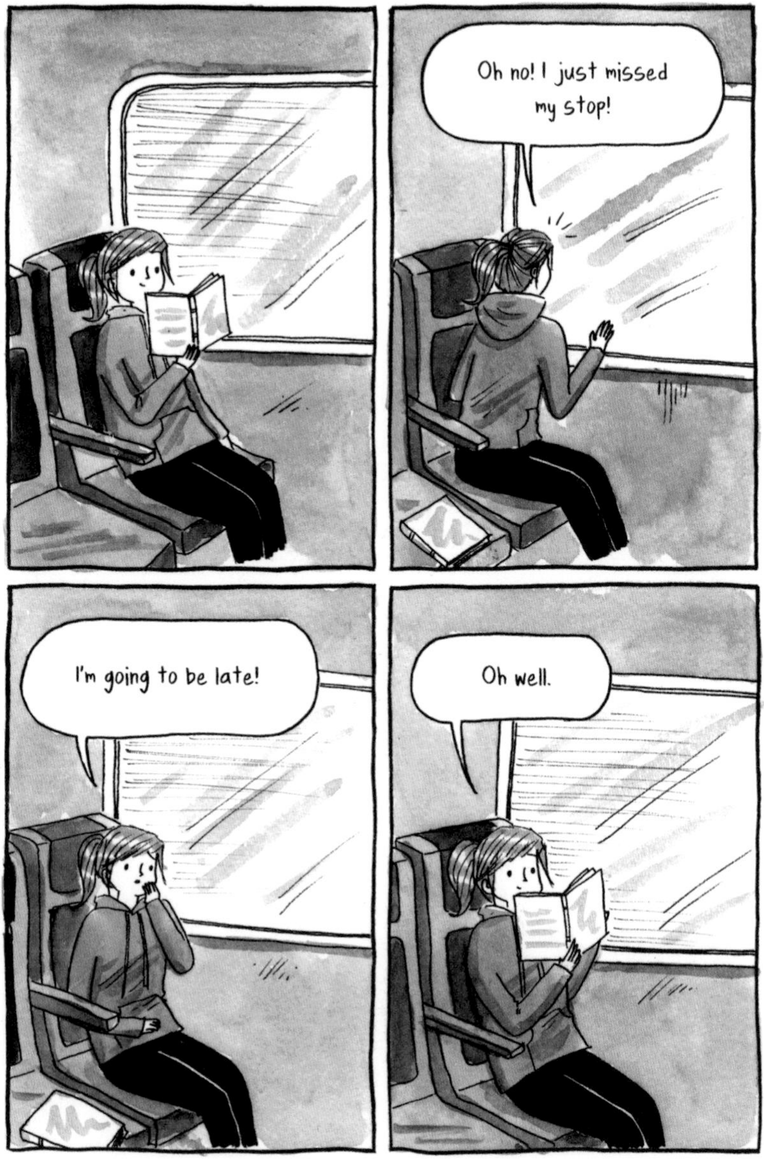
Oh no! I just missed my stop!
I'm going to be late!
Oh well.

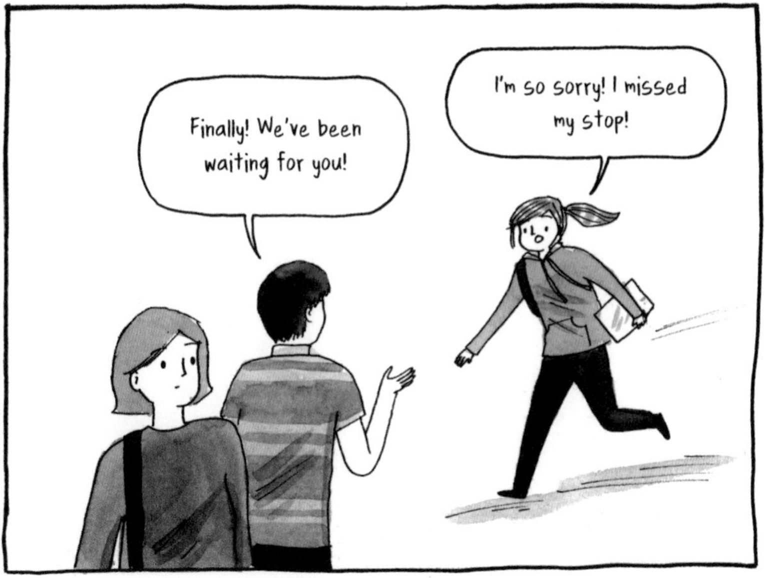
Finally! We've been waiting for you!
I'm so sorry! I missed my stop!

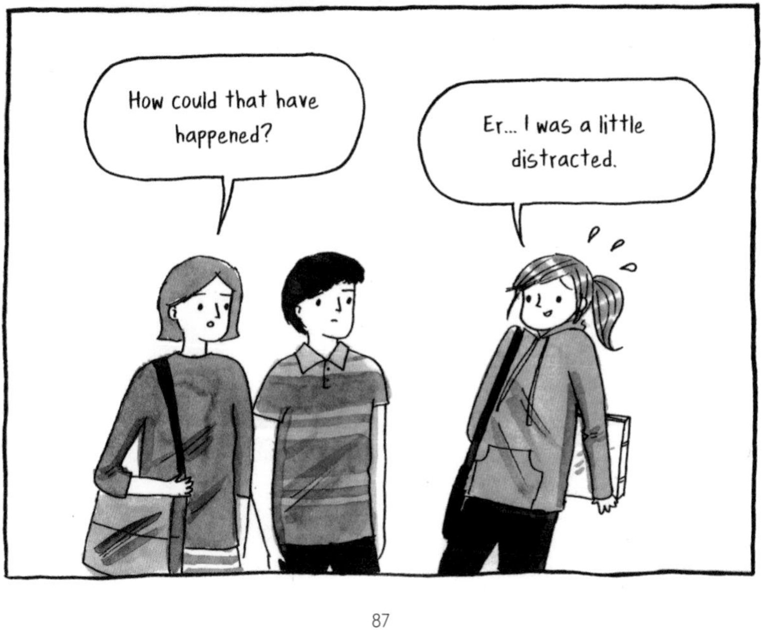
How could that have happened?
Er... I was a little distracted.

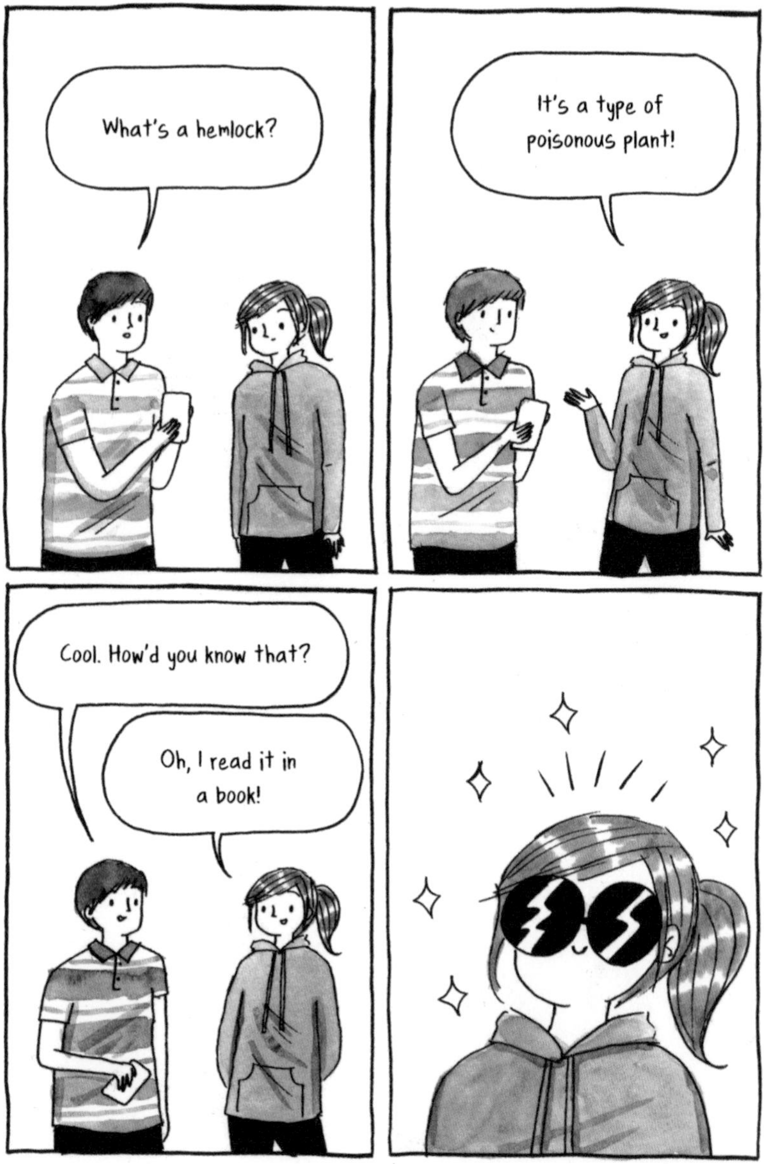
What's a hemlock?
It's a type of poisonous plant!
Cool. How'd you know that?
Oh, I read it in a book!

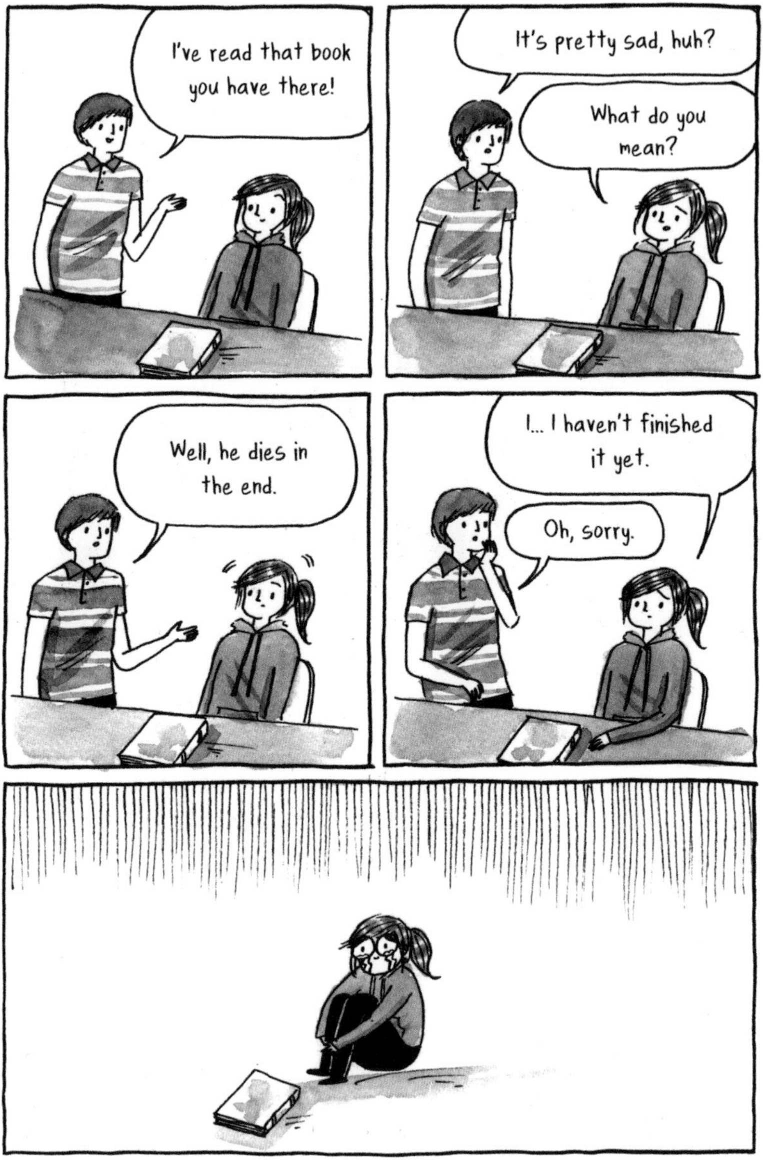
I've read that book you have there!
It's pretty sad, huh?
What do you mean?
Well, he dies in the end.
I... I haven't finished it yet.
Oh, sorry.

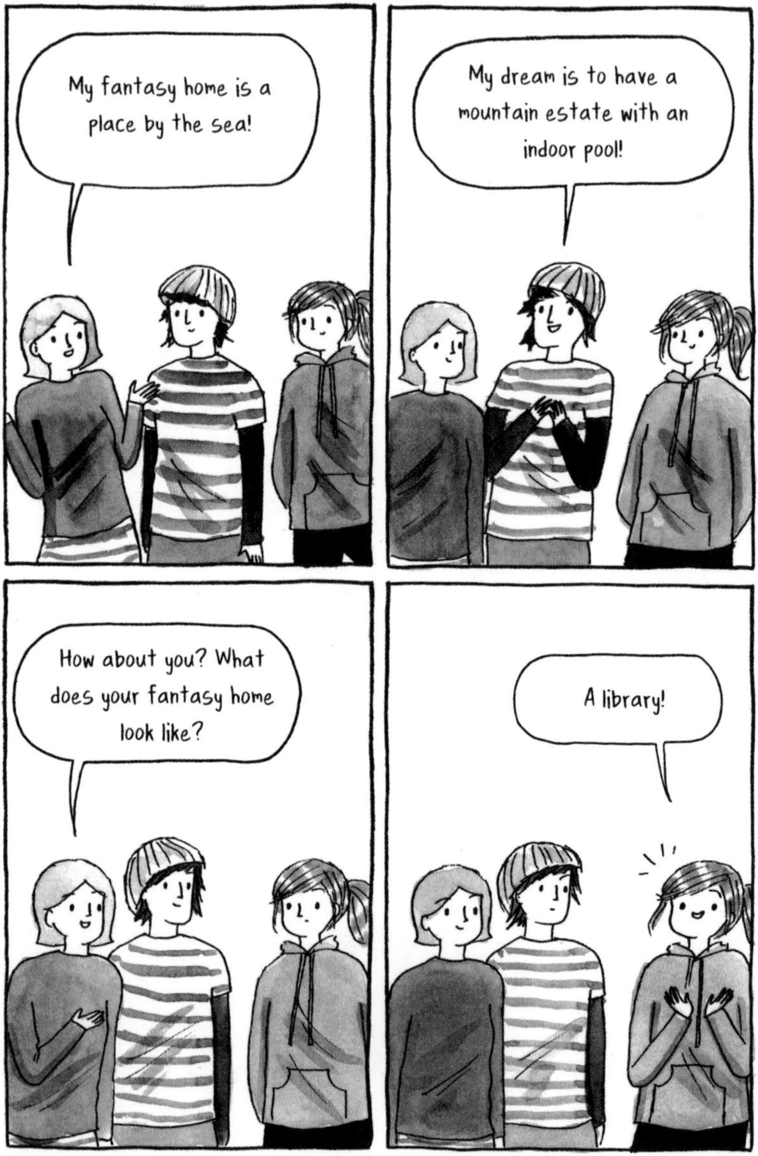
My fantasy home is a place by the sea!
My dream is to have a mountain estate with an indoor pool!
How about you? What does your fantasy home look like?
A library!

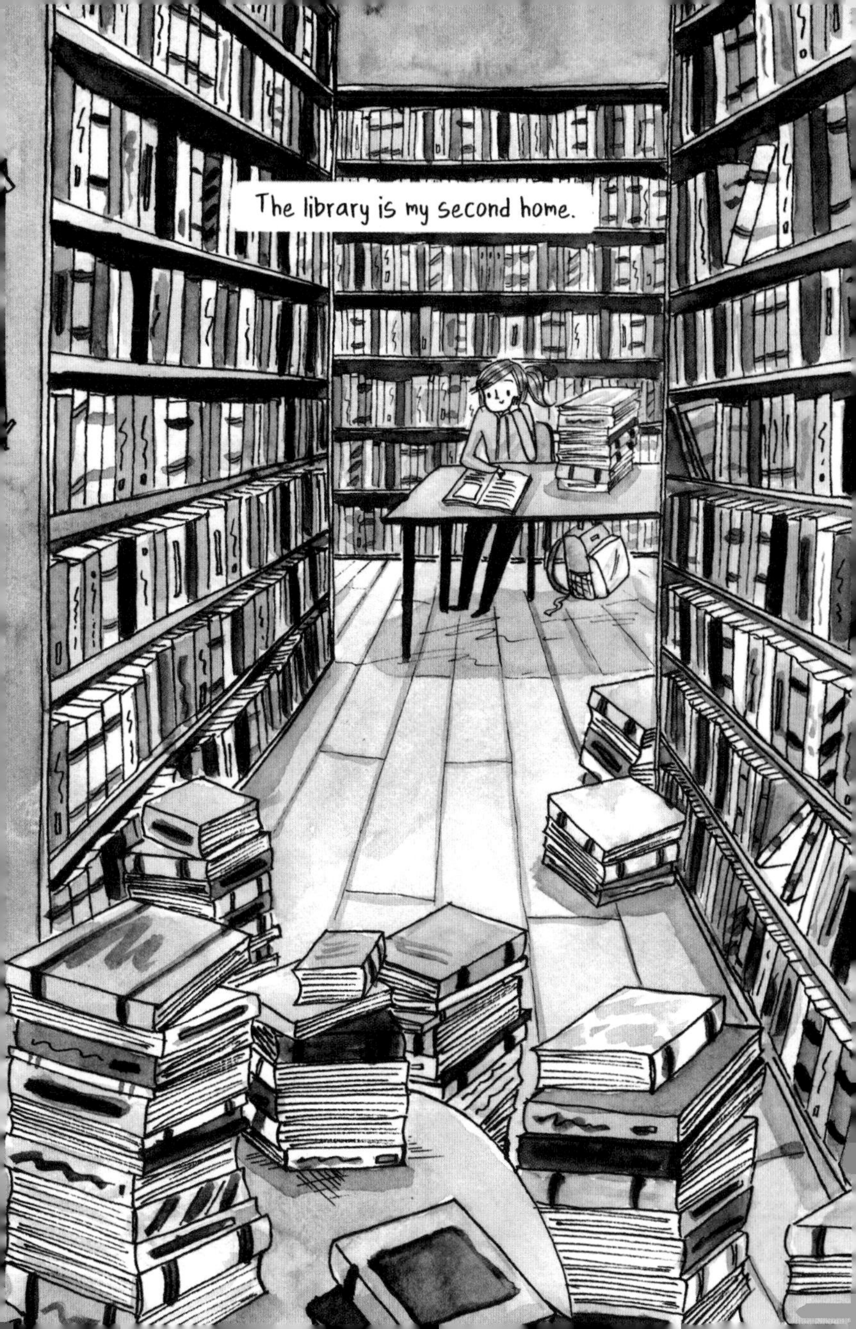
The library is my second home.

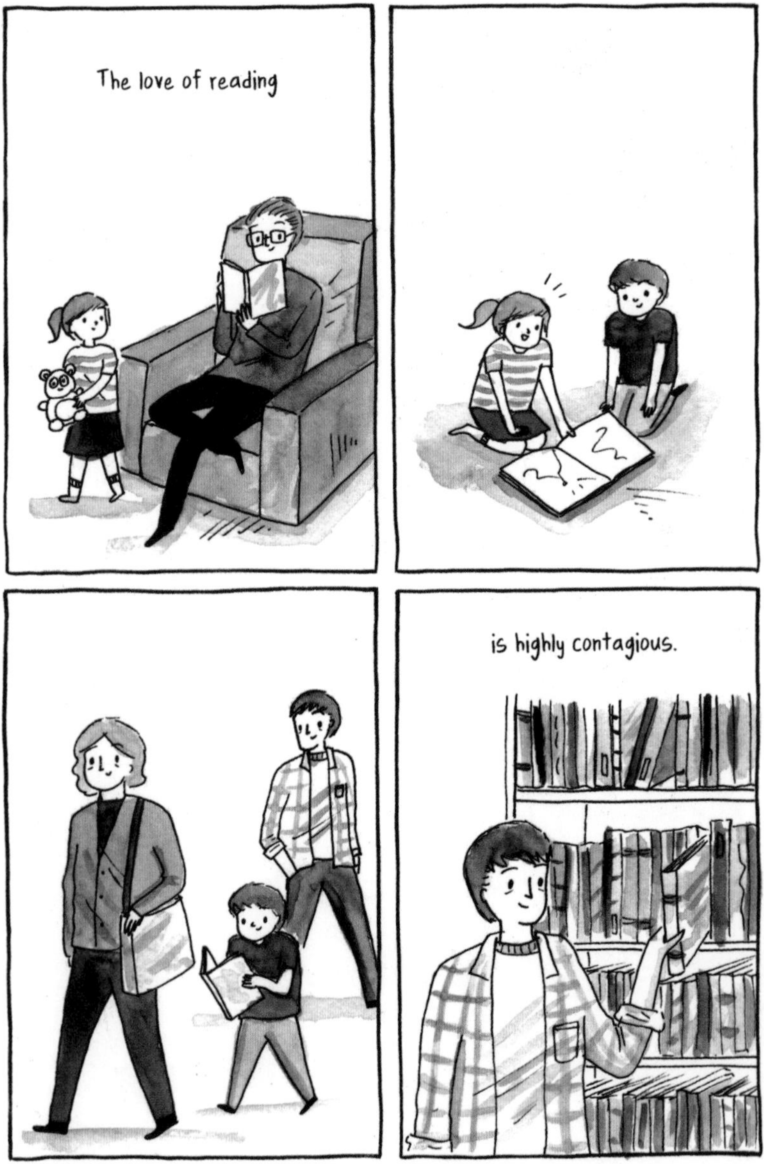
The love of reading
is highly contagious.

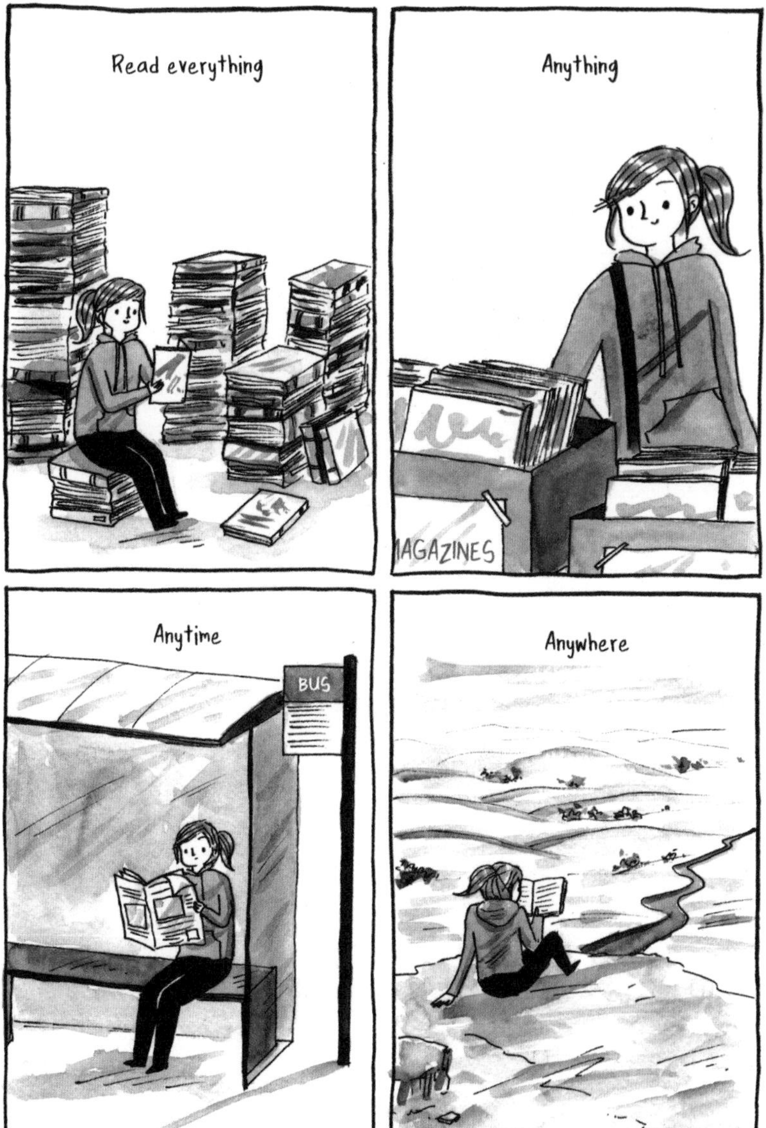
Read everything
Anything
MAGAZINES
Anytime
BUS
Anywhere

# Different Types of Libraries

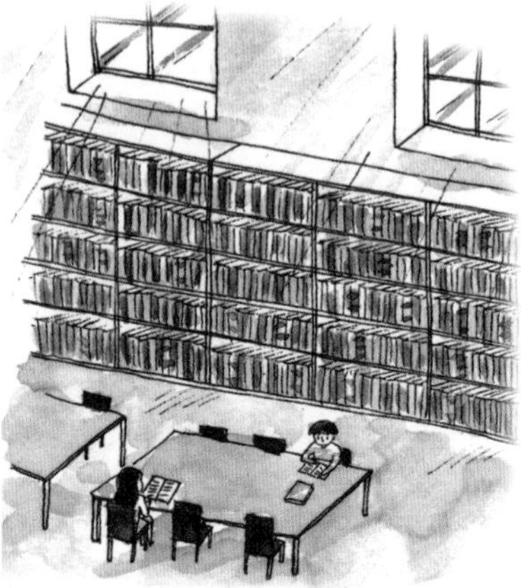

National library

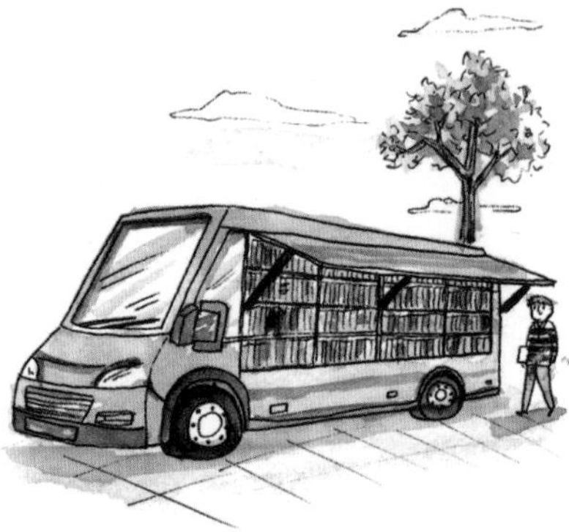

Mobile library

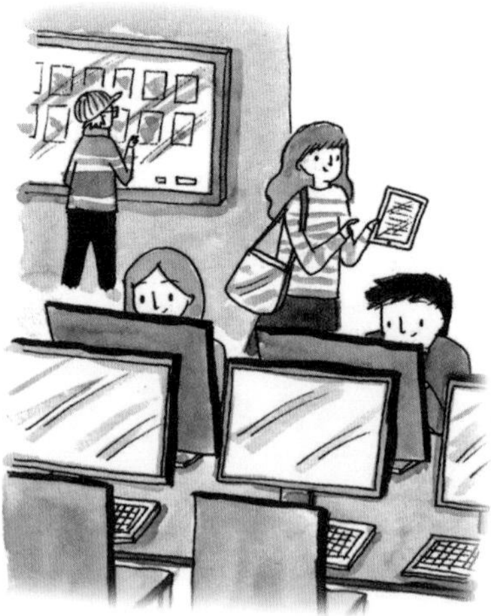

Bookless library

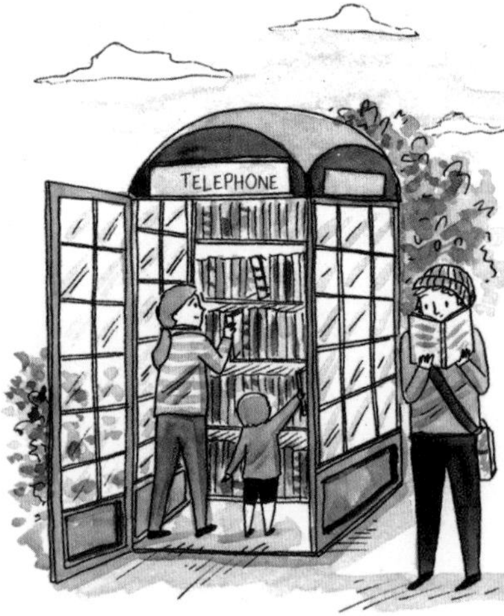
TELEPHONE

Phone booth library

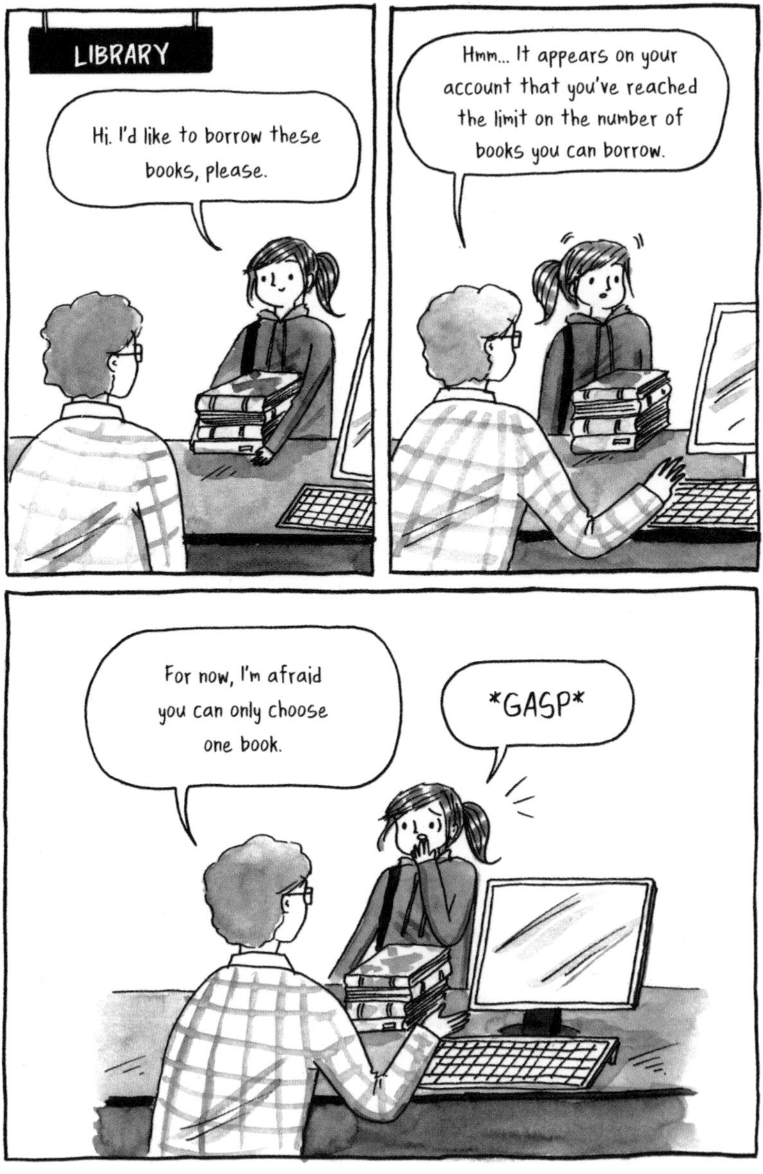
LIBRARY
Hi. I'd like to borrow these books, please.
Hmm... It appears on your account that you've reached the limit on the number of books you can borrow.
For now, I'm afraid you can only choose one book.
*GASP*

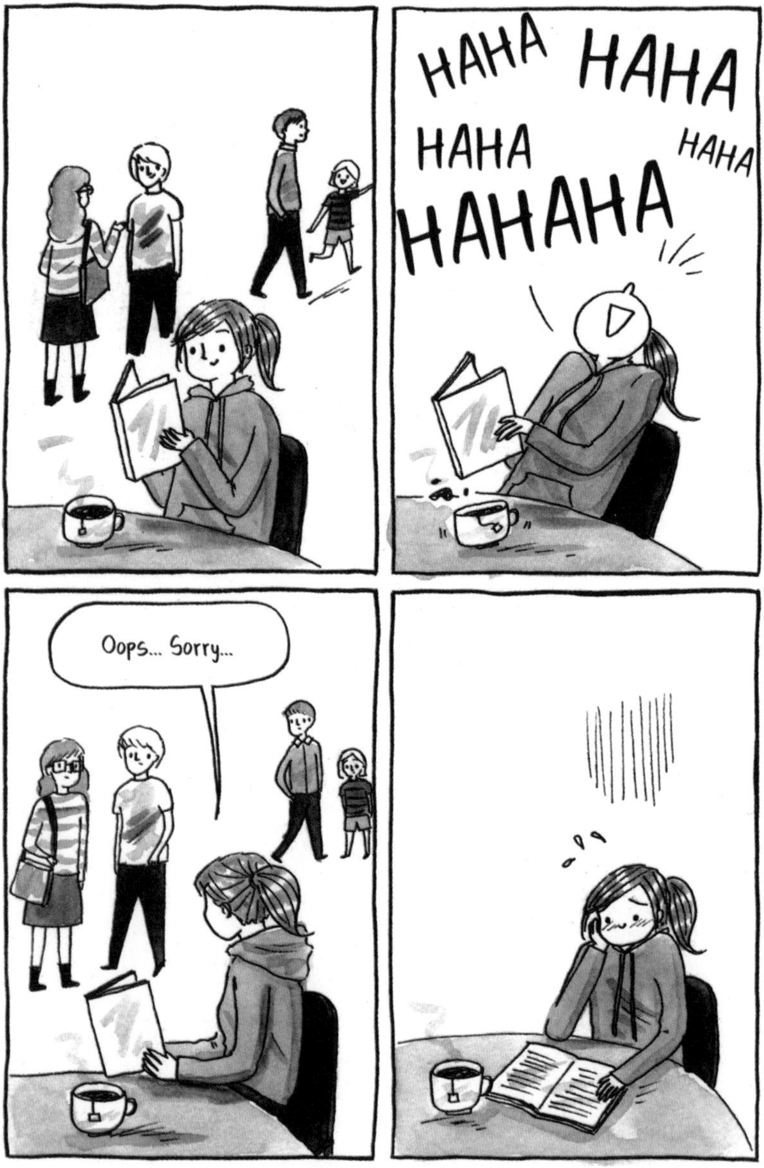
HAHA
HAHA
HAHA
HAHA
HAHAHA
Oops... Sorry...

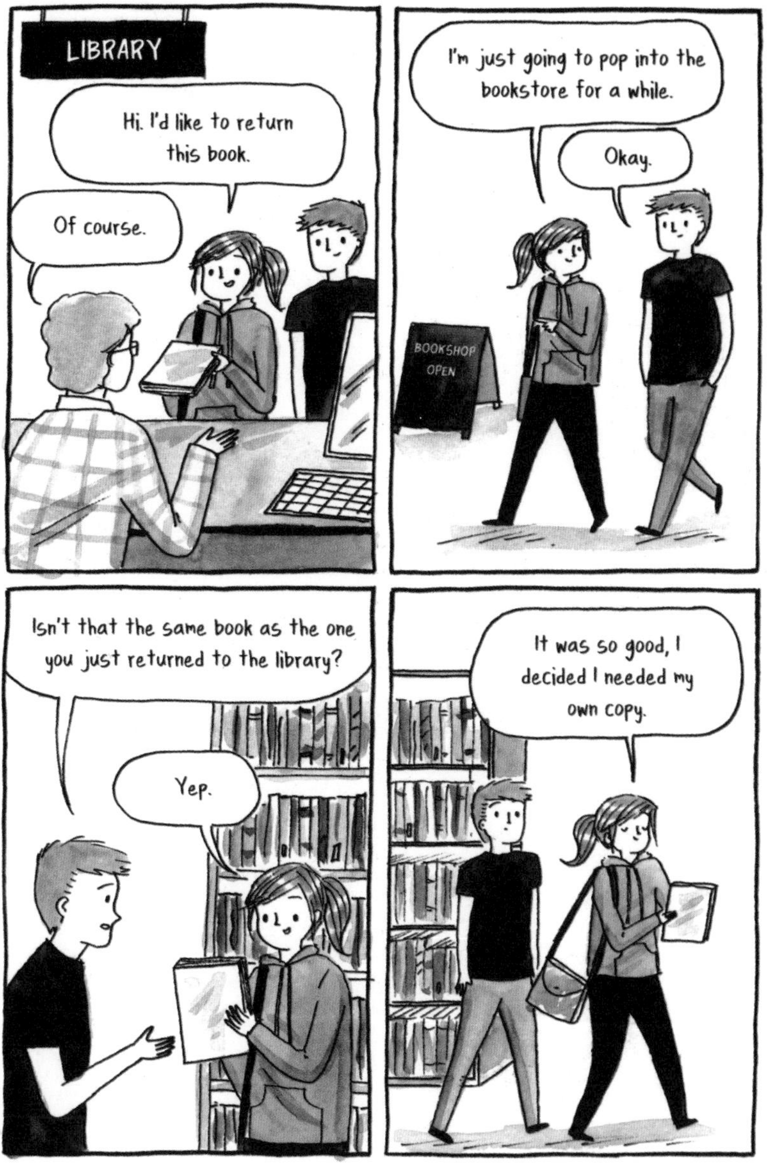
LIBRARY
Hi. I'd like to return this book.
Of course.
I'm just going to pop into the bookstore for a while.
Okay.
BOOKSHOP OPEN
Isn't that the same book as the one you just returned to the library?
Yep.
It was so good, I decided I needed my own copy.

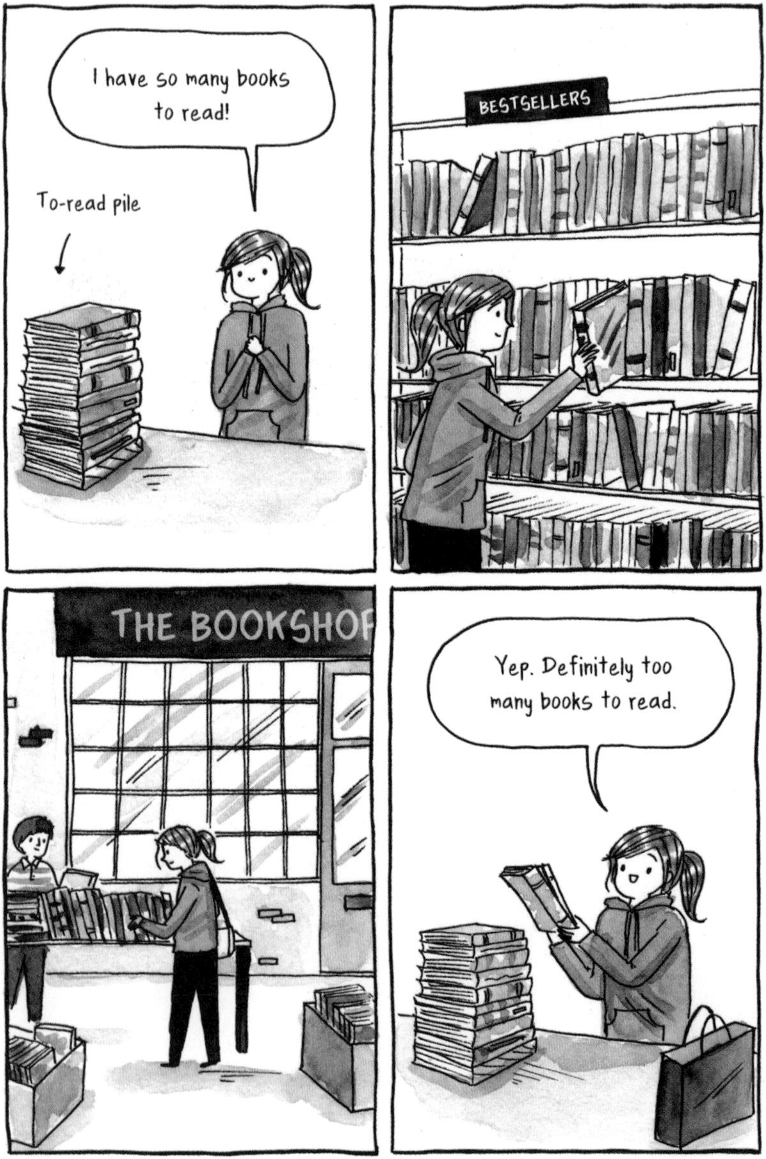
I have so many books to read!
To-read pile
BESTSELLERS
THE BOOKSHOP
Yep. Definitely too many books to read.

# Ways I Arrange My Books

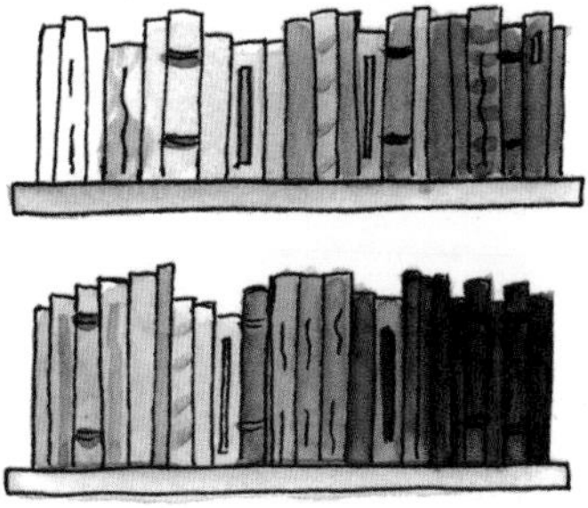

Color

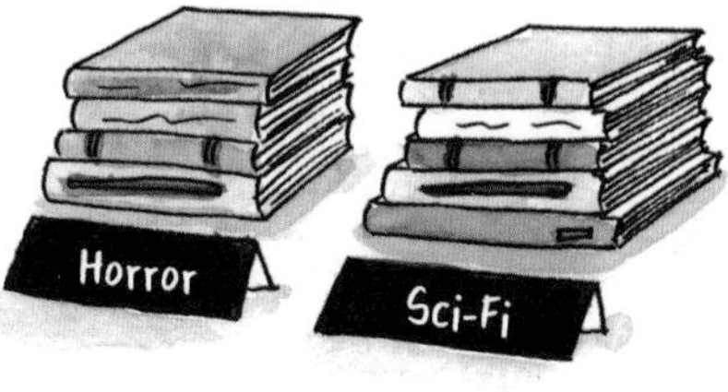
Horror
Sci-Fi

Genre

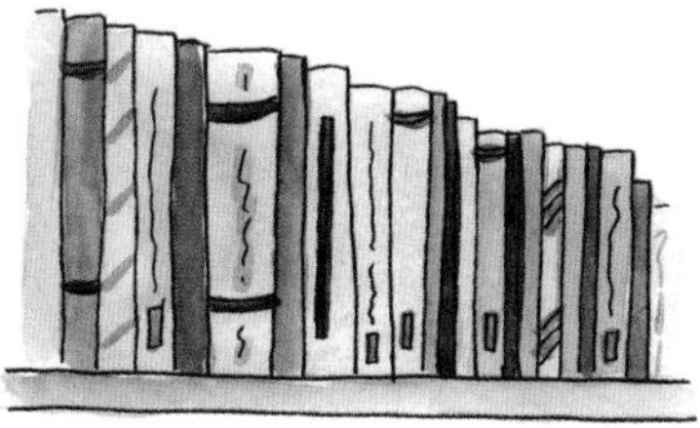

Size

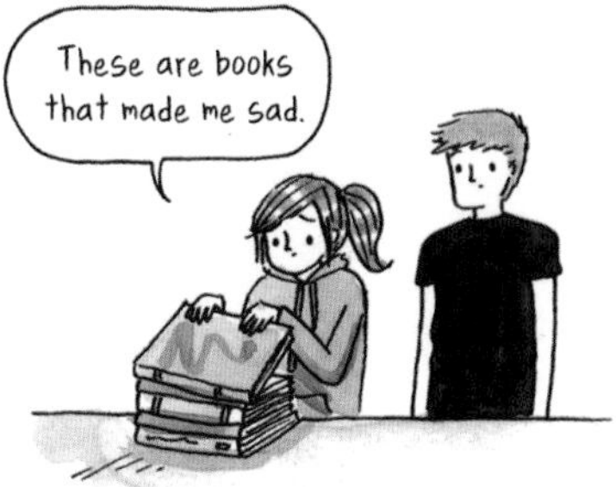
These are books that made me sad.

Emotions

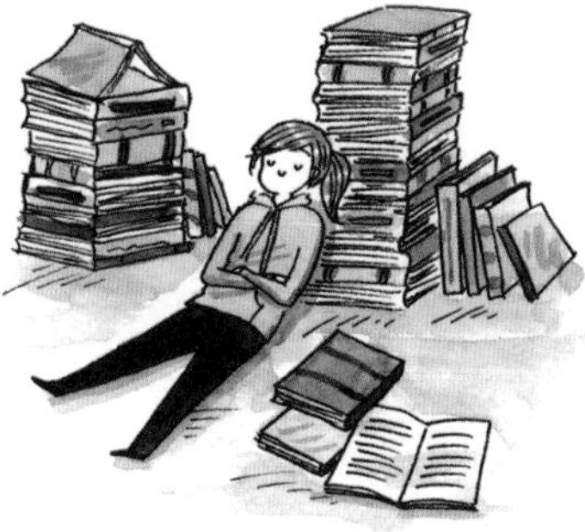

Complete and utter randomness

# How To Get Out of a Reading Slump

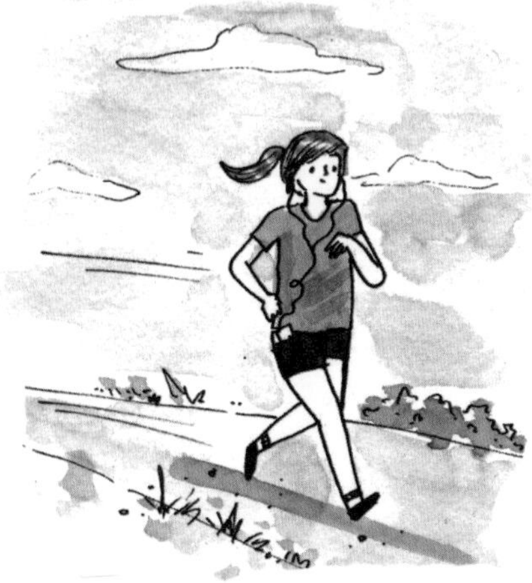

Take a break from reading and do something different for a change.

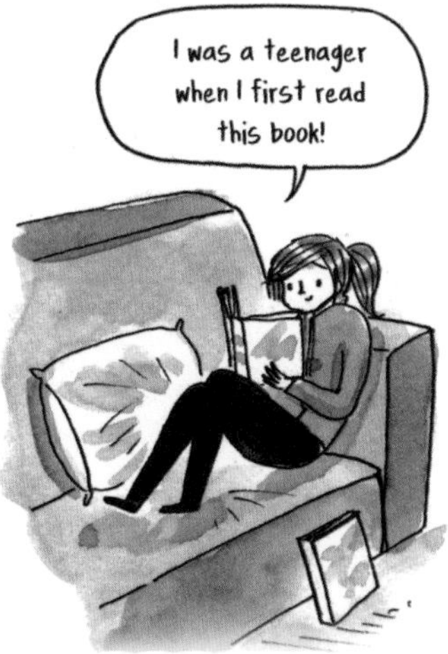
I was a teenager when I first read this book!

Reread some old favorite books, even if it's one from your childhood.

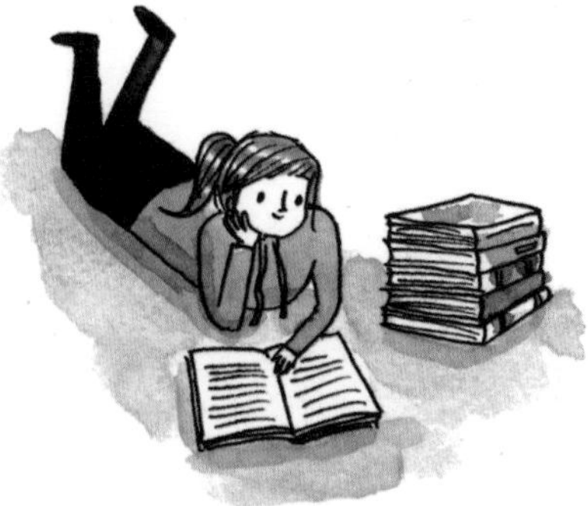

Go for light and easy reads that can ease you back into the habit.

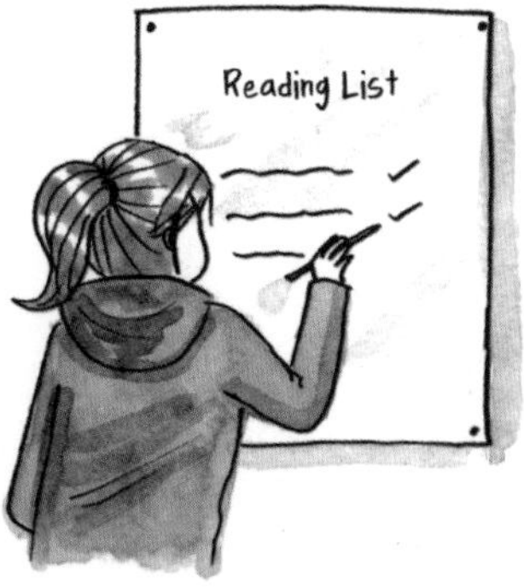
Reading List

Set reading goals and start with manageable targets.

# More Things You Can Do to Fall in Love with Reading

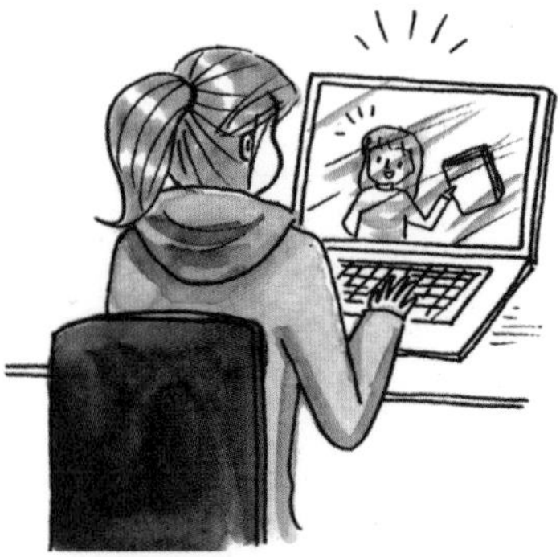

Watch book review and book haul videos online. Seeing people talk about books is a great way to find your next read.

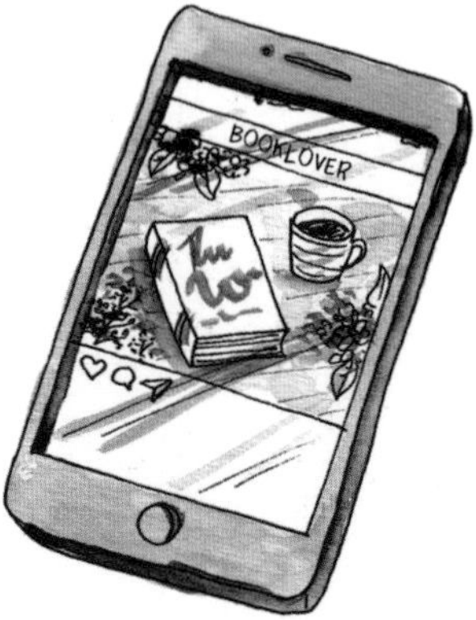
BOOKLOVER

Follow bookish social media sites. It's always nice to see beautiful photos of books.

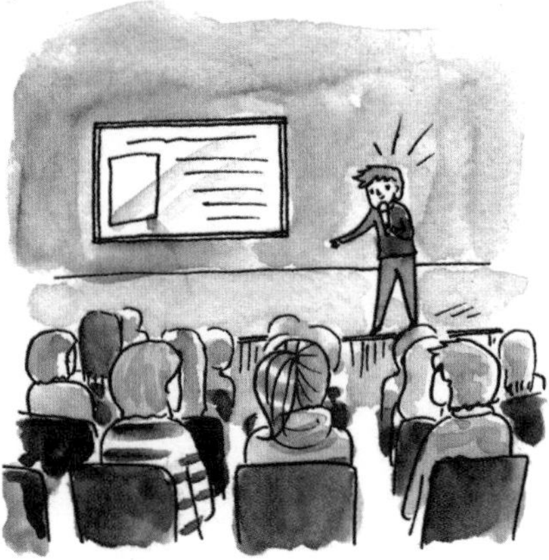

Attend literary events with presentations and workshops by authors to feel inspired.

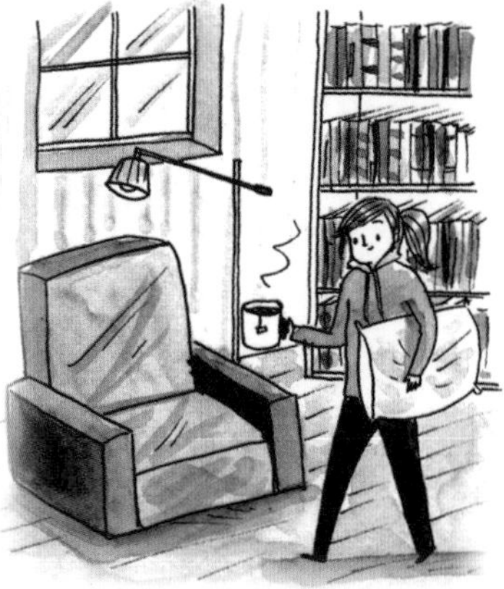

Build your own reading nook. It should be a space where you can turn off from the outside world.

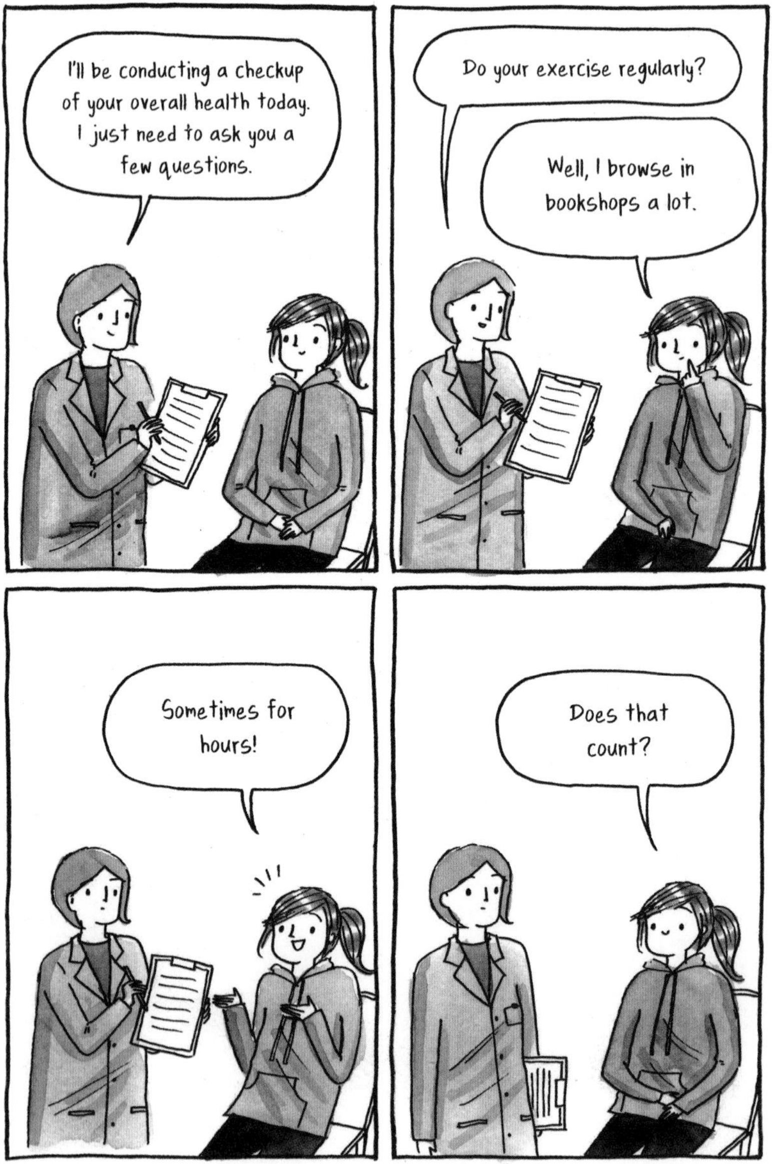
I'll be conducting a checkup of your overall health today. I just need to ask you a few questions.
Do your exercise regularly?
Well, I browse in bookshops a lot.
Sometimes for hours!
Does that count?

## Finding the Perfect Reading Position

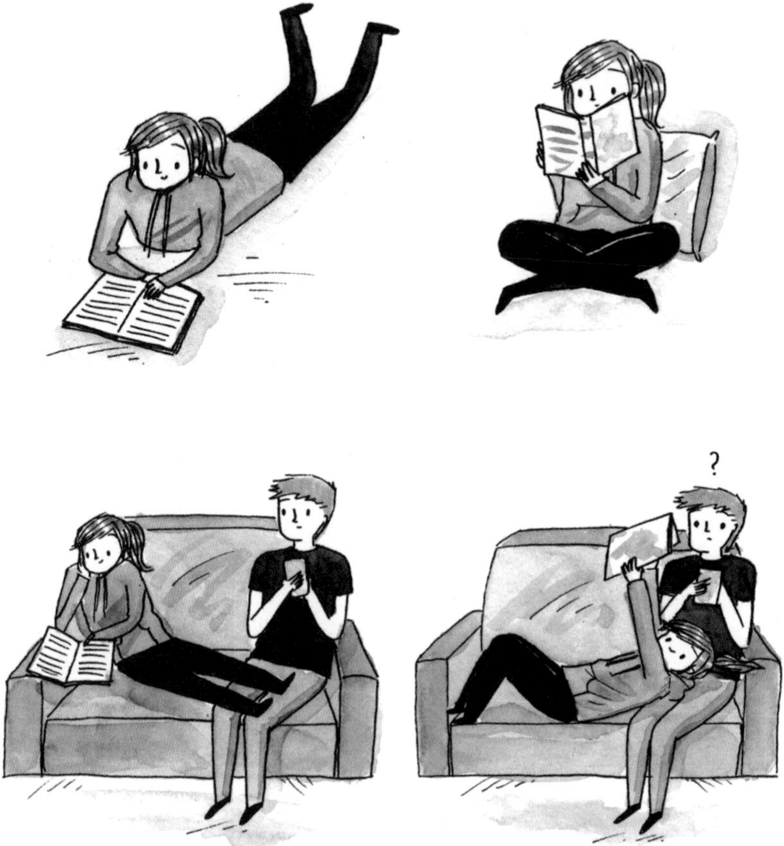
?

# Fitness for Bookworms

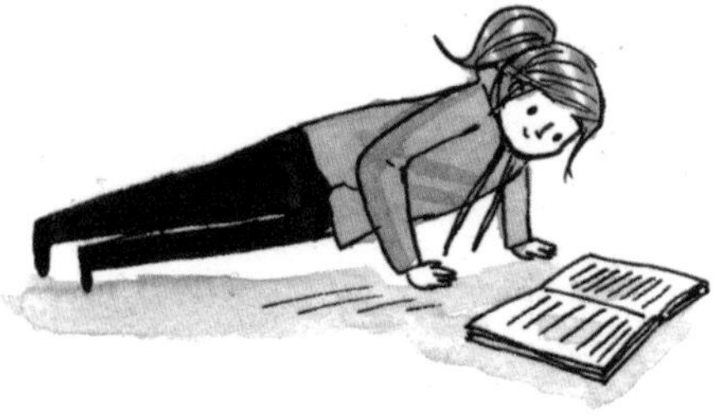

Push-up

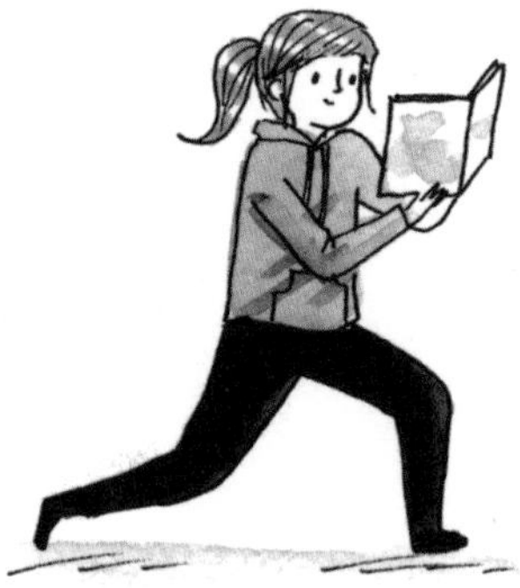

Lunge

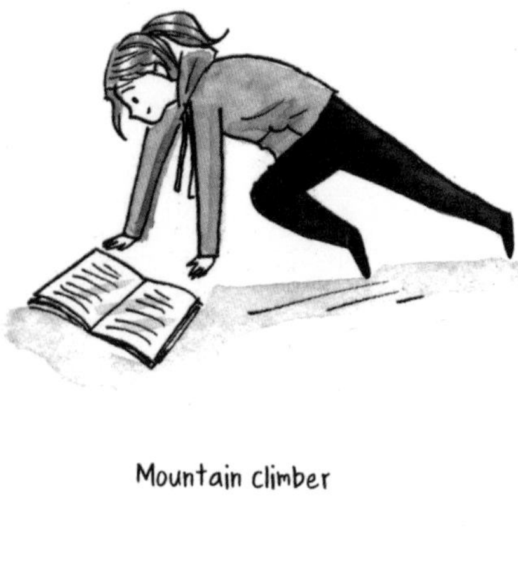

Mountain climber

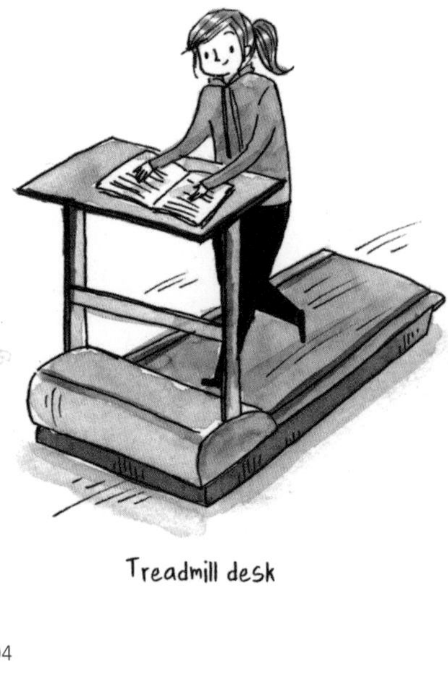

Treadmill desk

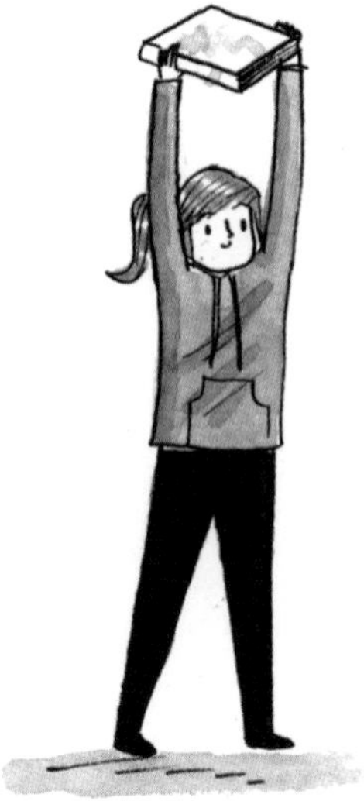

Overhead press

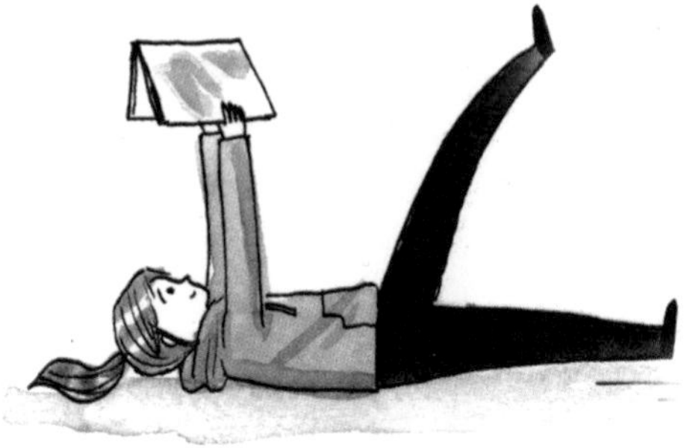

Leg raise

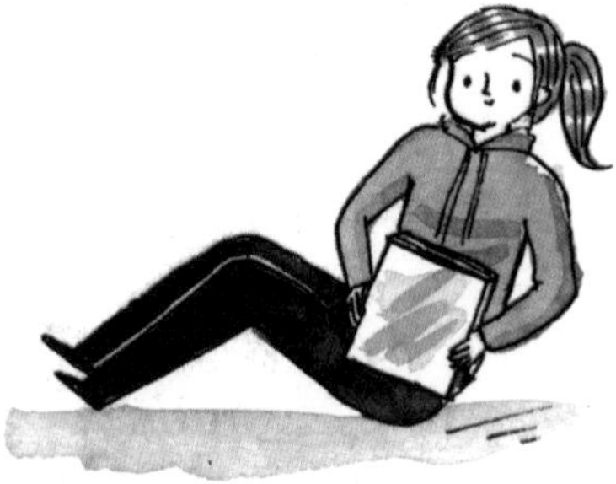

Oblique twist

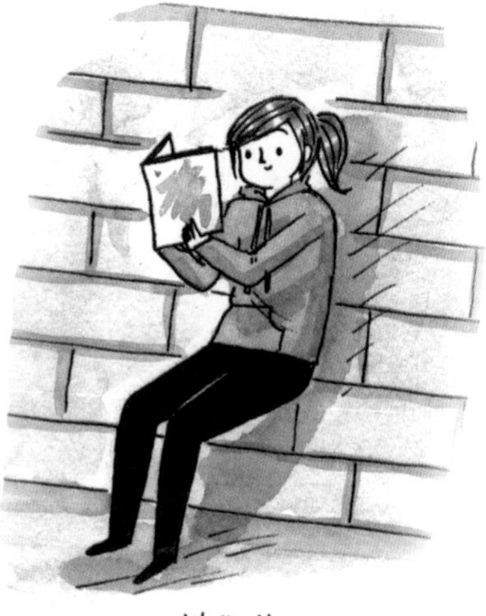

Wall sit

# How to Spot a Bookworm

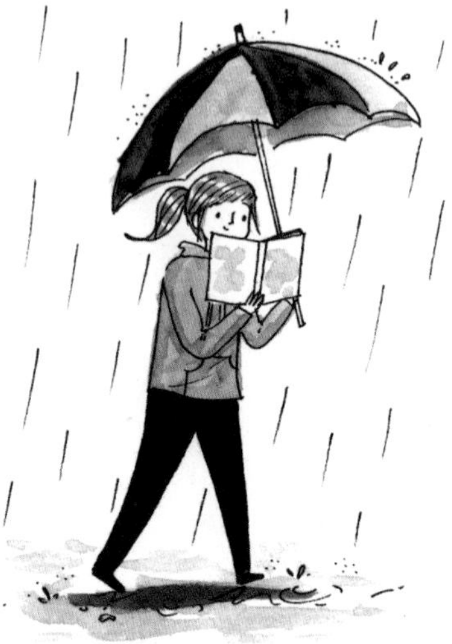

Always reading at any opportunity.

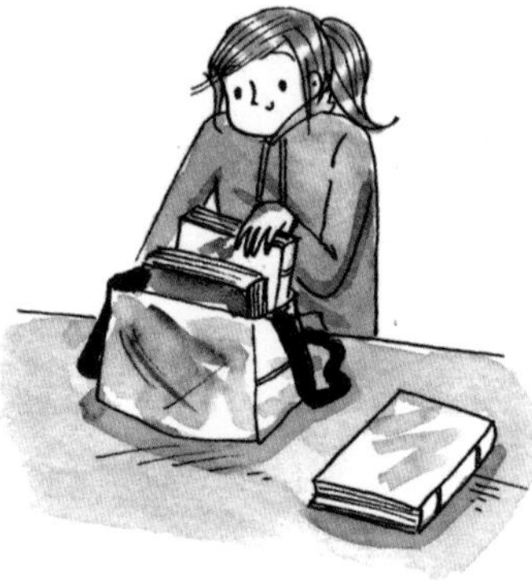

Carries a bag big enough to fit a book or two.

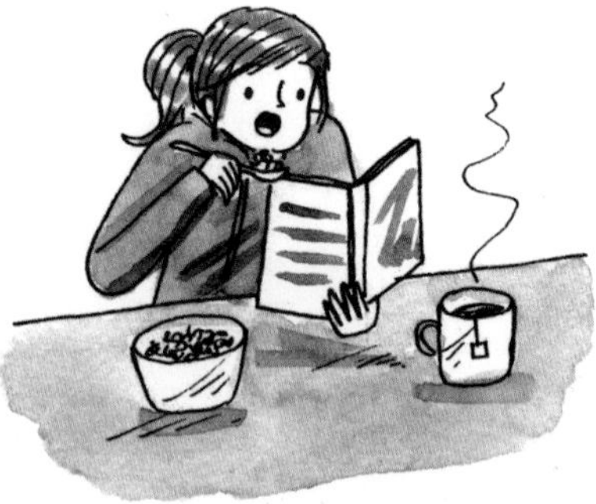

Trying to balance eating and reading at the same time.

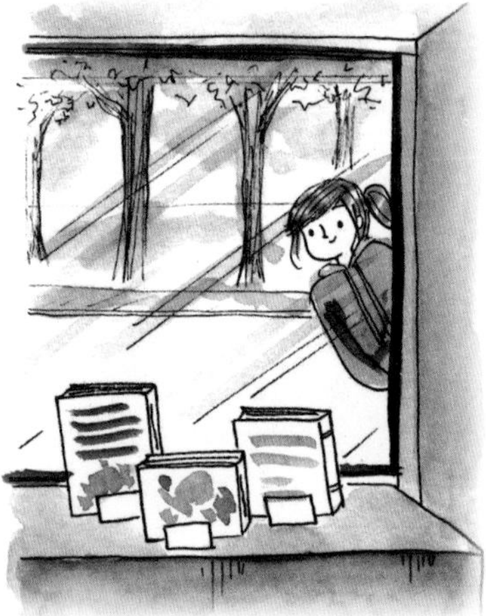

When passing a bookshop, head is turned toward the window display.

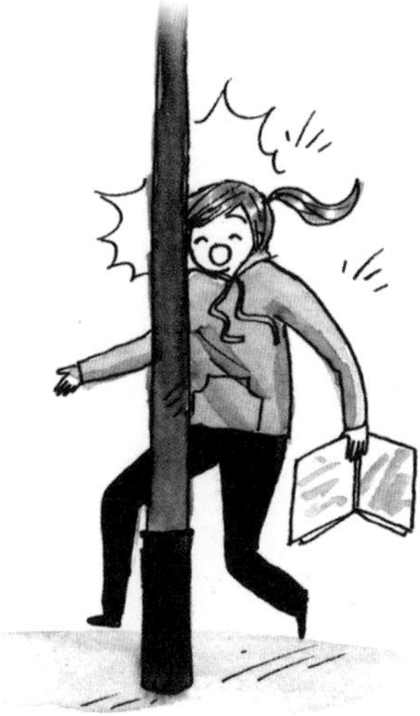

Occasionally walking into things.

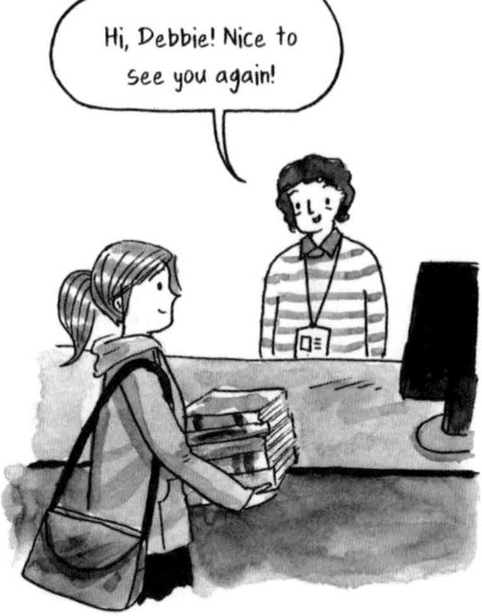
Hi, Debbie! Nice to see you again!

The staff at the local library knows them by name.

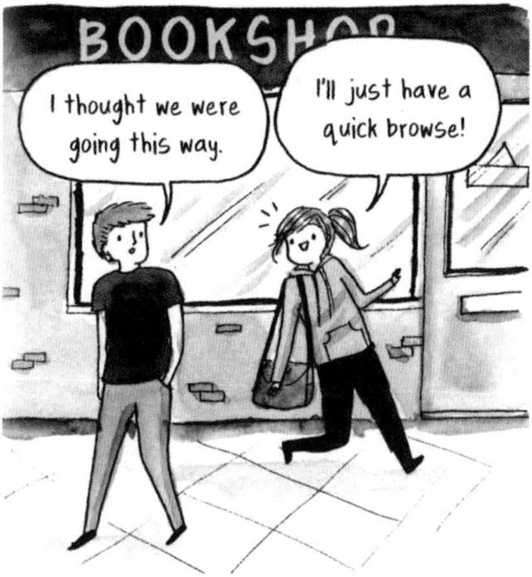
BOOKSHOP
I thought we were going this way.
I'll just have a quick browse!

Attracted to a bookshop like a magnetic pull.

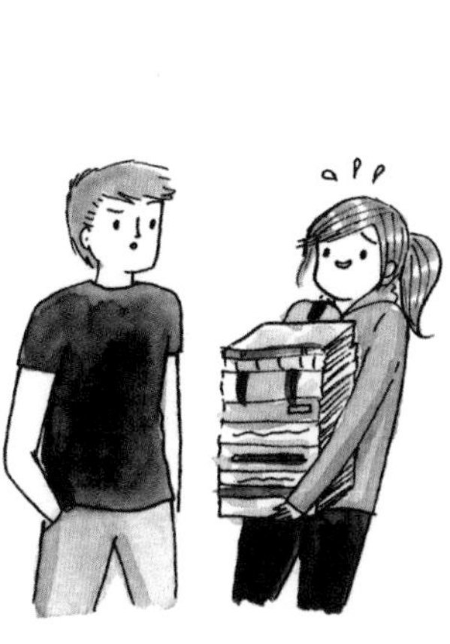

Saying they'll just have a quick browse but come out looking like they bought a whole shelf.

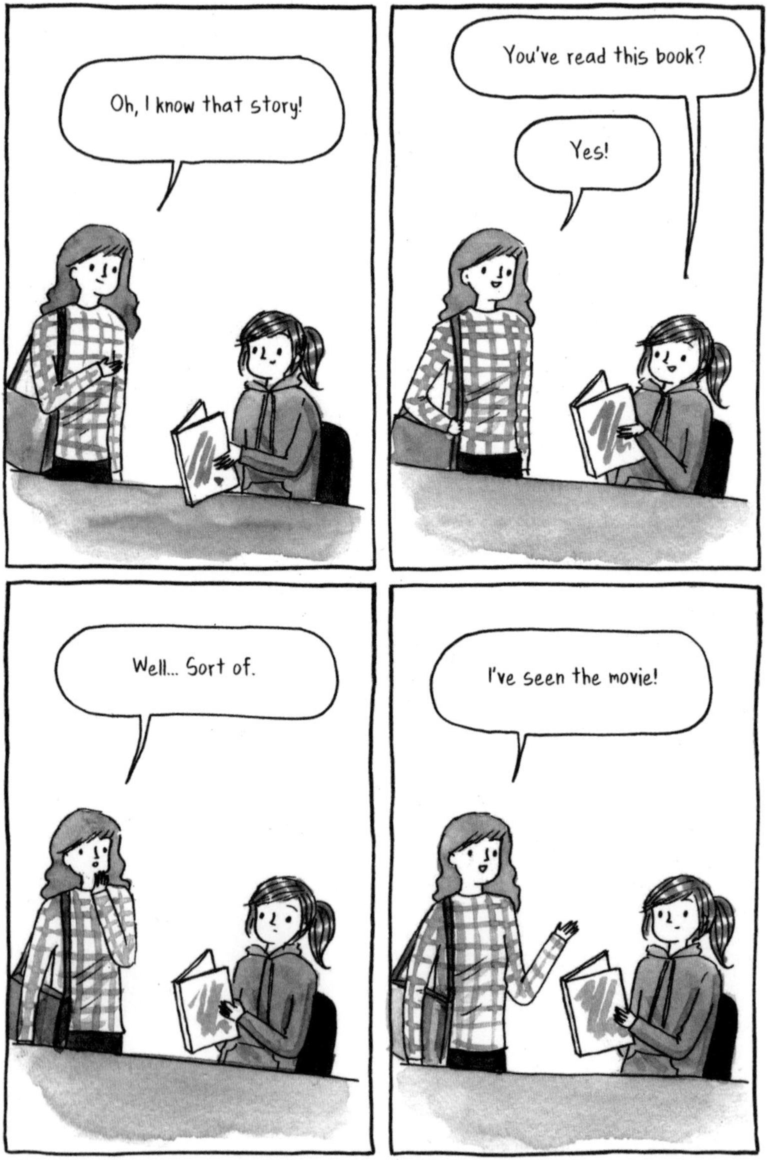
Oh, I know that story!
You've read this book?
Yes!
Well... Sort of.
I've seen the movie!

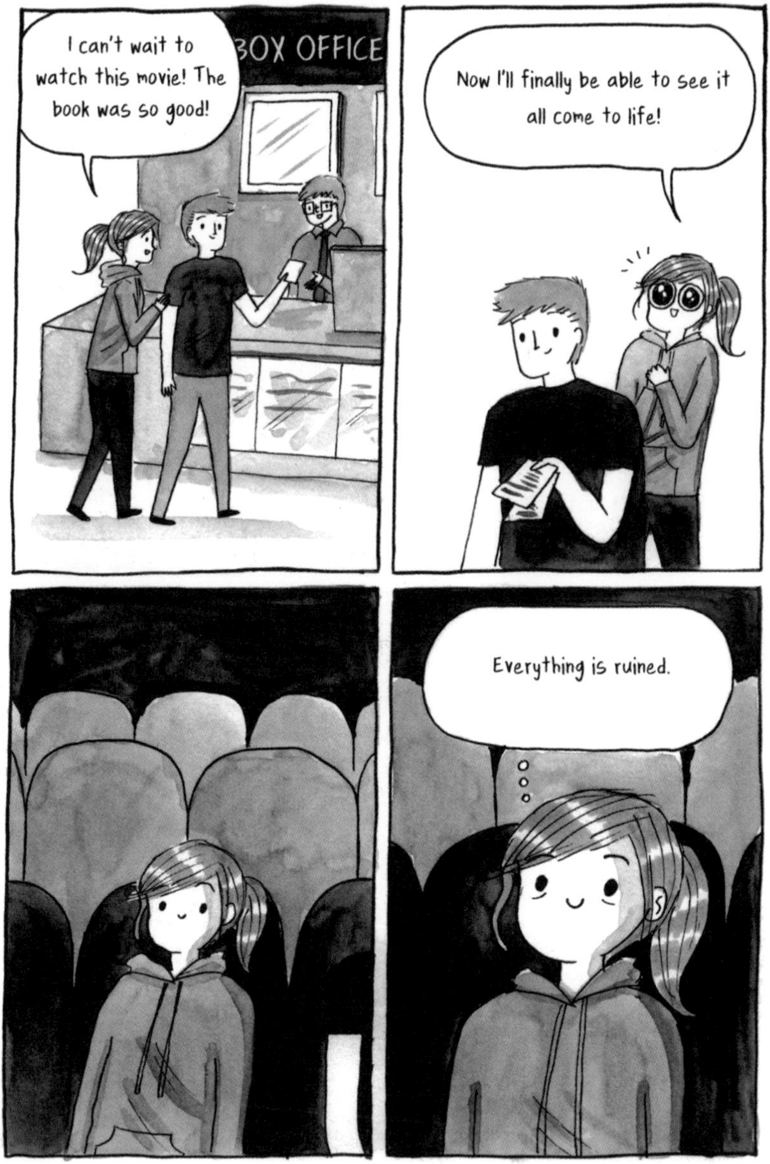
I can't wait to watch this movie! The book was so good!
BOX OFFICE
Now I'll finally be able to see it all come to life!
Everything is ruined.

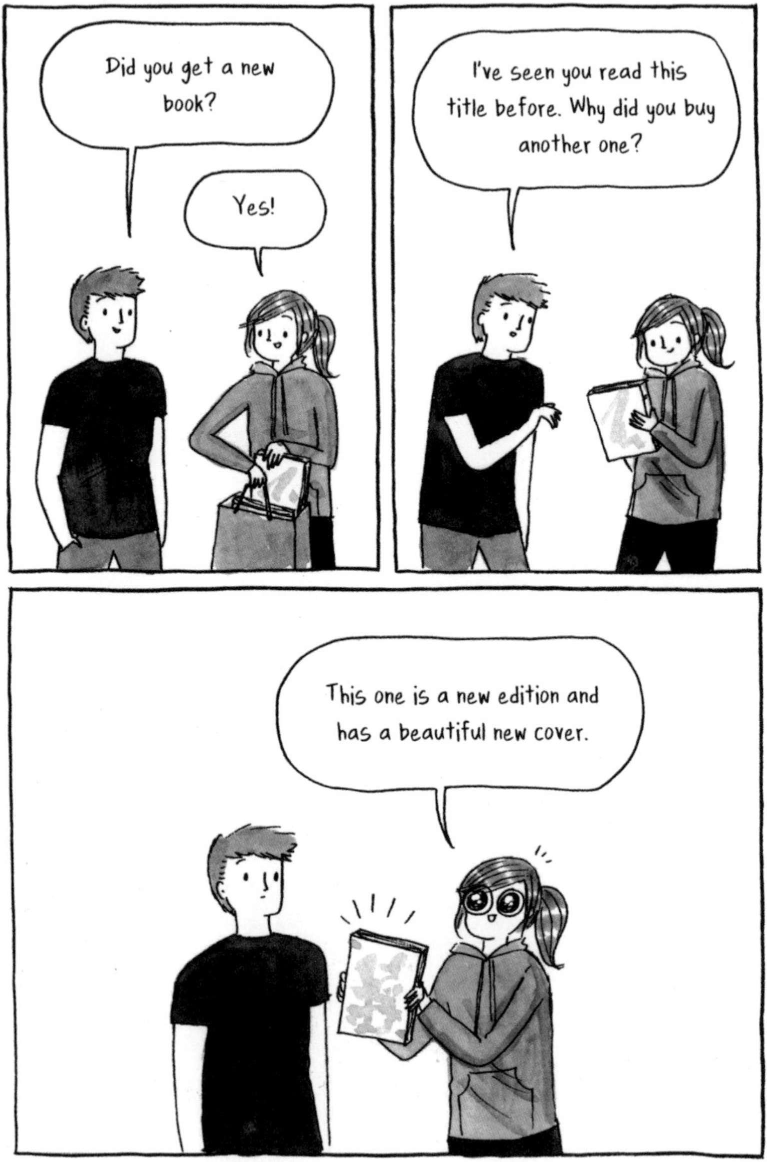
Did you get a new book?
Yes!
I've seen you read this title before. Why did you buy another one?
This one is a new edition and has a beautiful new cover.

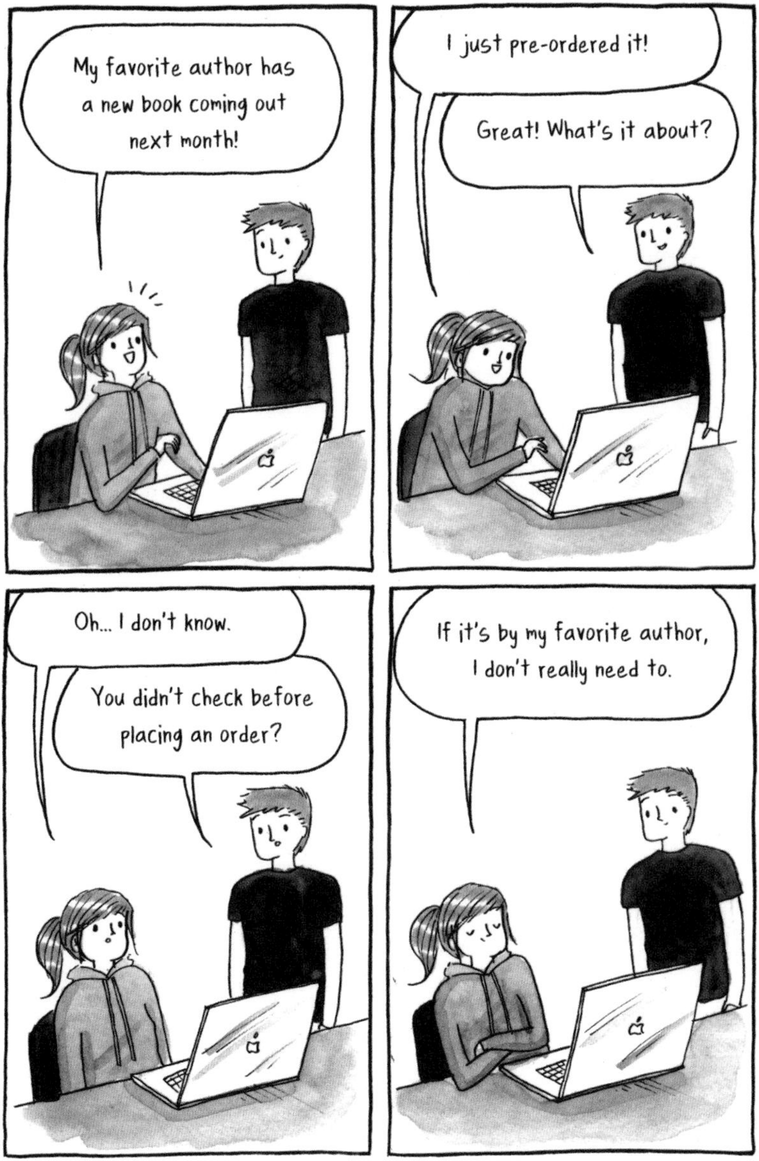
My favorite author has a new book coming out next month!
I just pre-ordered it!
Great! What's it about?
Oh... I don't know.
You didn't check before placing an order?
If it's by my favorite author, I don't really need to.

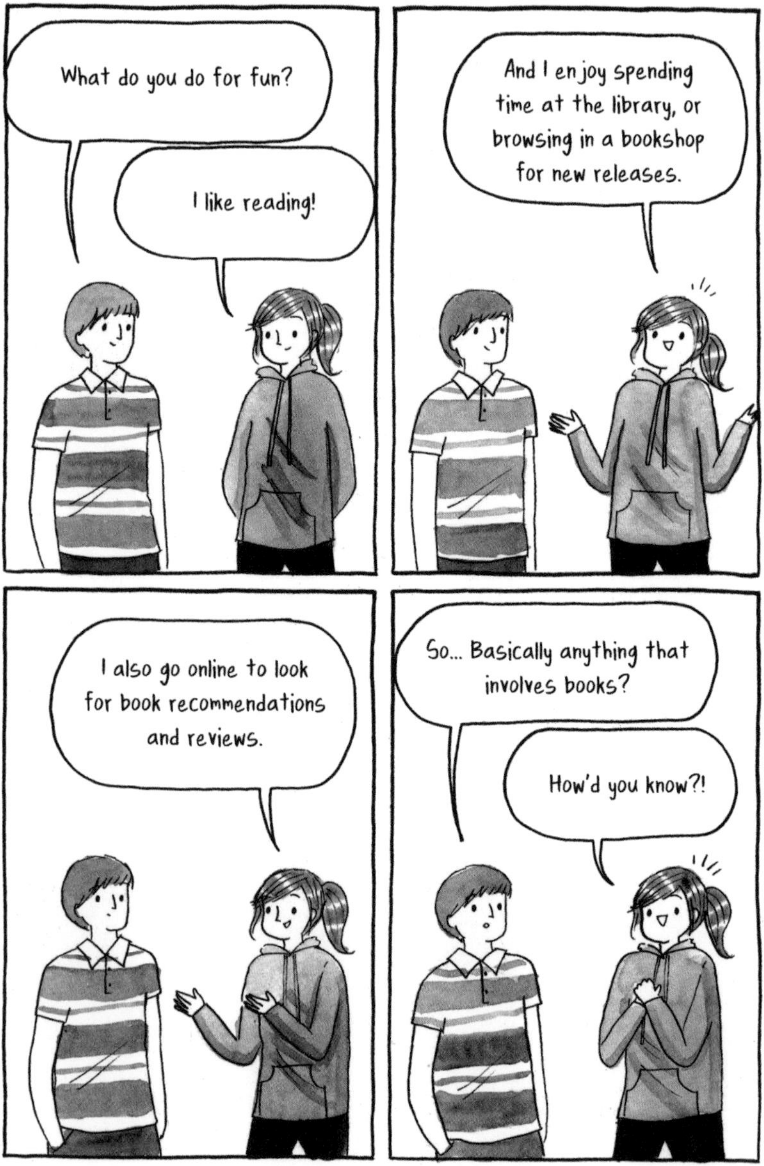
What do you do for fun?
I like reading!
And I enjoy spending time at the library, or browsing in a bookshop for new releases.
I also go online to look for book recommendations and reviews.
So... Basically anything that involves books?
How'd you know?!

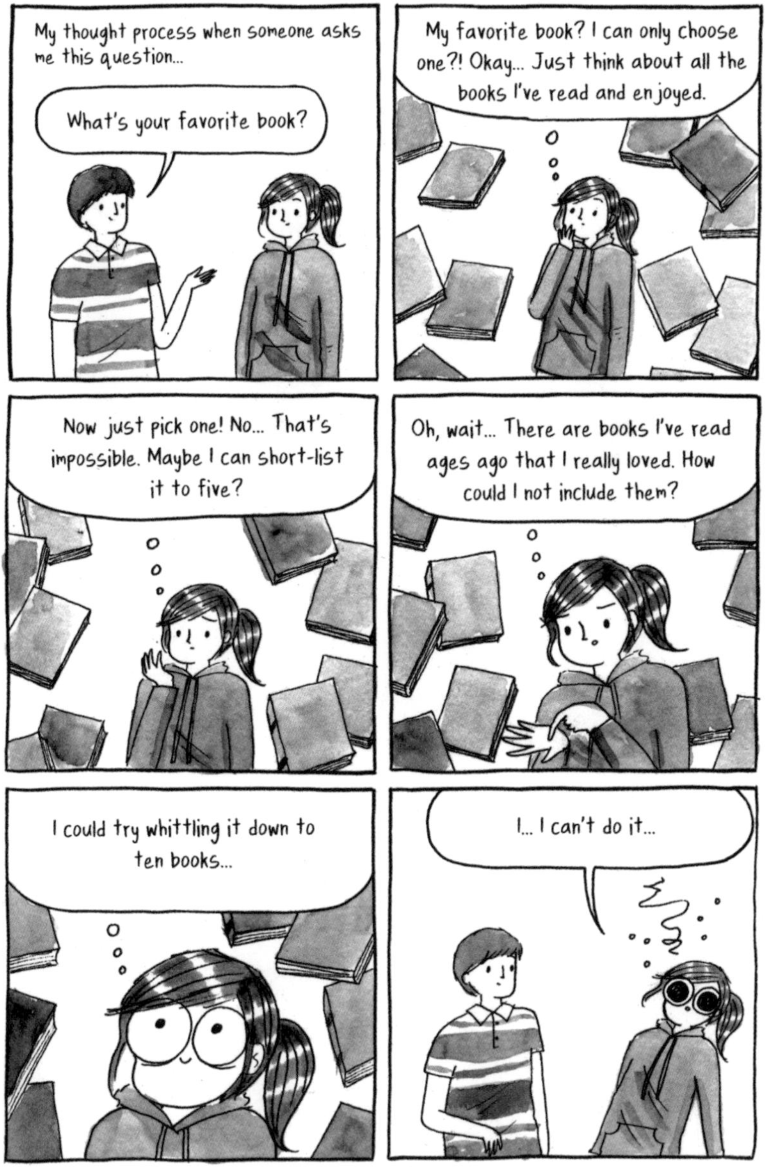
My thought process when someone asks me this question...
What's your favorite book?
My favorite book? I can only choose one?! Okay... Just think about all the books I've read and enjoyed.
Now just pick one! No... That's impossible. Maybe I can short-list it to five?
Oh, wait... There are books I've read ages ago that I really loved. How could I not include them?
I could try whittling it down to ten books...
I... I can't do it...

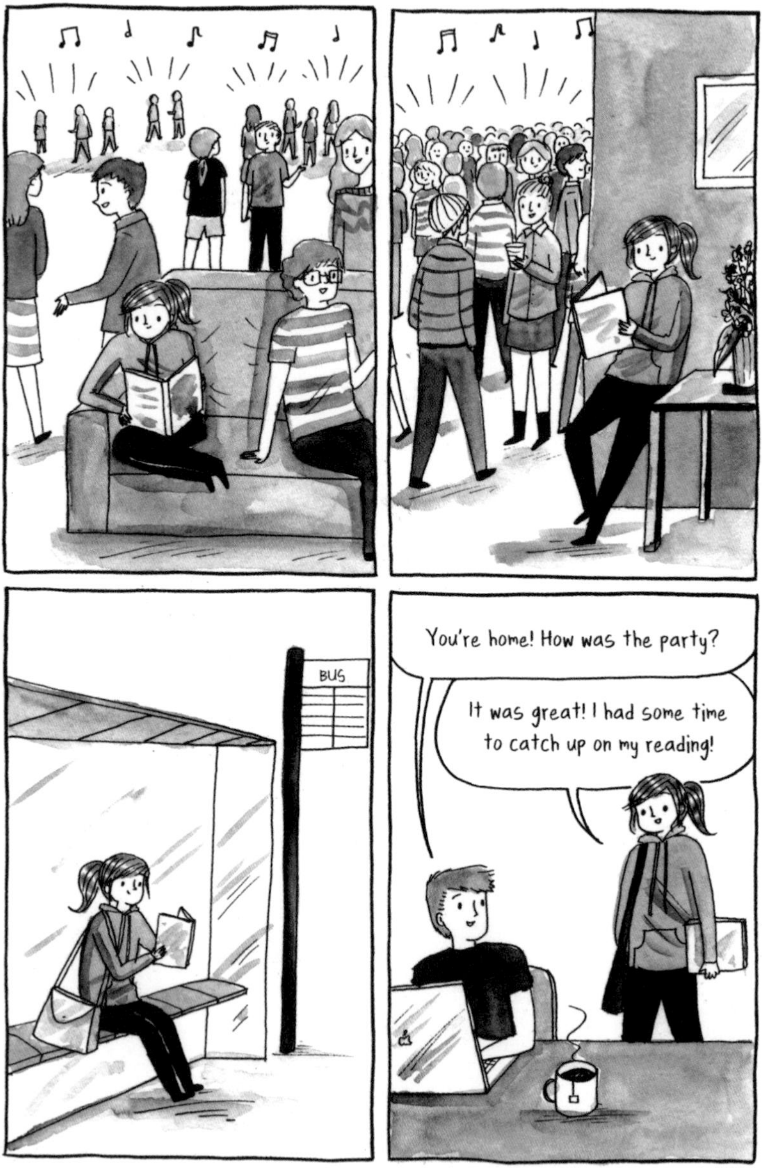
BUS
You're home! How was the party?
It was great! I had some time to catch up on my reading!

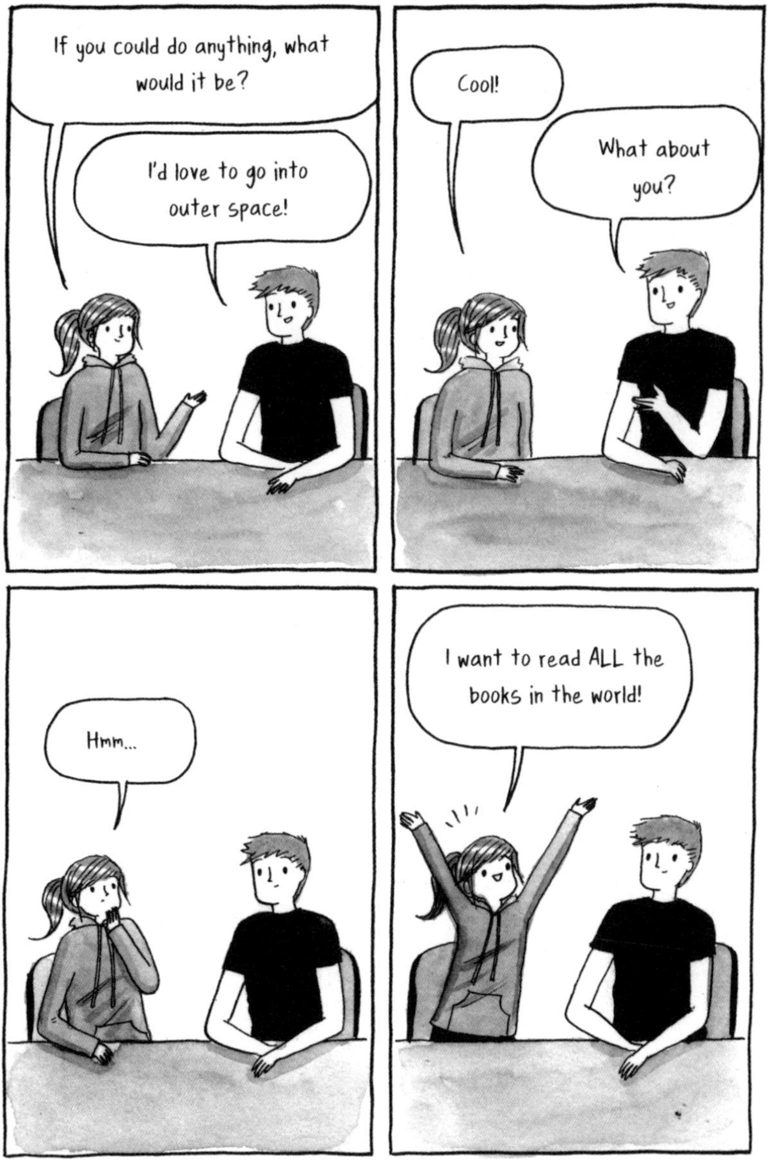
If you could do anything, what would it be?
I'd love to go into outer space!
Cool!
What about you?
Hmm...
I want to read ALL the books in the world!

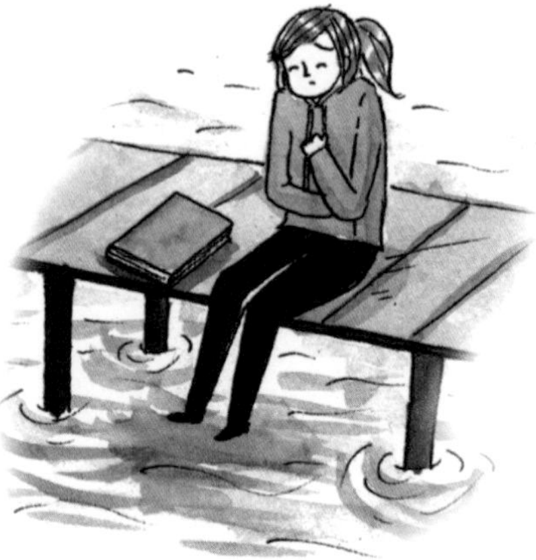

Books have helped me through tough times

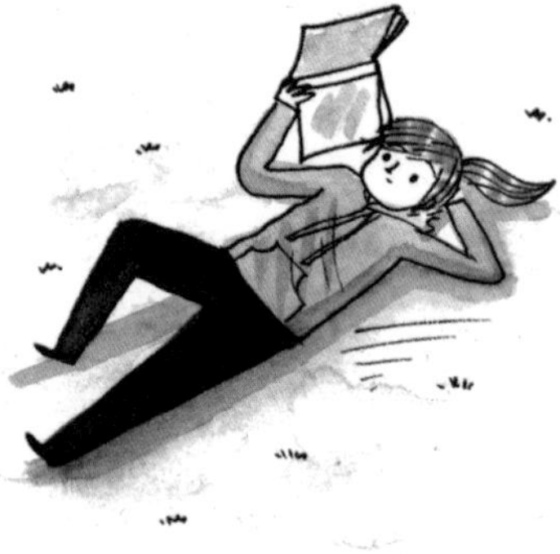

in moments of boredom

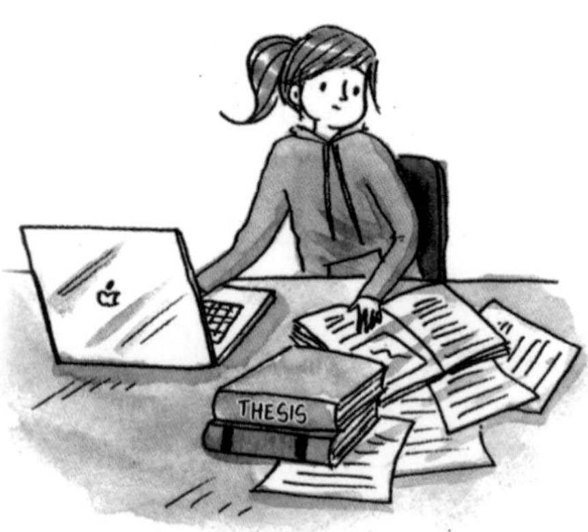
THESIS

and when I needed help.

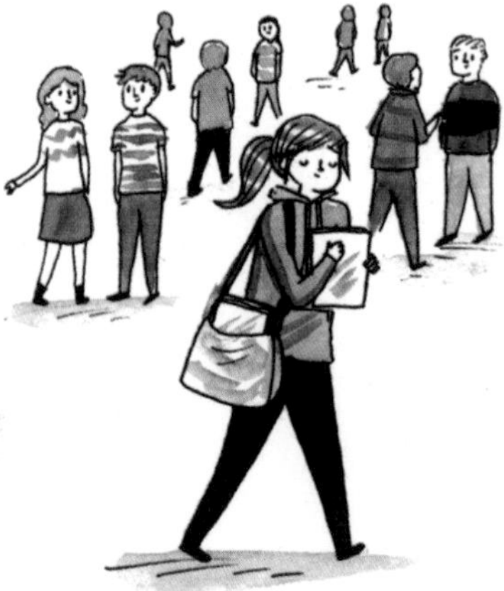

Books have been there for me when I felt like nobody else would understand.

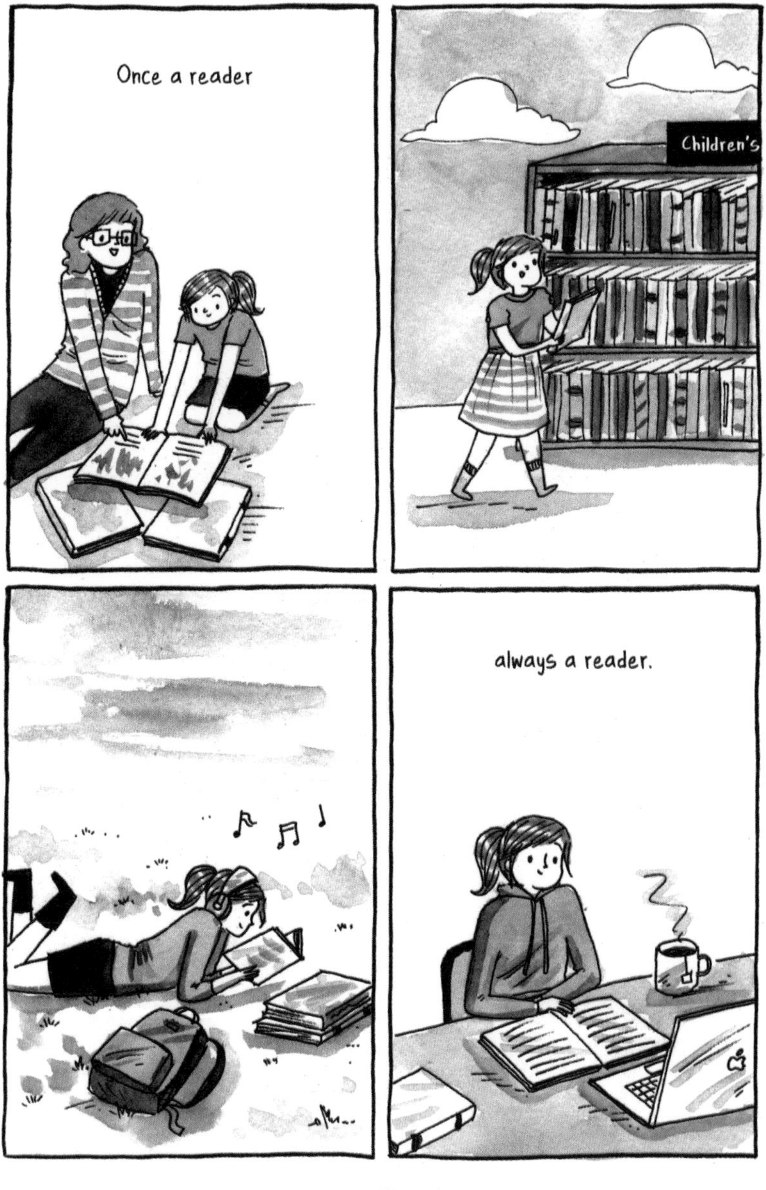
Once a reader
Children's
always a reader.

Levels of Accomplishment I Feel

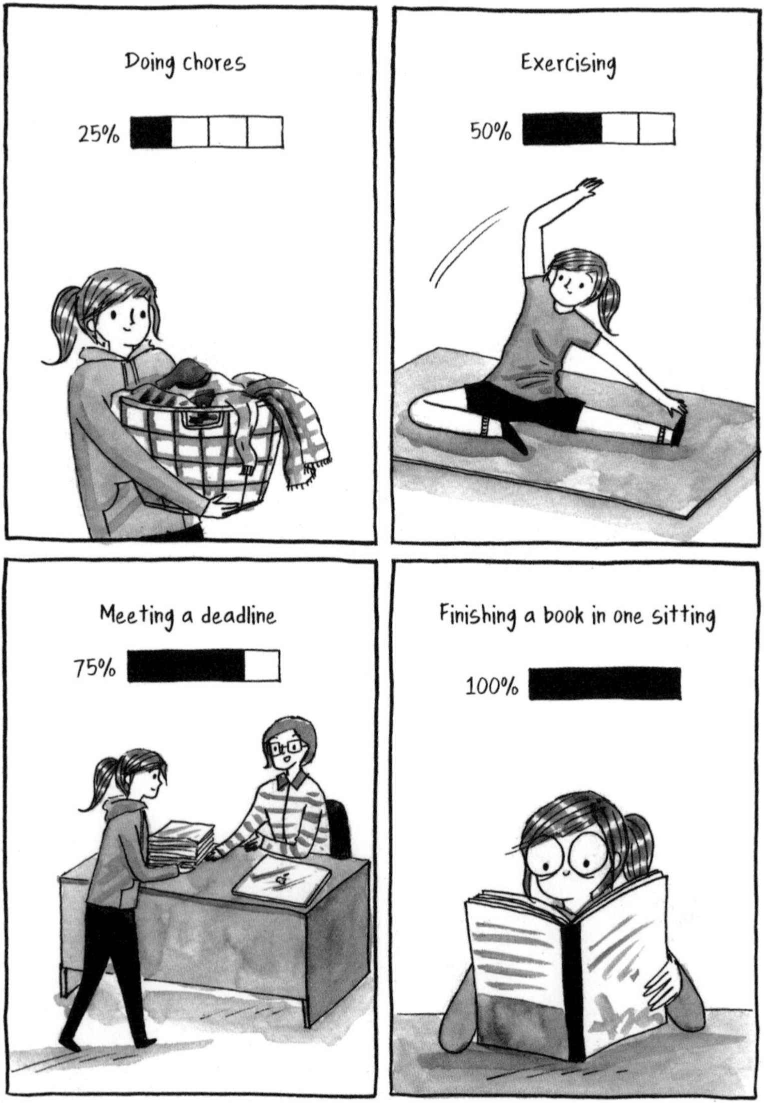
Doing chores
25%
Exercising
50%
Meeting a deadline
75%
Finishing a book in one sitting
100%

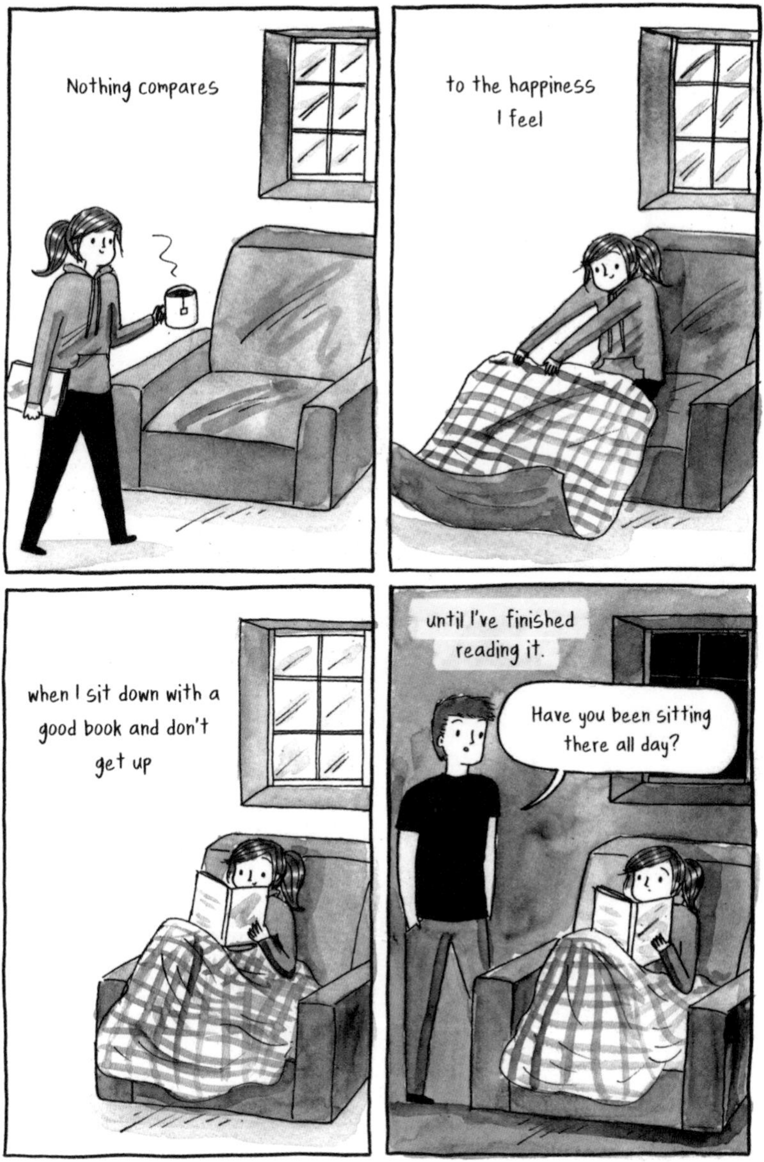
Nothing compares
to the happiness I feel
when I sit down with a good book and don't get up
until I've finished reading it.
Have you been sitting there all day?

# Places Where I Keep My Books

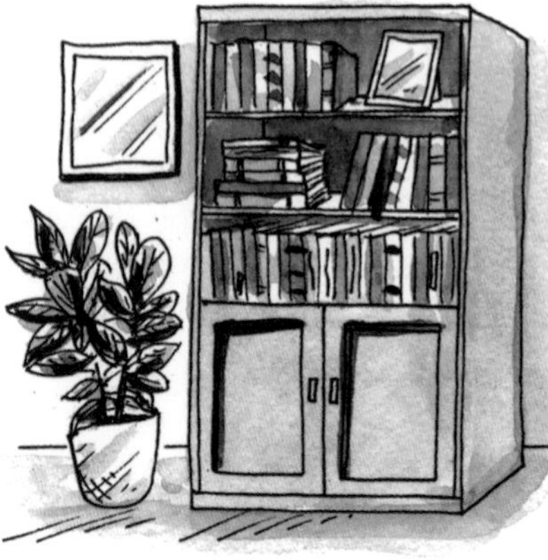

Bookshelf

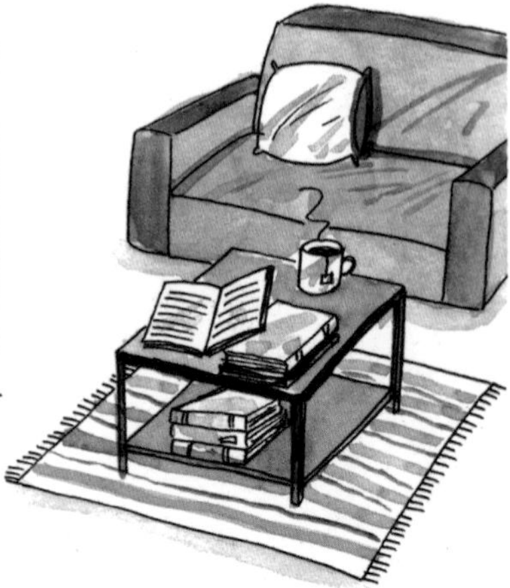

Coffee table

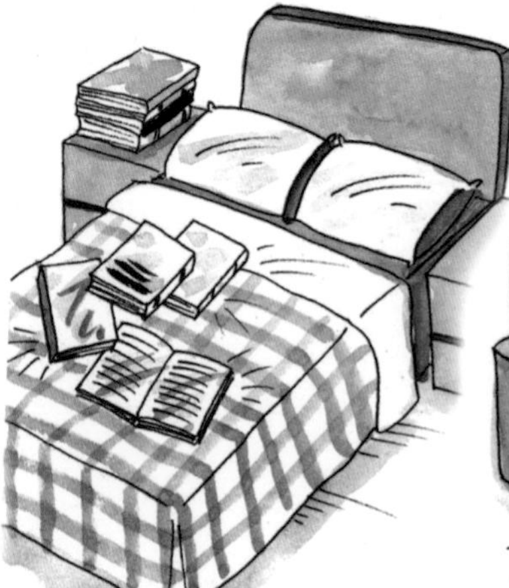

Bed

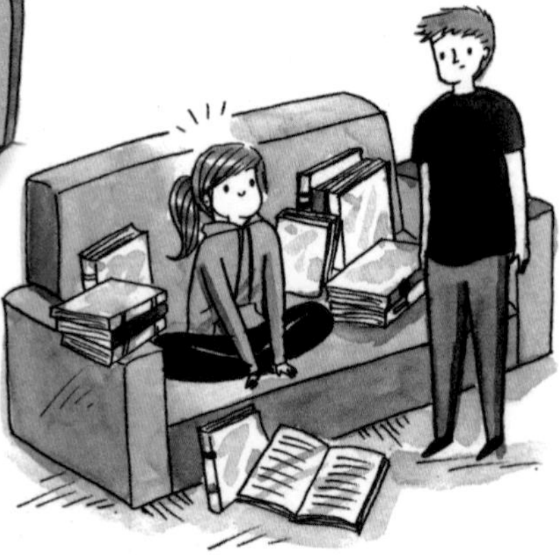

Any part of the sofa with available space

# Things I Use as Bookmarks

Old receipts

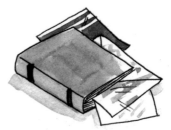

Junk mail

Pens

DENIM JEANS

Clothing tags

E-reader

Do you mind holding this page for me while I go to the bathroom?

Other people

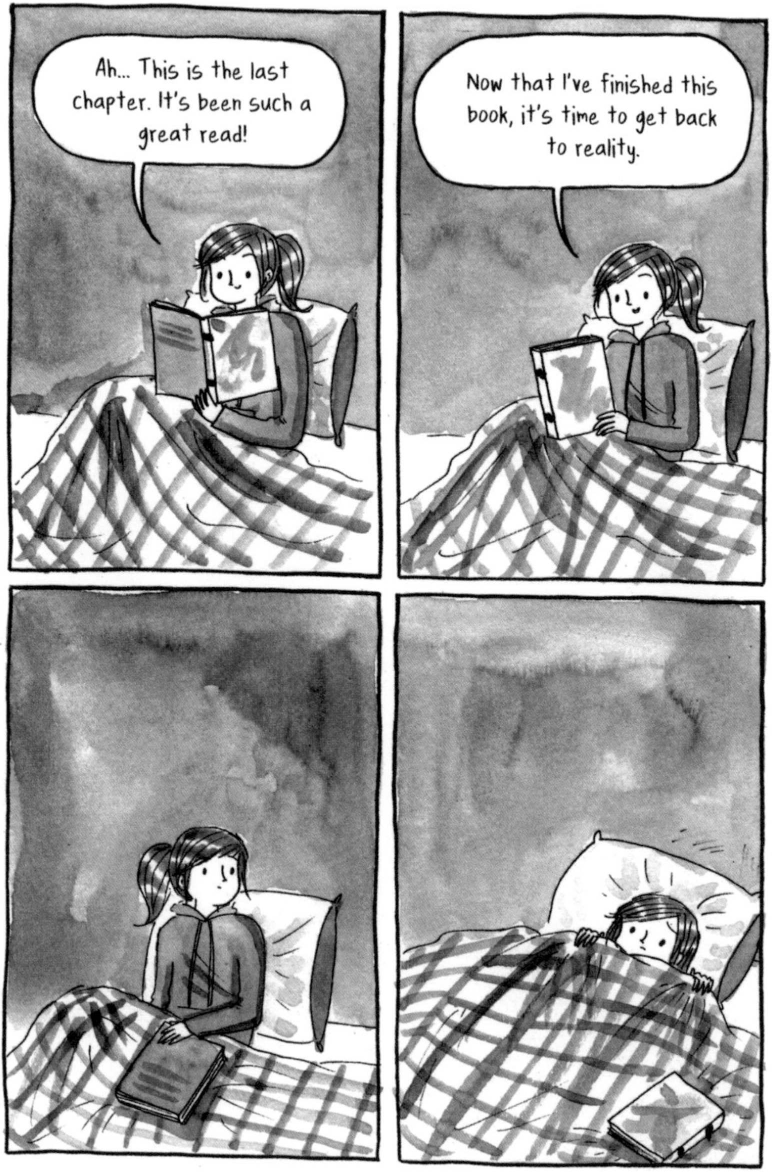
Ah... This is the last chapter. It's been such a great read!
Now that I've finished this book, it's time to get back to reality.

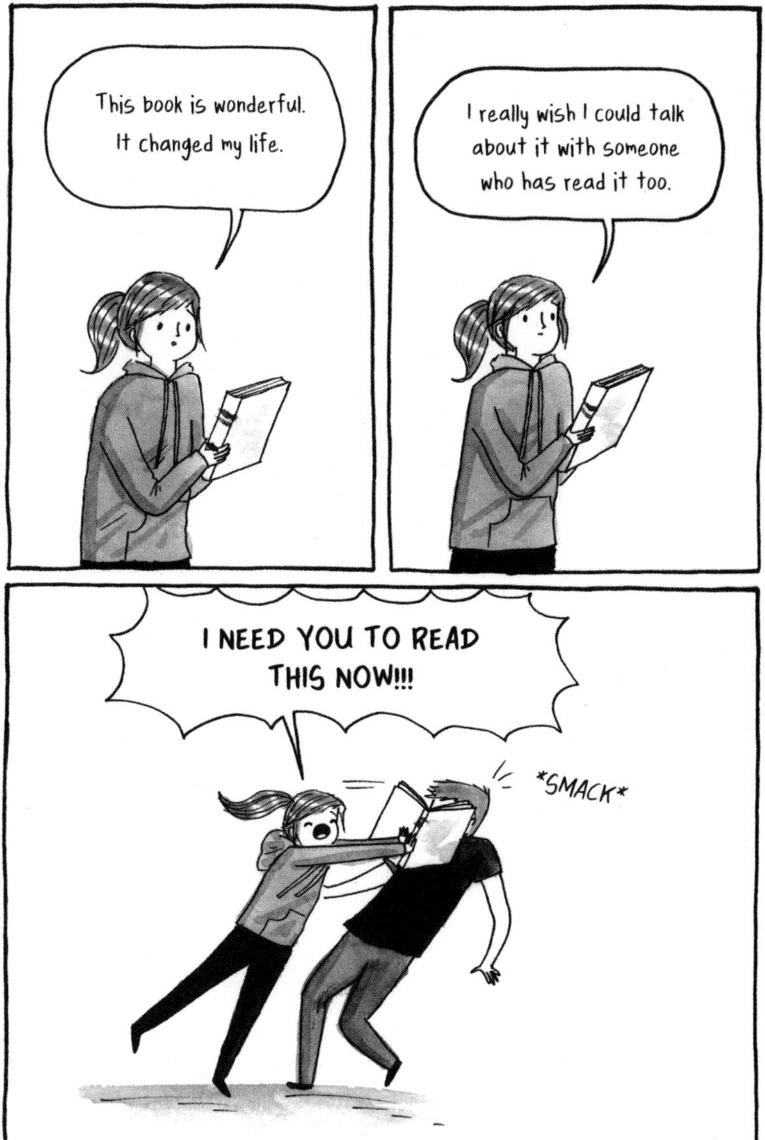
This book is wonderful.
It changed my life.
I really wish I could talk
about it with someone
who has read it too.
I NEED YOU TO READ
THIS NOW!!!
*SMACK*

# Different Ways of Reading

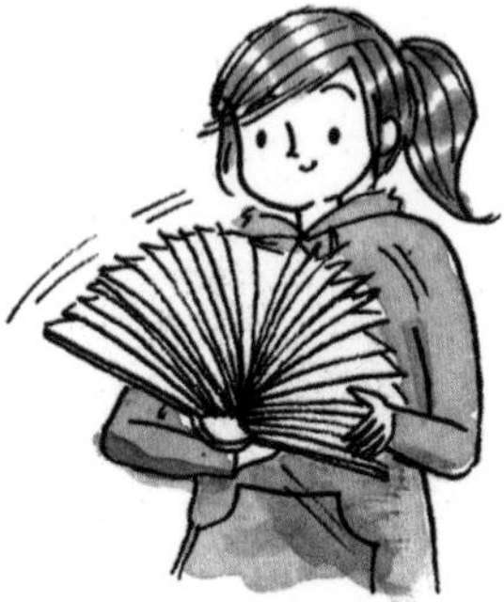

Speed reading

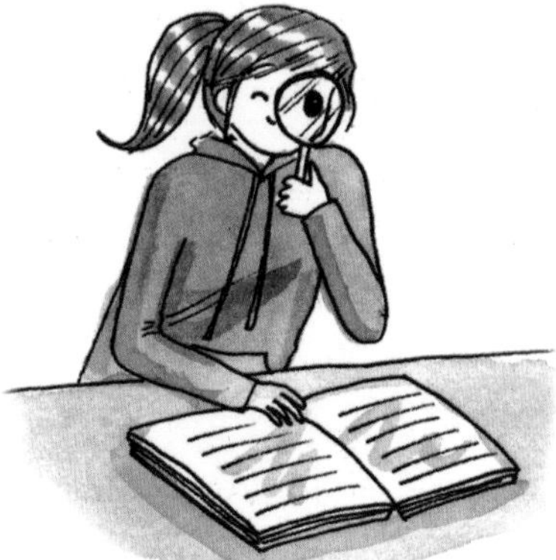

Close reading

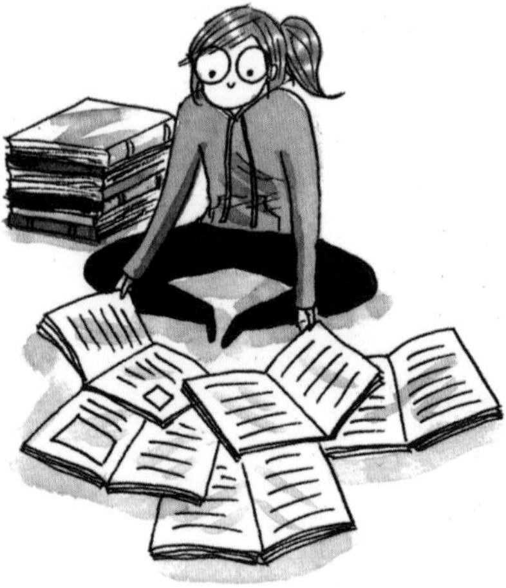

Extensive reading

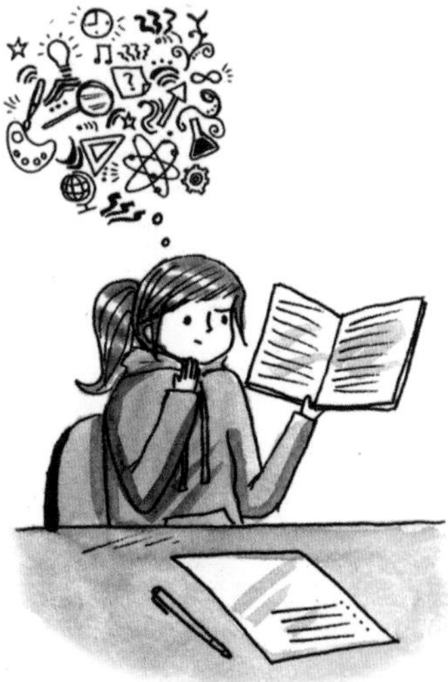

In-depth reading

# Every day is a good day for books

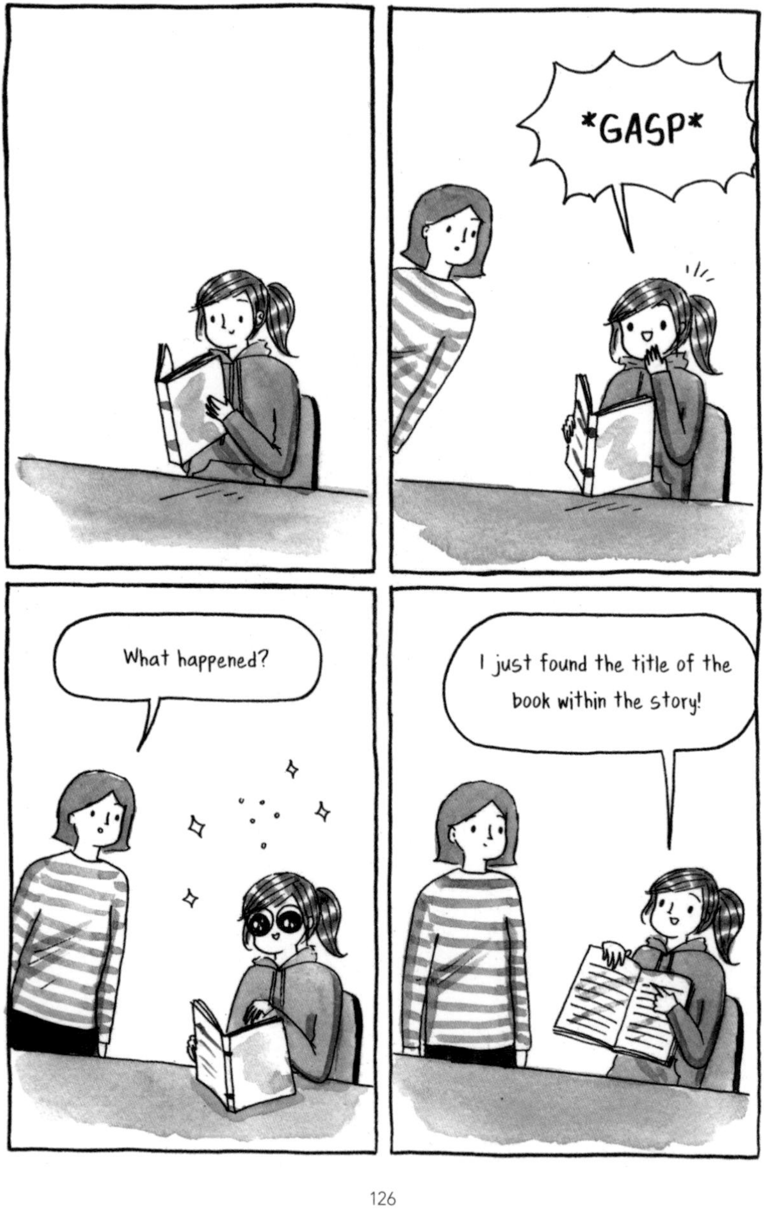
*GASP*
What happened?
I just found the title of the book within the story!

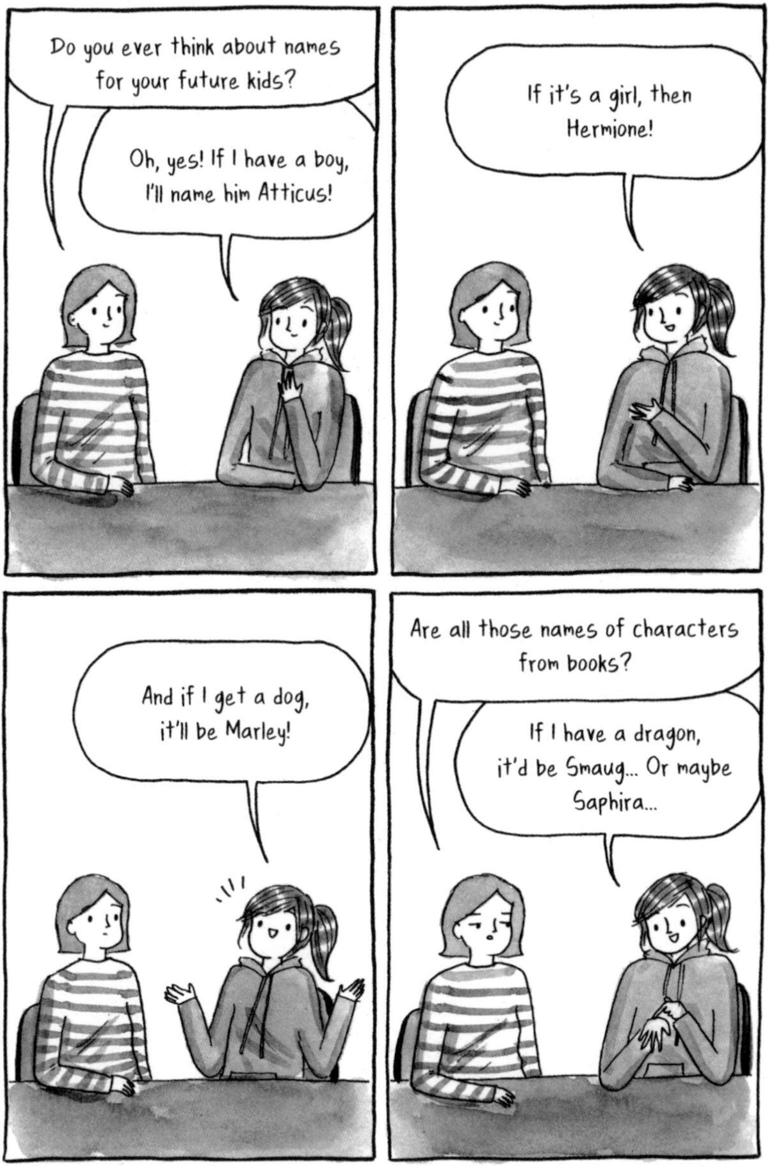
Do you ever think about names for your future kids?
Oh, yes! If I have a boy, I'll name him Atticus!
If it's a girl, then Hermione!
And if I get a dog, it'll be Marley!
Are all those names of characters from books?
If I have a dragon, it'd be Smaug... Or maybe Saphira...

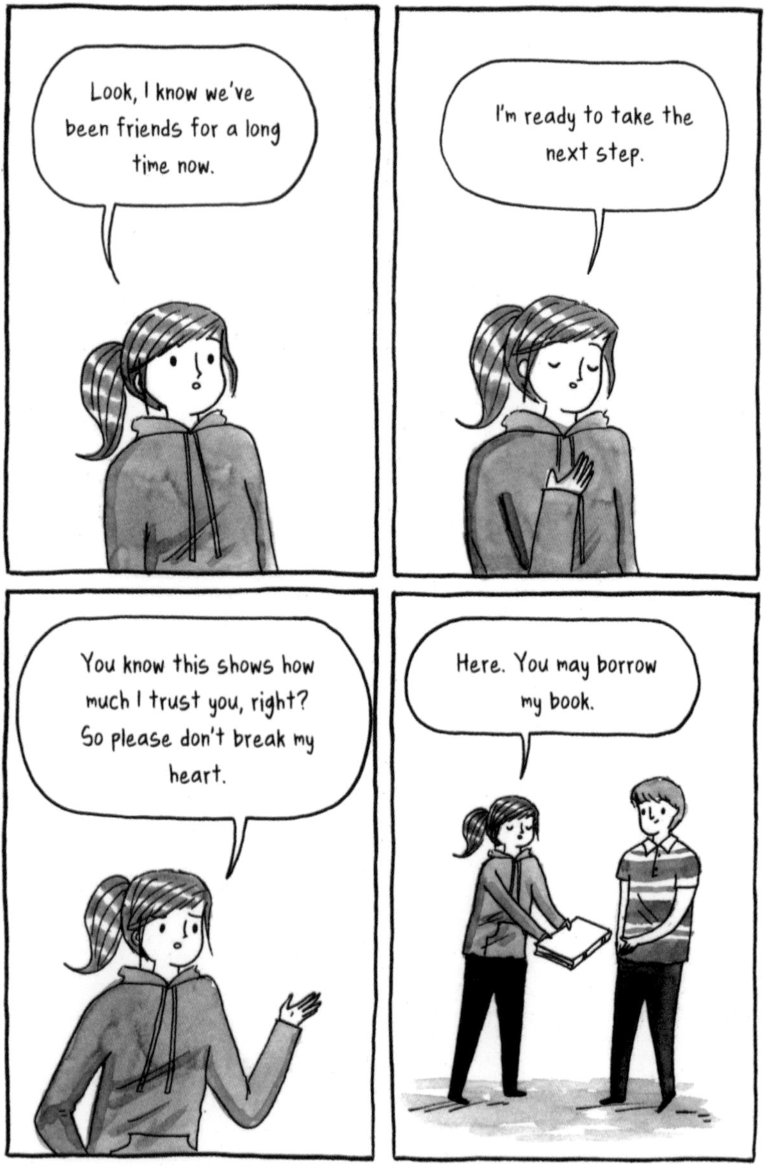
Look, I know we've been friends for a long time now.
I'm ready to take the next step.
You know this shows how much I trust you, right? So please don't break my heart.
Here. You may borrow my book.

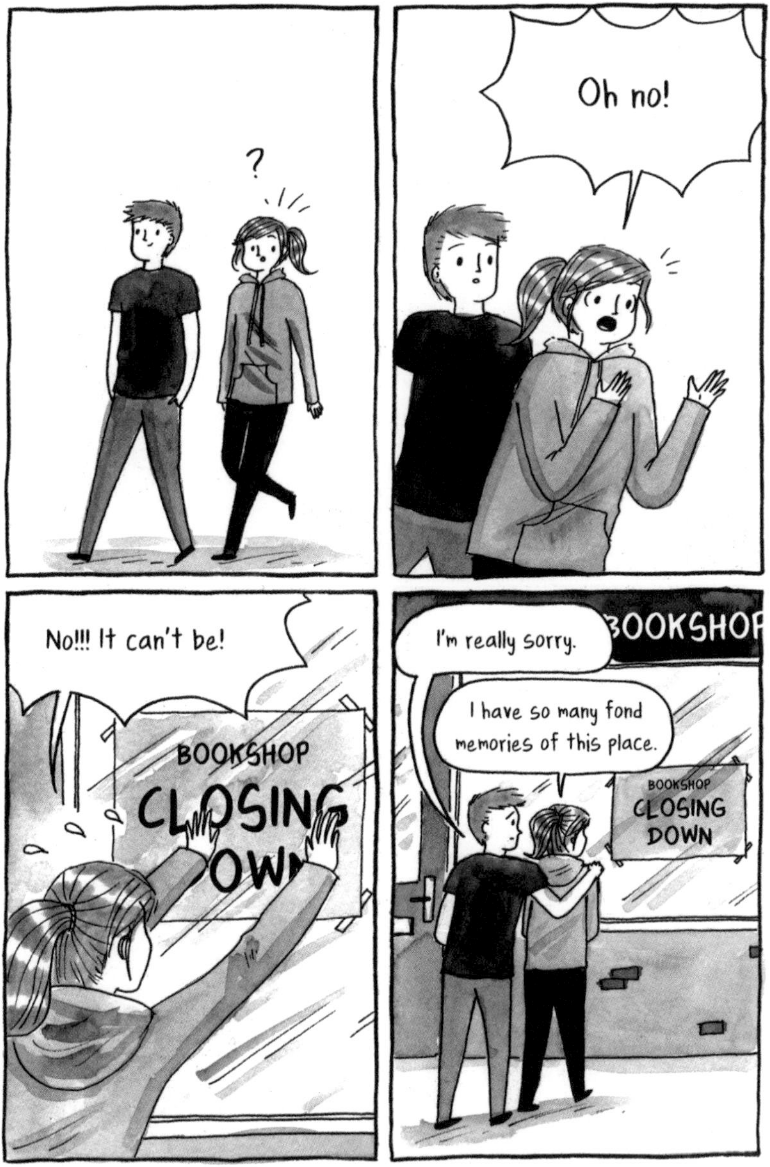
?
Oh no!
No!!! It can't be!
BOOKSHOP
CLOSING
BOOKSHOP
I'm really sorry.
I have so many fond memories of this place.
BOOKSHOP
CLOSING
DOWN

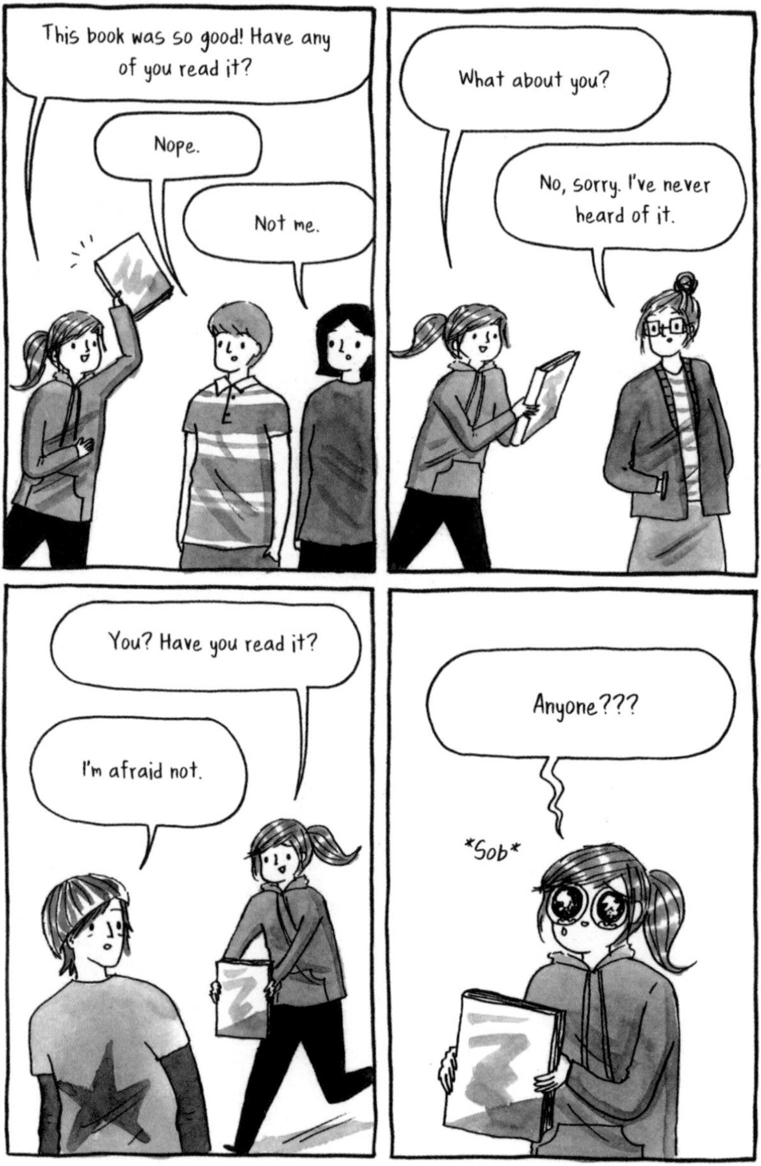
This book was so good! Have any of you read it?
Nope.
Not me.
What about you?
No, sorry. I've never heard of it.
You? Have you read it?
I'm afraid not.
Anyone???
*Sob*

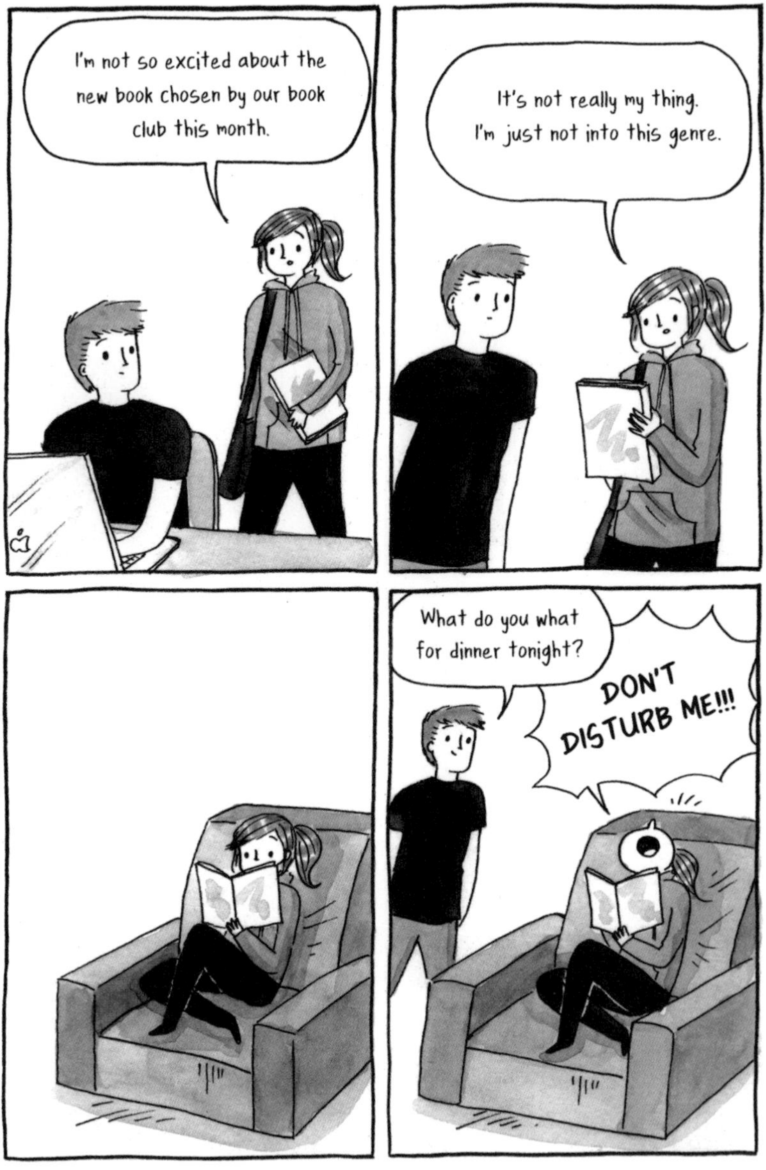
I'm not so excited about the new book chosen by our book club this month.
It's not really my thing. I'm just not into this genre.
What do you what for dinner tonight?
DON'T DISTURB ME!!!

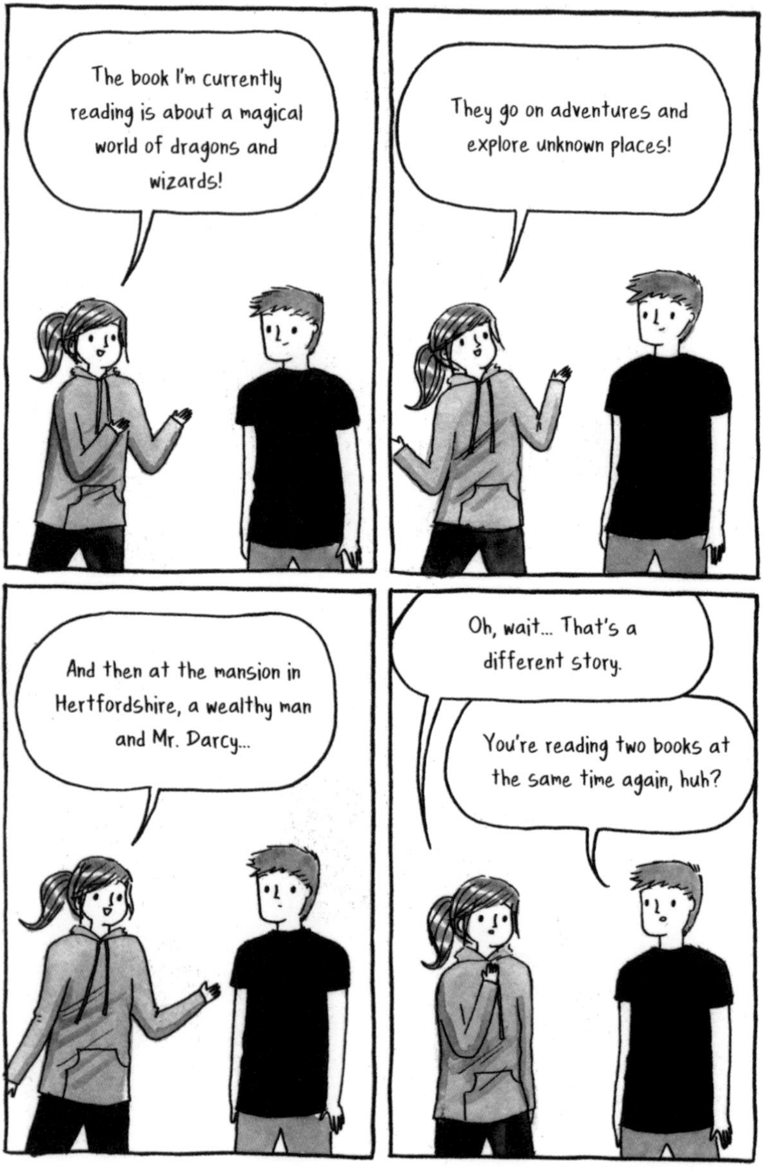
The book I'm currently reading is about a magical world of dragons and wizards!
They go on adventures and explore unknown places!
And then at the mansion in Hertfordshire, a wealthy man and Mr. Darcy...
Oh, wait... That's a different story.
You're reading two books at the same time again, huh?

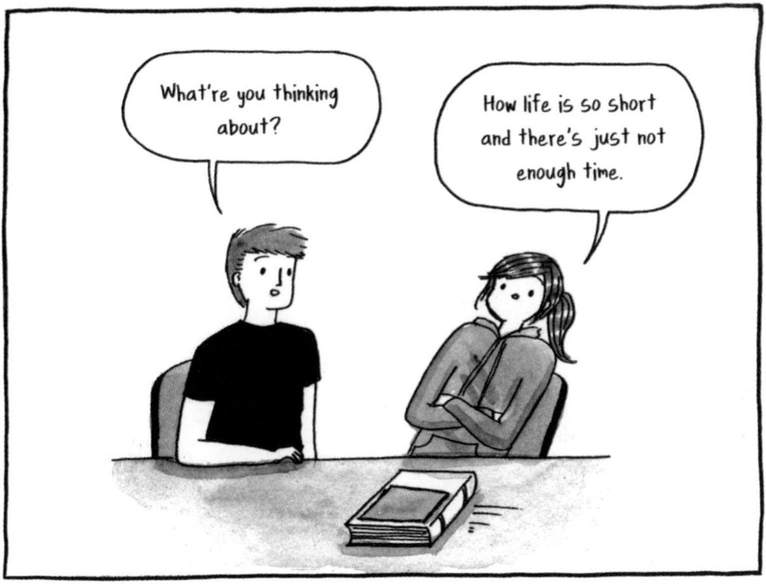
What're you thinking about?
How life is so short and there's just not enough time.

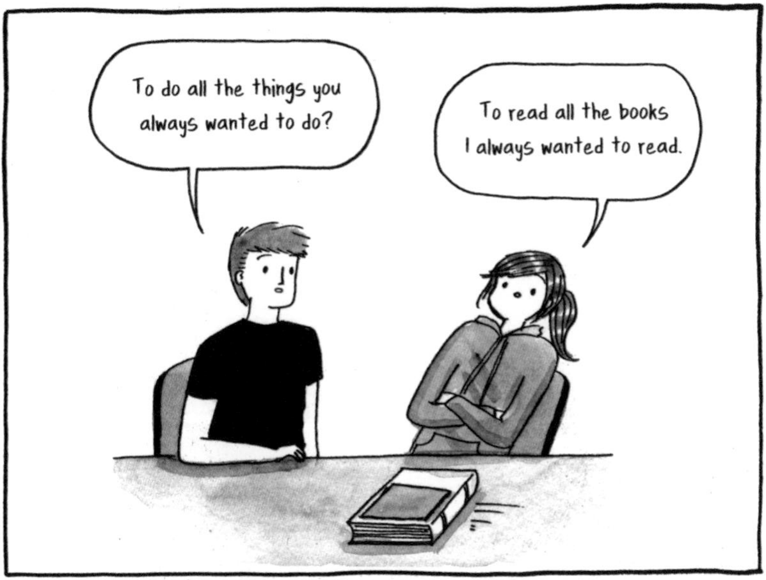
To do all the things you always wanted to do?
To read all the books I always wanted to read.

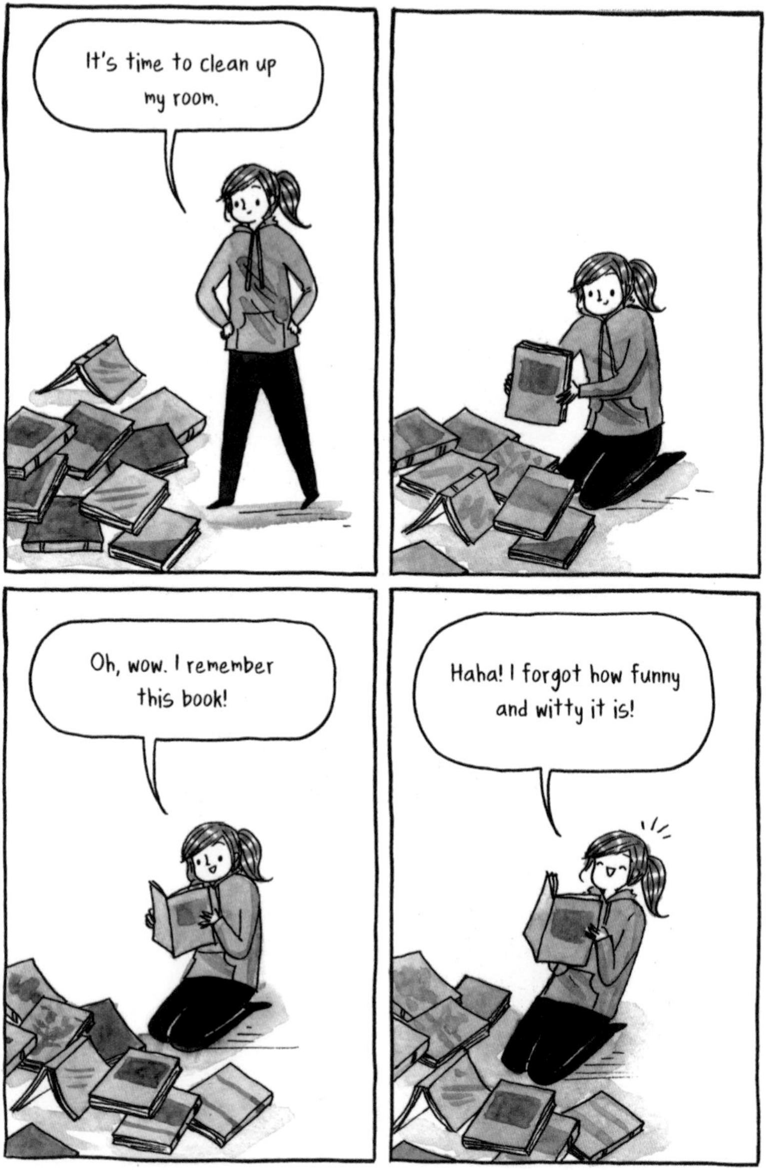
It's time to clean up my room.
Oh, wow. I remember this book!
Haha! I forgot how funny and witty it is!

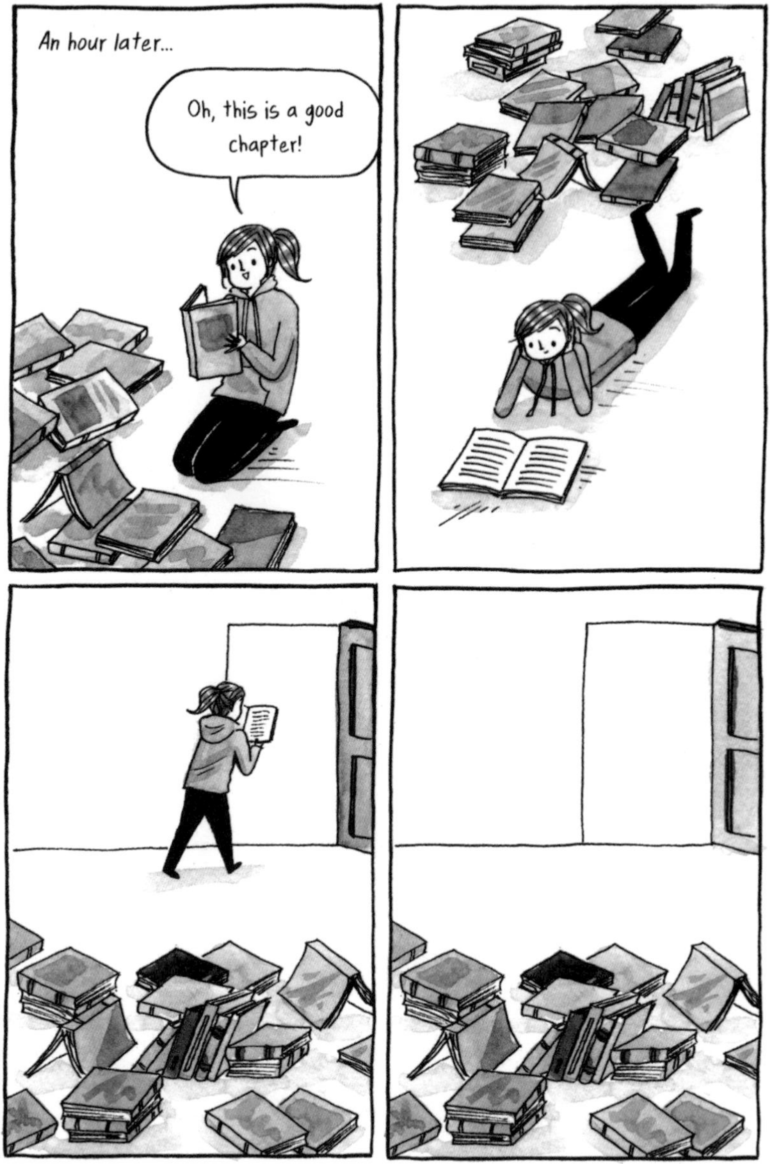
An hour later...
Oh, this is a good chapter!

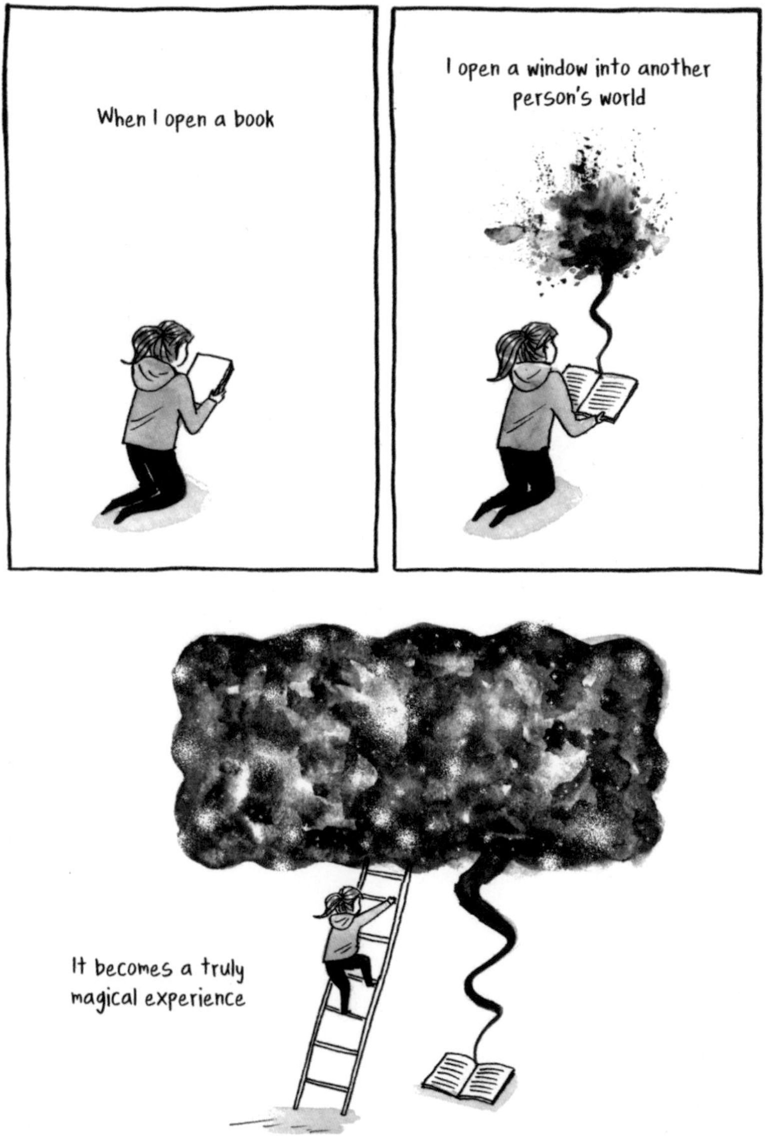
When I open a book
I open a window into another person's world
It becomes a truly magical experience

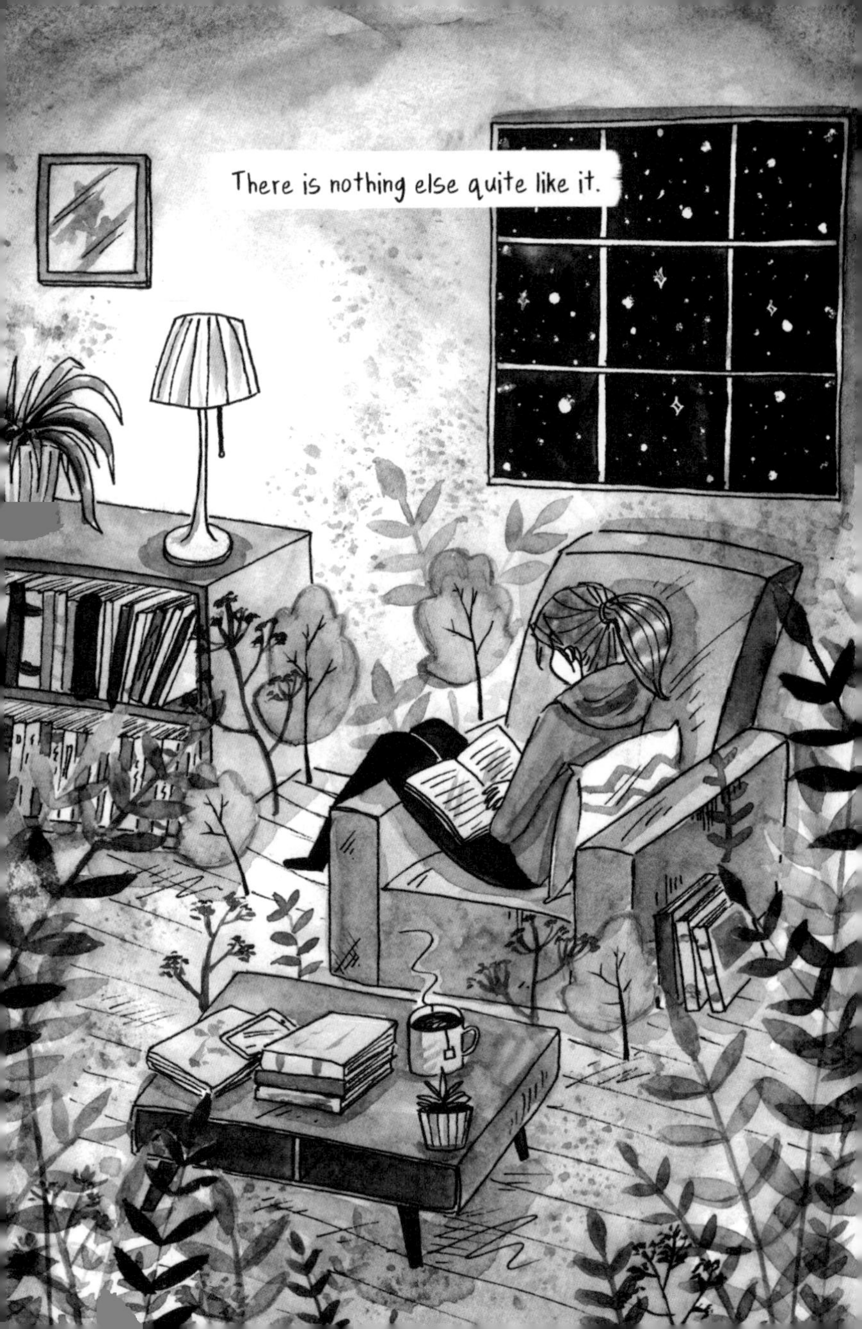
There is nothing else quite like it.

## About the Author

Debbie Tung is a cartoonist and illustrator based in Birmingham, England. She draws about everyday life and her love for books and tea at *Where's My Bubble?* (wheresmybubble.tumblr.com). Debbie is also the author of *Quiet Girl in a Noisy World.* Her comics have been shared widely by *Huffington Post, Bored Panda, 9GAG, Pulptastic,* and *Goodreads,* among others.

Andrews McMeel Publishing
a division of Andrews McMeel Universal
1130 Walnut Street, Kansas City, Missouri 64106

www.andrewsmcmeel.com

19 20 21 22 23 SDB 10 9 8 7 6 5 4 3 2 1

ISBN: 978-1-4494-9428-5

Library of Congress Control Number: 2018940985

**Attention: Schools and Businesses**
Andrews McMeel books are available at quantity
discounts with bulk purchase for educational, business,
or sales promotional use. For information, please e-mail the
Andrews McMeel Publishing Special Sales Department:
specialsales@amuniversal.com.